POETS' HANDWRITINGS
A graphological study

OTHER BOOKS BY THE SAME AUTHOR

Adam Mickiewicz, poète national de la Pologne. Étude psychanalytique et caractérologique, Bellarmin, Montréal and Les Belles Lettres, Paris, 1988, 878 p. Also in Polish (Warsaw, 1987).

Écritures de poètes de Byron à Baudelaire, Dervy-Livres and Chiron, Paris, 1977, 202 p.

Écritures de poètes. Graphologie et Poésie. Deuxième série: de Sully-Prudhomme à Valéry, Dervy-Livres and Chiron, Paris, 1981, 267 p.

Introduction aux systèmes asservis non linéaires [1977], 2nd ed., Dunod, Paris, 1984, 126 p.

Musique et Graphologie. Écritures de compositeurs de Beethoven à Debussy, Dervy-Livres and Chiron, 1978, 215 p.

Poésie, Musique et Graphologie. Écritures de poètes et de compositeurs : compléments, Dervy-Livres and Chiron, 1988, 232 p.

Four chapters of P. VIDAL (ed.), **Précis d'automatique**, Techniques de l'ingénieur, Paris, 1982-1990.

Psychologie de l'écriture. Suite à l'ABC de la graphologie [1969], 4th ed., Payot, Paris, 1989, 348 p. Also in Italian (Naples, 1990), in Spanish (Barcelona, 1991) and in English (London, 1992).

Systèmes linéaires. Problèmes avec solutions, Lidec, Montréal, 1992, 330 p.

Tempéraments psychobiologiques et Groupes sanguins. Expression graphologique et artistique, Frison-Roche, Paris, 1991, 334 p. Also in Italian (Castrovillari, 1991) and in Spanish (Barcelona, 1994).

Types de Jung et Tempéraments psychobiologiques. Expression dans l'écriture. Corrélation avec le groupe sanguin. Utilisation en psychologie appliquée, Maloine, Paris et Édisem, Québec, 1978, 196 p.

In collaboration with F. Lefebure :

Test de Szondi et Graphologie. 1: le Moi [1976], 3rd ed., Masson, Paris, 1990, 188 p.

Test de Szondi et Graphologie. 2: Dynamique des Pulsions [1980], 2nd ed., Masson, Paris, 1990, 234 p.

In collaboration with P. Decaulne and M. Pélegrin :

Feedback Control Systems. Analysis, Synthesis, and Design, McGraw-Hill, New York, 1959, 793 p. Also in French (1956), in Polish (1961), and in Russian (1961).

./....

OTHER BOOKS BY THE SAME AUTHOR (continued)

Théorie et Calcul des asservissements, Dunod, Paris, 1958; 3rd ed., 1963, 321p. Also in German 1960, 3rd ed.,1968), in Rumanian (1963), in Italian (1966), and in Spanish (1967, 2nd ed., 1971).

Les Organes des systèmes asservis, Dunod, Paris, 1959; 3rd ed., 1965, 463 p. Also in German (1962; 2nd ed. 1967) and in Rumanian (1963).

Problèmes d'asservissements avec solutions, Dunod, Paris,1959; 4th ed., 1971, 256 p. Also in Polish (1961) and in German (1963; 2nd ed., 1967).

Dynamique de la commande linéaire, Dunod, Paris, 1967; 9th ed., 1991, 524p.

Théorie et Calcul des asservissements linéaires, Dunod, Paris, 1967; 10th ed., 1991, 489 p.

Systèmes asservis non linéaires, Dunod, Paris, 1967; 6th ed., 1991, 3 vol., 163 + 151 + 219 p.

Introduction aux systèmes asservis extrémaux et adaptatifs, Dunod, Paris, 1976, 92 p.

In collaboration with M. Clique :

La Représentation d'état pour l'étude des systèmes dynamiques, Eyrolles, Paris, 1975, 2 vol., 192 + 109 p.

Calcul matriciel et Introduction à l'analyse fonctionnelle, Lidec, Montréal, 1979; 4th ed., 1989, 3 vol., 163 + 116 + 124 p. Also in Polish (1977; 2nd ed., 1986, 320 p).

Systèmes linéaires. Équations d'état, Eyrolles, Paris, 1984; 2nd ed., 1990, 203 p.

Calcul matriciel. Exercices et problèmes, Lidec, Montréal, 1984; 2nd ed., 1988, 223 p.

In collaboration with S. Wegrzyn and P. Vidal :

Introduction à l'étude de la stabilité dans les espaces métriques, Dunod, Paris, 1971, 73 p. Also in Polish (Warsaw, 1970).

Developmental Systems. At the Crossroads of System Theory, Computer Science, and Genetic Engineering, Springer-Verlag, New York, 1990, 120 p. Also in Polish (Gliwice, 1988; 2nd ed., 1992).

Dr. Jean-Charles Gille-Maisani

POETS' HANDWRITINGS
A graphological study

Foreword by Renna Nezos

***Translated by* Robert Laversuch**

Edited by Lorraine Herbert

an imprint of
The British Academy of Graphology
London

English Edition Copyright © 1995
SCRIPTOR BOOKS,
an imprint of
The British Academy of Graphology (Limited by Guarantee)
75 Quinta Drive, Barnet, Herts. EN5 3DA

Editorial Office: 1B Limpsfield Avenue, London SW19 6DL

A CIP catalogue record for this book is available from the British Library.

ISBN 1-899653 15 5

Typesetting and layout by

EuroBuro '92 Brigitte Froud
London, Tel 0181-788 3289

Printed and bound in Great Britain

CONTENTS

FOREWORD

This book contains the complete graphological analysis of the handwriting of eight poets known world-wide.

It has been essentially written for students in graphology with a view to providing them with eight samples of handwriting analyses according to the method which has been adopted and is recommended by the British Academy of Graphology. The method is based on four main approaches :

1. The French graphological school (Crépieux-Jamin and his followers, which insists on orientation syntheses (organisation, harmony, irregularities and inhibitions) and on interpreting all signs (species) only by relating them to the whole of the handwriting.

2. The German authors who have introduced the concepts of rhythm and formlevel (Klages), of tension (Pophal), of form, movement and spatial layout (Gross, Heiss) and of the relation of form to movement (Müller-Enskat).

3. The typologies which help to situate the writer within the frame of different psychological systems. The author here resorts to Hippocrates-Galen's temperaments, to mythological types, to Jungian types and to Szondi's vectors.

4. Finally graphometry, which adds a quantitative touch and makes objective validation easier.

These approaches are systematically applied by Dr. Gille-Maisani (the first three to all eight poets, the fourth to the French poets only because the graphometric scales used have been established on the base of contemporary French handwriting). Writings dating back to different eras of their lives are analysed in order to show the evolution of personality with age. The fact that the writers are famous people with strong personalities, who devoted their lives to the expression of their inner life and to their view on man and the world, should help the graphology student associate the graphic aspects of writing with personality traits.

All the analyses presented in this book have been constructed in a most thorough manner, which is so characteristic of the author in all his work. It is a unique manual and I am sure that it will be of great interest, not only to all graphologists, but also to those people who would simply like to understand the soul of the great poet.

Renna Nezos
The British Academy of Graphology

PREFACE

Les poètes doivent être la grande étude
du philosophe qui veut connaître l'Homme.
(Gaston Bachelard, *L'Air et les Songes*) (1)

On s'attendait à trouver un auteur
et on trouve un homme.
(Blaise Pascal, *Pensées*) (2)

This book is a companion to *The Psychology of Handwriting*, previously published by Scriptor Books.

In *The Psychology of Handwriting* thirty-three "new" species of handwriting have been used to unfold a method of study which is broadly that of most French graphologists at this end of the twentieth century. The book is an inventory of writing characteristics, their dividing into groups helped by orientational syntheses, by psychobiological interpretation and by the light given by psychoanalysis and typologies.

The object of this present book is to help English-speaking graphologists to learn and to apply this method by putting eight complete analyses at their disposal.

These concern the handwriting of poets. Eight analyses have been chosen from the twenty-one that have appeared in three of my books (in the edition Dervy-Livres of Paris in the 70's and 80's). They treat two English Romantic poets, Byron and Keats, the Russian, Pushkin, and the five French poets who seem to be the best known in England : Vigny, Baudelaire,

(1) Poets must be the great study of the philospher who wants to understand Man.
(2) One expected to find an author and one finds a man.

Mallarmé, Verlaine and Rimbaud. As far as possible scripts coming from different periods of their lives have been studied in order to illustrate the development of personality.

Each of these eight studies has been made by the method outlined above. There is also a graphometrical study [3] for the last four French poets only, because our graphometrical scales having been set up for contemporary Frenchmen, it would have been imprudent to apply them to Vigny, born in 1798, or to the English or Russian poets. Lastly, the study of each handwriting is followed by a summary of analyses made by graphologists since the start of the science.

This work makes no literary claim. Occasional references to poetic work or to works of criticism are subordinated to a psychological purpose. As far as literature is concerned, one should note the opportunities afforded to literary critics to appreciate literary works by situating their authors in their biographic context. Nowadays they have recourse to the notions of modern psychology. Graphology should be a part of this fruitful disciplinary convergence.

*

Thanks are due to all those who allowed the inspection and reproduction of scripts and gave access to former works of graphology now out of print : writers, graphologists and librarians from Paris, Charleville, London and Moscow.

I also wish to thank the graphologists who contributed to my work. The typological diagnoses were approved by the best authorities in this domain, viz. Mesdames Elisabeth Koechlin (H. Saint-Morand) for the mythological types, Ania Teillard

---

(3) An appendix at the end of the book (after the Bibliography) explains the graphometric technique used.

for the Jungian types, Fanchette Lefebure for the Szondian vectors, André Lecerf for Galen's temperaments and Jacques Genevay for the psychobiological temperaments of Léone Bourdel. The calculations in the graphometrical analyses were performed by Mesdames Marie-France Leclère and Marie-Thérèse Prénat.

I express my gratitude to Robert Laversuch, who translated the text competently and conscientiously and to the staff of Scriptor Books, in particular to Mrs Lorraine Herbert and Brigitte Froud for their courageous and meticulous work, and to Mrs. Renna Nezos, Principal of the British Academy of Graphology, for her support and her valuable advice.

All that remains is to express the hope that this book will help English-speaking graphologists to become acquainted with Continental graphology.

Romagne, July 1993

Nota bene :

1. An asterisk (*) identifies the examples of which we have seen the originals and can guarantee their correct size. All other examples are from facsimiles (faithful in principle, though not always in fact) or from other documents. The origin of the scripts cited is given on pages 263 and 264.

2. As regards the reproduction of samples, the reader should be aware that on occasions we either had to "crop" the original samples or accommodate them on two consecutive pages in order to reproduce them at their at original size. Any reductions we *did* have to make are clearly stated in the captions.

1

George Gordon Lord BYRON (1788 - 1824)

Toi, dont le monde encore ignore le vrai nom,
Esprit mystérieux, mortel, ange ou démon,
Qui que tu sois, Byron, bon ou fatal génie.
J'aime de tes concerts la sauvage harmonie.[1]
(Lamartine, *L'Homme*.)

In his time, Byron was the idol of a whole generation. His poetical works exercised a major influence over the Romantics, who from France to Russia, looked upon him as a father. The first writer to be printed widely, he heralded the era in which literature was to touch social layers hitherto unreached. His death in the war for Greek independence made him the hero in the cause for national liberty.

Many enthusiastic causes are today forgotten. Byron has become the man of another epoch. Although everyone is familiar

(1) You, whose real name the world still does not know,
Mysterious spirit, mortal, angel or demon,
Whoever you are, Byron, good or evil genius,
Of your concerts I love the savage harmony.

with his name, knows that he had a club foot, that his private life was sometimes scandalous and that he died at Missolonghi, most educated people do not read him and picture him as the proud, brooding Byronic hero. He is taken for a poseur and both his poetry and his departure for literary Greece are considered as a pose.

I have turned to graphology for light on these questions. Figures 1.1 to 1.6 are specimens of Byron's handwriting. The first two are from letters dated from his youth. The third is an extract from a letter to a friend when he was twenty five, about a year after the sensational publication of *Childe Harold* (cantos I and II), which made Byron famous overnight. The rest are from letters to his publisher. Figure 1.4 was written in Venice. After his liaison with Augusta Leigh and his unhappy marriage, Byron left England for Switzc1rland and then Italy. Letter 1.5 dates from the time when Byron was with the Countess Guiccioli in Ravenna. The last example was written by Byron during his illness at Missolonghi, a few weeks before his death.

*

1) With reference to ORIENTATING SYNTHESES :

Byron's writing is very *evolved,* with simplifications and some combinations.

Its *harmony* is lowered by the indifferent quality of the stroke and the exaggerations (thrown and invading writing).

The writing shows *above average vitality* by its speed, rightward slant, prolongments, invading layout, its angles and cruciform gestures; but the pressure, continuity and direction are irregular.

Forms are neglected for the sake of the greater *movement* which is impulsive, sustained, strongly rhythmic, but disharmonic (the upward movement from the middle zone leads to exaggerated strokes), irregular (too uneven, imprecise, big difference in height between the middle zone and the upper extensions) and disturbed (interruptions, retouching sometimes). The rhythm of the spatial layout is strong and sustained though a little disturbed. The rhythm of form creation is poor.

The *tension*, according to the Pophal scale is IVa, dissolving to IVb (angles becoming thread-like, letters narrowing, occasional crossings-out and wavering of the stroke).

2) With reference to DEFINITION, we note first :

A handwriting that is *rapid, right-slanted, superelevated, sharp-pointed and resolute.*

Irregular in every category (except for slant), especially speed and continuity.

Well-nourished and *congested.* In several examples there are spasms, reversed pressure and blurred downstrokes.

Angles tend to be *threadlike*, some shapes are imprecise.

3) With reference to FREE MOVEMENTS :

T-bars are generally sharp-pointed.

Accents are well nourished, rapid, often crescent-shaped.

The *signature* is like the text, but larger, discordant in pressure, whip-like, centripetal and followed by a full stop.

The initial impact of the writing is one of power and overall superiority. The graphologist may guess that he has before him the work of a great poet. In any case, he will recognise a person of the first order. But it is equally obvious that this power lacks unity, that the personality is in many respects untamed. To quote from *Manfred* :

> "It is an awful chaos - light and darkness,
> And wind and dust, and passions and pure thoughts
> Mix'd, and contending without end or order".

First, the surge that carries the writing towards the right (rapidity, flying strokes, slant, no right-hand margin) indicates a nature that is daring, determined to win, enthusiastic and carried to extremes. The frequent crosses show his combativity, the sharp points his causticity and the spasms (note the superelevations) his authoritarian anger. This impulsiveness is regardless (recumbent and angular). The question is, to what purpose is this surging energy directed? Will it be successful and creative?

Notice first of all that this energy is not consistent (the writing looks resolute, but it is very uneven). Threadlike, imprecise strokes appear near the angles : lack of certainty. In this spasmodic writing the downstrokes are sometimes blurred and the pressure is deviated: this shows a lack of structured unity and an activity that is forced. Lively signs (speed, cruciform strokes) are there along with banal, even vulgar forms, with centripetal movements, showing a mean secretiveness. Such a graphic context suggests over-compensation because of the superelevations and the free swing. Byron's provocative and exaggerated self-assertion hides an abiding unease and his enthusiasm covers much bitterness and mistrust. Disappointment and despair make him into a destroyer.

Can graphology shed light on this chaos? I will attempt this, relying mainly on typological considerations, illustrated when needed by biographical details.

Notice first that the pressure of Byron's writing shows an overruling and unbalanced sensuality (spasms, ink-filled and sometimes blurred) manifested early : "My passions were developed very early - so early, that few would believe me, if I were to state the period and the facts which accompanied it".

At the age of nine Byron was in love with one of his cousins and became ill when hearing of her marriage. He still longed for her fifteen years later. At sixteen he fell for a young neighbour, Mary Chaworth, and was ill for several months because she mocked his crippled condition. The experience affected his attitude to women for a long time. I will return later to another aspect of this uncontrolled sensuality.

The psychology of Byron is made clear by two classic notions in psychiatry that have been long applied to the study of handwriting. The first, introduced into graphology by Dr. R. Monpin is the DISHARMONY of Regis. Here it is seen in the lack of control and the idiosyncrasies of the rhythmic movement in a very evolved graphic context. Byron had the "personality of a psychopath", was a "superior degenerate" (that is, unbalanced) in the meaning of the term in classic French psychiatry. His forebears were unstable, his eccentric father being a debauched spendthrift who killed himself. On his mother's side there was a history of murders and suicides. From childhood he displayed a nature that went to extremes in every respect, being affectionate, violent and irascible. His schoolmaster noted the contrast between his exceptional intelligence and his lack of judgement. His life with its sudden changes of direction was certainly disharmonic. No one has expressed that better than André Maurois in his classic, *Byron*. Wondering why Byron, in spite of his qualities of courage, realism and precision, was not a successful man of action, the author explains : "Byron's indecisiveness condemned him to a life of dreaming. He wanted to be both the people's defender and a great free-thinking lord, a husband as well as a Don Juan, a disciple of Voltaire and also a Puritan. He fought against English society and expected favours from it. [...]*He always lacked that unity of thought and conduct* which alone assures the execution of great plans".

The second psychiatric notion is that of PARANOIA introduced into graphology by Crépieux-Jamin. Byron's handwriting has three direct elements of this psychopathy. Pride (free, superelevated writing) and inadaptability (angles, monotonous slant, stable rhythmic basis) are in the foreground of the picture. A hostile wariness of others is displayed in the signs of mistrust (centripetal strokes, a full stop after the signature) and of active persecution (thrown and sharp-pointed, recumbent writing), for those who persecute are always the victims of persecution too.

The life of Byron eloquently confirms this diagnosis, the element of proud revolt being the most apparent. In primary school he used to defy the caretaker. At college he became at seventeen the leader of a pupils' revolt, tearing off the bars in front of their new master's window. He made up satirical verses against the master and adopted "Liberty or Rebellion" as his motto. This behaviour was permanent with Byron. His visit to Bonnivard's cell on Lake Geneva inspired the *Prisoner of Chillon* which was composed in one night. At thirty five, Byron stated that he was faithful only to two emotions : a great love for freedom and a horror of hypocrisy. In *Don Juan* he wrote "I was born for opposition". This meant that he was opposed to tyranny. Byron claimed that he would try to teach the very stones to rise against the tyrants of the earth! In the reactionary Europe of the time that meant the fight for the liberty of different peoples. His protest also took the form of a Rousseauesque contrasting of nature and civilisation and a defiance of socially conforming morality and religion.

This Englishman's admiration of Napoleon, with whom he identified (he thought of himself as "the great Napoleon of the kingdom of rhyme" and noted that Noël Byron has the same initials as Napoleon Bonaparte), reflects his pride and his opposition to his circle. Byron's signature (fig. 1.5), is, it seems to me, not unlike Napoleon's, having the same flying initials. The Polish poet, Mickiewicz, who admired both men, thought of Byron as the spiritual son of Napoleon.

Byron's poetry naturally reflects these tendencies. The Byronic hero and his general psychology has been thoroughly studied by critics : Giaour, Selim, Conrad and Lara are dark, misanthropic and solitary ("strangers to the world"), like the Harold of the first cantos. Moreover, they are fearless, lawless and wildly passionate, full of culpable desires with an admixture of feelings of remorse or vengeance. Critics have found it easy to show how this kind of hero, while having literary ancestors (for example, Prometheus, who fascinated the child Byron), has his roots in the very character of Byron and in his experiences. The psychologist, familiar with the study of personality through the intermediary of works of the imagination, will come to the same conclusion and will see in the above characters a reflection of Byron's own psychology, especially his paranoic syndrome as typical as that of Don Quixote or Emma Bovary.

Byron's TEMPERAMENT is above all Nervous (irregularity, speed, jerkiness) and Sanguine (exaggerations, flying strokes). The Bilious element comes next (angular, spasms and sustained slant). There is a Lymphatic touch (imprecisions).

We are therefore dealing with a *Nervous-Sanguine* type, with pretty well all the characteristics that are conferred by this relatively rare alliance between opposing temperaments : anxiety, enthusiasm coexisting with a critical sense, need for interchange and for solitude and finally subjectiveness with a note of intransigence.

A *Bilious* nature overlays these contrasts, gives energy and daring, without however bringing complete self-control. The whole make-up would be terrible, were it not softened by a touch of *Lymphatic* dreaminess and whimsy.

MYTHOLOGICAL TYPES shed light on the personality.

Naturally, *Mars* dominates the picture because of the energy, the cruciform movements and the spasms, already interpreted as the sign of an impulsiveness capable of exaggeration and spite. It is noteworthy that Byron's military vocation was apparent in childhood. In Aberdeen he was interested in the wars of antiquity and dreamt of raising a regiment of black knights on black horses, named Byron's Blacks whose deeds would be world famous. He was never happier than in Cephalonia in 1823 where he lived the simple, rough life of a soldier.

The Mars type, as has been seen, is modified by the unevennesses and occasional signs of a low vitality, constituting with the other mythological types the basis for numerous possibilities of orientation which show the powerful adaptability of this typology.

The strongest types, after Mars, are Sun, Mercury and Moon. *Sun* appears in the superelevations : desire to exalt the self and give orders, dignity and even arrogance. The aeration in the writing extends this, suggesting a global perception. The combination of Mars-Sun, noticeable in particular in the high arcades of the signature, correspond to a haughty and intransigent nature.

Mercury appears in the combinations and irregularity of continuity, the speed and sharp-pointedness. This shows quick understanding, an exacerbated critical sense and a streak of satire. Relevant also are both the smallness of the middle zone and the jerky movements : the dissatisfaction of a disappointed cynic. The combination Sun-Mercury supplies the verve of expression.

Moon is present in the significant white spaces, the breaks in continuity and in the shape of some accents. It adds a note of receptivity and aesthetic feeling, and shows a deep and vulnerable sensitivity behind the facade of Mars. To sum up, the association Sun-Moon is typical of poetic intuition, the expression of which will be brilliant (Mercury), but aggressive (Mars). The combination Mars-Moon is, by the way, characteristic of explorers and famous travellers.

Saturn, Jupiter and Earth are present to some degree. *Jupiter* appears in the exaggerated upper extensions and signature : pride and concern with appearances. It is related to the solar elements (personal desire to rise in the world). Mars, Sun and Jupiter produce exaltation and the wish to be in control ... and this with somebody who controls himself only with difficulty.

Sober, angular and "black" writing indicates *Saturn*. There is a dark, taciturn and vindictive fire, fanned by Mars. We recognise the metaphysical pessimism of Byron who was brought up with the Calvinistic doctrine of predestination. The ascetic side of his nature is evident from the strict dieting he imposed on himself to combat obesity.

Earth appears with its banal forms, occasionally rustic and crude, close to those of Mars. This pragmatic element counterbalances the exaltation of Sun-Jupiter. As Dr. Corman has underlined, the partnership Sun-Earth means creativity.

In this extremely rich compound, only *Venus* is *lacking*. The writing is angular, sober, with trenchant and sometimes blurred strokes, with no concern for neatness. This shows little tact or friendly adaptation. We should not be surprised to learn that Byron was capable of extreme boorishness, especially towards women (Mars-Saturn-Earth).

*

From the ANALYTIC point of view, the *libido* is strong (large, homogeneous, angular, well-nourished writing), but one must take into account the uneven lower extensions, ends of lines that go down and deviations in pressure, all of which indicate a certain basic fragility. *Extraversion* (right-slanted, prolonged, rapid, with flying strokes, signature to the right) much more than introversion, nearly touches hysteria (exaggeration).

The *Jungian functions* are *all strong, but not harmonised* : *Sensation* seen in the stroke, the basic stability of the rhythm and the banal forms : *Thinking* in the simplifications, combinations and sharp points, *Sentiment* in the width and the "pathos"; *Intuition* in the grouped, irregular writing. The writing could be labelled an introverted Sensation type, with a strong Thinking auxiliary function.

This judgement conforms with the biography and literary criticism. Byron, unlike other English romantic poets, led a worldly existence. He loved life and had an acute awareness of reality. At the beginning of *Childe Harold* he states that his literary method will be experimental and will take public reaction into account. His poetry abounds in exact descriptions and his accounts of travel (notably in Albania) have the ring of well-documented reporting. In Greece, Byron knew how to make a sober judgement of men and his strategy was objective. One understands his literary enmity for Keats whose type was introverted Intuition Sentiment, therefore his complete contrary. Byron spoke of him without indulgence and sometimes in unrepeatable language. Keats, for his part said less truculently of Byron that he "describes what he sees", whereas "I describe what I imagine - mine is the harder task", Finally, Byron's Intuition, although strong, presents certain characteristics that Janet would say were of an inferior function. He was superstitious (number 13, etc.), was interested in coincidences (dates, initials) and in predictions and was something of a fetishist. In a word, he lacked true spirituality.

It must be understood that Byron, with his four strong but disharmonic functions, was forever a contradiction, living now one way, now the other. The descriptions, *disharmonic* (Regis) and *Nervous* (Le Senne), dissatisfied and unsettled, express this. Byron did not exaggerate when he said, "If I know myself, I must say that I have no character [...] am so volatile that I am everything at the passing moment and nothing permanently. I am such a mixture of good and evil that it would be hard to describe me"[*].

This sequence of contrasts expresses, in SZONDIAN terms, the characteristics of the *Fugitive Ego* A_2C (*Sch* = *k*+/- *p*-). The "pulsional dangers" that Szondi warns of in this profile of the Ego - the impulse to kill or to flee in order not to kill the loved or hated object, the Oedipian, childish Cain, these surely describe Byron's "Shadow".

In the handwriting, the ambivalent reaction *k*+/- is visible in the unevenness of the middle zone and in the vigorous but careless forms. The charged *p* factor corresponds to animated writing and the general tendency to narrowing evokes, typically, the reaction *p*-.

In life, as well as in literary work, the reaction *k*+/- (desire to detach oneself) shows itself in the passion for freedom and the hatred of tyrants. The reaction *p*- (whilst *p*+[2] is much more widespread with poets) corresponds in poetical work to the fact that Byron often expresses himself, not directly, but through the intermediary of a narrator, of characters on whom he projects himself, without being really conscious of it[3]. More generally, this reaction *p*- entails a definite immaturity of the Ego. Byron lived his passion for freedom (*k*+/-) as a flight from moral and social

---

(*) *Translator's Note* : These lines have been retranslated from the French, the original English text having been undiscovered. The reader is asked to pardon their relative inexactness.

(2) High hopes and their verbal expression. Most poets have a *p*+ reaction, while the *p*- reaction is found among painters and sculptors.

(3) Byron insisted that *Childe Harold* was *only* "a *fictitious character* [...] introduced for the sake of giving some connection to the piece [...]. Harold is the *child of imagination*".

constraints, from stable situations, as an escape into action, whereas with Schiller - another *k+/-* poet, but with a *p+* reaction and a mature Ego ("The Self seeking an ideal" B_2D) - this passion takes on an idealistic aspect and expresses itself directly, with the demands of a strong and structured ethic.

The *general appearance* of the writing is marked by the reactions *hy+* (predominance of movement over form, exaggerations), *p-* (animated, squeezed writing) and *d+* (connected writing with form sacrificed to speed).

In the *Paroxysmal* vector the reaction *hy+* is obvious. There is a predominance of movement over form, exaggerations, the Nervous-Sanguine temperament, all indicative of the desire to be noticed. In the *e* factor there is both an *e+* reaction (heavy, clinging stroke, sustained rhythm and slant) and an *e-* reaction (angles, sharp strokes and some tangling, negative Mars and Bilious). As a result, there is contrasting behaviour: enthusiasm and criticism, constructiveness and revolt, an attempt at self-control and debauchery.

Apparent also is the co-existence of two sub-profiles *e+hy+* and *e-hy+* :

a) The sub-profile *e+hy+* (resolute writing, but exaggerated, irregular and animated) expresses a considerable emotional upsurge ("a storm of feeling"). A certain capacity for generosity results from the conjunction of the *e+* tonicity (strength of the stroke) and of the desire to please *hy+* (large, superelevated writing), but there is a danger of the theatrical, since the Ego is immature (*hy+* : attracting attention, striving after effect).

b) The other sub-profile *e-hy+* is that of the "Cain-like leader". Aggressive and malicious revolt (slant, needle-points, heavy stroke and congestions : *e-*) is spectacularly manifested (large, exaggerated writing : *hy+*) as is the desire to come first (superelevated writing).

The profile *e+/- hy+* can also be interpreted as the presence of aggressive tension (*e-*) in a haughty person (*e+hy+*), the display of the conflict that sets off the ambivalent reaction *e+/-* (ending with *e0 hy+* : the desire to be noticed).

The profile of the *Sexual* pulsion is typically *h- s+/-*. The ambivalence *s+/-* results from the co-existence of signs of creative activity (*s+*) (writing of above average vitality, Pophalian tension IVa, right slant, needle-points) and of anxious "giving up" *s-* (diminishing and threads, the Nervous-Bilious side of the temperament). The reaction *h-* adds a note of ruthlessness (thin, angular, simplified writing with a dry stroke).

Here also the vectorial profile can be looked upon as made up by two sub-profiles uniting :

a) The sub-profile *h-s+* confers a macho element with a fear of defeat, a concentration of strength upon a clearly defined action (wide, angular, resolute, with a regular right slant) - these signs are accompanied by violence (charged *e*) and exhibitionism (*hy+*), because of the immature Ego.

b) The sub-profile *h-s-* tempers aggression (signs of sensitivity, hesitation, anxiety) and adds a note of humanity, although it is not really sublimation because of the indifferent quality of the stroke and of the presence of many complexes (disharmonious rhythm, over-compensated inferiority complex, sexual complexes, anality).

One must conclude that there is a considerable amount of practised and preoccupying sado-masochism (masochistic dependence and sadistic aggression).

In collaboration with Fanchette Lefebure, I have written the following lines [4] on the subject of the profile *h- s+/-* and they apply here precisely :

> The many-sided sadistic reaction (*s+/-*) is deeply felt because the subject has got to the stage of repressing (*h-*) individual tenderness.
>
> The crisis of insecurity can therefore be much more violent, the

(4) *Dynamique des pulsions. Introduction aux pulsions de Szondi. Leur expression dans l'écriture,* Mont-Blanc, Geneva, 1980, p.130; 2nd édition, Masson, Paris, 1990, p.124.

subject being no longer able to resolve it by looking for a genuinely affectionate support (choice of a partner to whom he can be really attached).

A deep affective shock is very often the basis of this reaction. It arises from a parental, conjugal or loving context..., and the subject, his tenderness wounded (*h*-), and his behaviour undecided (*s*+/-), finds himself in a situation which he wants and does not want to escape from.

He can attempt to find a truly human solution, if his personal make-up lets him transform his aggressivity (*s*+) without repressing it, thus tending towards the solution *h-s-*, but this transformation, as has been seen, requires not only a strong Ego, but also a solid ethic permitting the regaining of the lost security.

This is very hard. The most frequent solution is instead a violent reaction, which has the merit of getting a momentary relief, without, however, solving the underlying problem.

Finally, in the *Contact* vector the accentuated *d*+ reaction (connected, accelerated, form, neglected for the sake of speed) is associated with a non-reaction of the *m* factor (*m*0 : lack of orality), visible in the comfortable stroke, in the reduction of tension IVa to IVb (angle becoming a thread, narrowing of letters, small crossings-out and a disturbance in the stroke), in the imprecise forms and in the dryness of the stroke. In terms of behaviour, there is a considerable agitated search for new objects (large, right-slanted, rapid and invading writing), but without the ability really to "latch on" to them (instability of size and tension). From this we deduce dissatisfaction and feelings of non-fulfilment, avidity and protest (Szondi's depressive contact). The association with the fugitive Ego accentuates the tendency to dispersion, the reaction *p*- aggravating the feeling of protest. The strong positive charge of the factor *hy* brings a compensatory note of erotic disturbance.

*

When dealing with Byron, the topic arises of a 'mixed' NEUROSIS with *obsessional* signs ("anality" of the stroke, rigidity and monotonous right slant) and *hysterical* signs (exaggerations, threadlike tendencies). This suggests, on the one hand, a propensity toward fixed ideas and anxiety, and on the other, a love of the theatrical. The study of COMPLEXES will clarify this.

There are many. In the foreground is a huge, overcompensated *inferiority complex* (superelevations, enlarged signature, centripetal strokes, Mercury with Saturn). One known cause was the club foot that made Byron limp and needed painful medical care. Would there be a direct graphological expression of this in the irregular lower extensions which are sometimes "atrophied"? Such a conclusion would be premature before a thorough study of the association between physical characteristics and writing has been made. It is safer to limit oneself to the psychological aspects of the complex, as learnt from biographers.

His inferiority was well compensated for on the physical side, because Byron learnt to fence and to box and crowned his swimming career by crossing the Hellespont. He was ambitious, dreamt of greatness, identifying himself with Napoleon. With this Lord who was very proud of his title (*Persona*) the complex took a *theatrical* form (visible in the handwriting by the signs of hysteria and narcissism), with the desire to astonish others or just attract attention. In his youth, Byron took part in amateur theatricals, and when still a student and under age, he borrowed a horse and chaise. Among his other eccentricities he had a tame bear at Cambridge. When Byron was sulking shamefully in a house to which he had been invited, his friend, Hobhouse, explained to the host that he would continue his behaviour while attention was being paid to him. This has been called the Byronic "pose", which can be looked upon either as a neurosis or a fundamental character trait.

This theatrical complex, as Ch. Baudouin has insisted, is close to *narcissism* (free writing with centripetal strokes and enlarged signature). *Manfred* is the Tragedy of a man who cannot come out of himself and for whom hell is an interior drama (guilt, narcissism and inferior introversion).

Anality is nearly as distinct as the inferiority complex (character of the stroke, angularity, exaggerated and pointed *t*-bars, monotonous right slant, Mars and Saturn types with

Venus lacking). Most of the corresponding character traits are present.

Byron was often tight-fisted. In Venice, when he was rich and behaved generously from time to time, he skimped on the day-to-day running of his home, checking meticulously the expenses of his servant and filling a money-box with minor savings. Byron's sado-masochism and its literary counterpart, "Satanism", are too well known to be treated here. Some childhood details are however worth recalling. At an early age he was fascinated both by the story of Cain (about whom he was to write in 1821) and by the Devil, a prominent feature in his Protestant education. In prep-school he was deeply affected by a novel by Moore and was haunted by the fear of imitating its hero who had killed his pet sparrow and later strangled his own child. Byron's appetite for domination and, more generally, his paranoic syndrome are also connected with his anal complex.

Sexual complexes are to be seen in the writing, which is congested, irregular, spasmodic, by turn firm or slack and with uneven lower extensions. We have already seen how the early awakening of Byron's sexuality was strong, but disordered. The graphologist will consider the probability of homosexual anomalies in the discordances of pressure, the intense anality and narcissism and finally in the existence of a paranoic syndrome, which is often associated with homosexual tendencies, as Freud and his disciples, Ferenczi and Stekel, have shown.

This point is confirmed by historians who note the constancy with which Byron protected boys younger than himself, his passionate and tormented friendships, some of which were long-lasting. This unsociable man loved living with his friend, Hobhouse, who came to him in Switzerland and Venice. His fear of women is relevant. At one time he would count up to seven before being introduced to one. His marriage was a drama. He put it off from week to week and finally from day to day. It was in order to flee from women that he used to leave England; when he was twenty one it was to avoid his mother and the married Mary Chaworth and in 1816 it was to escape from his wife.

This brings us to say a few words about Byron's *relationship with his mother*. His parents lived separated in Aberdeen and quarrelled violently when they met. When young George was scarcely two, his father left for France where he committed suicide. So the mother played an all-important role in forming the character of her only son. Biographers describe her as a mean, courageous, irascible Scot, alternately tender or rough. She adopted the motto "Je ne change qu'en mourant". Her handwriting (fig. 1.7) is astonishingly similar to her son's with a like mythological picture (Mars, Saturn, Earth, with Venus deficient) and with the same dominant complexes, but without the superiority. Here we have a fine example of *identification.* We have known, since Freud, that identification is always ambivalent. Contemporaries noticed how much Byron hated the 'dowager', avoiding her from his fifteenth year, but also how much he imitated her, modelling his behaviour on hers.

This identification deserves a closer look. It lies behind many facets of Byron's personality, namely his attitude towards women, his mixed feelings for England, and lastly his attitude towards nature, which he never considered to be benevolent, as did Wordsworth or Shelley. Confirmation would be found there of the Oedipian origin of his passion for his half-sister Augusta. Rank maintained this as did, with reservations, Ch. Baudouin. This thesis is confirmed by several historical details. According to all the biographies, Augusta pandered to Byron's self-love, gave in to all his wishes and while she was with him protected him, as Leslie Marchand wrote, like a *motherly elder sister.*

Anima is powerful, but unconscious and hidden, because the poet is almost ashamed of his sensitivity (angular, simplified and resolute writing) which is intense (irregularities, lack of proportion). In the last period of his life his handwriting seems to indicate the beginnings of integration or at least an acceptance of the Anima.

*

Literary critics have studied the EVOLUTION of the themes in Byron's poetry. After *Hebrew Melodies,* they broadened, ceasing to be negative, praising the indestructible human mind, the creative power of love and personal and national freedom. It would be interesting to study at the same time Byron's psychological evolution and to ascertain how after the crisis of

1816 and the cathartic third canto of *Childe Harold* and *Manfred*, Byron matured while remaining true to himself.

The handwriting reveals little on this subject, his evolution between the ages of eighteen and thirty-six being less striking than with many other writers. Most of the characteristics of fig. 1.1 pointed to the end. All the same, fig. 1.6 shows a break, in the sense of greater harmony, the writing being aerated and softened. It is true that the document was written in a period of great exhaustion (ten days after an attack of a kind of epilepsy, witness the blurred stroke). But it is likely that this harmony had a deeper cause, although to be certain, other writings from 1823 would need inspection, but are unavailable. The expedition to Greece was a great step towards the integration of a hitherto immature personality, bringing together the major tendencies Mars, Moon and Sun, the start of the integration of the Anima and the union of ideal and action.

Other poets, notably his admirers Lamartine and Mickiewicz, felt this and said so. Besides, there is confirmation from Byron himself. "I feel as if the eleven long years of bitterness I have passed through since I was here, have been taken off my shoulders". A critic has pointed out that the start of the bitterness was not the separation in 1816, but really the success in 1812 of *Childe Harold.* When near to death in Missolonghi, Byron said to Peter Gamba : "There are things which make the world dear to me (Io lascio qualche cosa de caro nel mondo), for the rest, I am content to die". He spoke also of Greece, saying, "I have given her my time, my means, my health and now I give her my life! - what more could I do?"

*

Byron was not responsible for his heredity, for his lameness, nor for his mother's character or the fact that his father abandoned them, nor for his social position in the England of the time. So his personality took shape painfully and irreversibly. What did he make of the margin of liberty that the determinism of temperament and education leaves to every human? That is how he must be judged. It is only then that in reply to the questions brought up at the beginning, that his tragic greatness will be perceived and there will be no temptation to accuse of insincere posturing, a man whose handwriting reveals his constant faithfulness to himself, a man who fought for a great cause and gave his life for it.

*

BIBLIOGRAPHY

Jean-Hippolyte MICHON, *Système de graphologie. L'art de connaître les hommes d'après leur écriture.* (1875), 4th edition, *La Graphologie*, 1878, 323p : see pp.160, 203-204, 216, 272, (123, 153, 161, 204). The numbers in brackets refer to the pages of the edition of 1944, published by Payot, 234p.
- Intuitiveness and deductivity (letters juxtaposed in connected writing), disdain (signs of ill-will, hardness) and bitterness (varying slant, strange forms), mistrust ("legal flourish"), anger (ascending bars).

Rosa BAUGHAN, *Character Indicated by Handwriting. A practical treatise in support of the assertion that the handwriting of a person is an infallible guide to his character, with illustrations taken from autographic letters of statesmen, lawyers, soldiers, ecclesiastics, authors poets, musicians, actors and other persons*, 2nd ed., Upton Gill, London 1886, 139p : see pp.107, 115-116, (By.)
- Signature analysed, remarkably profound for the time. Careful character (dot after the name), changeable moods (varying signature). Passionate tenderness (slant) stands out above other signs, forgetfulness of self (no paraph), idealism (no join between *r* and *o*). Ardent temperament (soaring finals), imagination (capitals).

Henry FRITH, *How to Read Character in Handwriting, or, the Grammar of Graphology described and illustrated*, Ward and Lork, London, 1890, 138p : see p.134.
- Byron, literary man with impulsive imagination (illegibility).

I.F. MORGENSHTERN, *Psikho-Grafologiia ili nauka ob opredelenii vnutrenniago mira cheloveka po iego pocherku* (Psychographology, or the science of determining a man's inner life from his handwriting), Neierman, St. Petersburg, 1903, 593p : see p. 478.
- "A gifted artist. Suffers unconsciously from his vacillating will.

Prudence joined to great strength. Good natured, sociable, open. Fertile imagination. Believes in predestination and fatalism".

Magdalene THUMM-KINTZEL, *Der pychologische und pathologische Wert der Handschrift*, Paul List, Leipzig. 1904, 208p.
- Combined (*re*print, p.49) : mental power. Aesthetic double curve (*m* p.52, *h* p.57, *y* p.58) : aesthetic sense. Curved connections (*q* p.80) : humour. Right-turning connections (*And* p.87) : wit. Predominance of abductive strokes, tall writing with concave strokes facing right (*r* p.104) : good humour. Signature right-slanted (p.142) : warmth of feeling. Irregular slant (p.155) : violent, irascible nature.

Magdalene KINTZEL-THUMM (IVANOVIC) *Der pychologische und pathologische Wert der Handschrift*, Fowler and Wells, New York, 1905, 149p : see pp.36, 39, 40, 43.
- Signs of intelligence, curve of an artistic gift.

Herbert GERSTNER *Schule der Graphologie,* Felsenverlag, Buchenwald-Baden, 1922, 142p : see p.80.
- Heavy, right-slanted writing.

Robert SAUDEK, *The Psychology of Handwriting*, Allen and Unwin, London, 1925, 2nd ed., 1954, 288p : see pp.42-43, 57.

Robert SAUDEK, *Wissenschaftliche Graphologie,* Drei Masken Verlag, Munich, 1926, 347p : see pp.47-48.
- Byron's pasty writing: sensuality.

G.-E. MAGNAT, *Poésie de l'écriture*, Sack, Geneva, 1944, 108p : see p.89.
- Byron's handwriting, as wilful as that of Chateaubriand.

Broder CHRISTIANSEN and Elisabeth CARNAP, *Lehrbuch der Handschriftendeutung*, 2nd edition, Reclam, Stuttgart, 1947, 192p : see p.175.
- Sensuality (pasty), but torment and depression (fall in direction). "Outward drive" on *j*'s and *t*'s : the expedition to Greece was not merely an adventure, but made an ideal into a reality.

Huntington HARTFORD, *You are What you Write*, Peter Owen, London, 1973, 380p : see p.106.
- Contrary to Saudek, Byron's writing is not pasty (sensuality), but neat and clean, with the ebb and flow of a strong rhythm, with accidents here and there. Byron may have been sensual, but it is hard to deny him the title of the greatest Romantic of his time.

Eva DIETRICH, *Astro-Graphologie. Der neue Schlüssel zur Charakterdeutung und Selbsterkenntnis. Was die Synthese von Sternbild und Schriftbild über Wesen und Schicksal des Menschen verrät,* of which certain copies are headed, *Schicksal und Lebenserfolg in Sternbild und Schrift : was Sterne und Handschrift gemeinsam über Charakter und Chancen, Herkunft und Zukunft eines Menschen verraten; ein neuer Weg, andere und sich selbst zu beurteilen und zu verstehen,* Scherz, Berne and Munich, 1978, 308p : see p.115.
- Irregular writing : enthusiasm, impatience with restraints; lived an exceptionally agitated life; Aquarius.

Marie BERNARD, *The Art of Graphology,* Whitston Publishing Co., Troy (New York), 1985, 416p : see p.243.
- Reared signature : struggle against society, disappointment.

Dr. Jean RIVÈRE. *Le monde de l'écriture,* Gonon, Neuilly-sur-Seine, 1958, 294p : see p.34.
- The *B* in Byron, referred to without commentary.

Augusto VELS, *La selección de personal y el problema humano en las empressas,* Luis Miracle, Barcelona, 1970, 564p. Translated into French : *La Sélection du personnel et le problème humain dans les entreprises,* ed. Mont-Blanc, Geneva, 1973, 444p : see p.147.
- Writing connected, right-slanted and pasty: appetite for contact, adherence to and union with the object, rooted in the appetites of the senses and the body (sensual and sexual excitability).

Suzanne BRESARD, "Intuition Imagination", *La Graphologie* no.118, pp.39-43, April 1970.
- Quotes four lines of writing with the heading "Byron's Intuition".

* Dr. J.-Ch. GILLE-MAISANI[5], "A propos de l'écriture de Byron", *La Graphologie* no.121 : pp.74-85, January 1971.
- First draft of the present chapter with some minor differences.

F. LEFEBURE and Dr. J.-Ch. GILLE, *Introduction à la psychologie du Moi. Les seize profils du Moi de Szondi et leur expression dans l'écritures,* Mont-Blanc, Geneva, 1976, 159p: see pp.103-108.
- Byron, probably the fugitive Ego. 3rd ed., *Graphologie et Test de Szondi. Volume 1 : Le Moi,* Masson, Paris, 1990, 182p.

(5) An asterisk means a complete graphological analysis, as opposed to remarks limited to a few writing peculiarities or some character traits.

Dr. J.-Ch. GILLE-MAISANI, *Psychologie de l'écriture. Suite à L'ABC de la graphologie*, Payot, 1978; 4th edition, 244p - Ch.8, 15 .
- The disharmonic rhythm of Byron's writing. The blurred writing in Missolonghi.
In English : *The Psychology of Handwriting*, Scriptor Books, 1992, 462pp : see pp.62-63, 118.

Dr. J.-Ch. GILLE-MAISANI, "Il test di Szondi", *Il gesto creativo. Studi grafologici*, no.1/2, 11-16, 1985-1986, see pp.15, 18, 25.
- Profile of the Ego *k+/- p+* (emphatic middle zone, constructed rhythmic forms, strongly paranoic).

Marie BERNARD, *Graphologie. Eine Einführung mit 800 Beispielen*, Sphinx-Verlag, Basle, 1990, 329p : see pp.202-203.
- Reared signature : the writer destroys what he has created.

Marie BERNARD, *Sexual Deviations as seen in Handwriting.* Whitston Press, Troy (New York), 1990, 408p : see pp.151-153.
- In an address written at the age of twenty-nine, the boundless will for conquest is apparent (explosive, straight-lined, simplified writing), as is a talent for satire (sharp-pointed *t*-bars). Deceit appears in the backward stroke in the signature.

Guiseppe COSCO, *Dimmi come scrivi e ti dirò chi sei (Manuale pratico dei grafologia)*, Sarva, Imola, 1991, 127p : see p.82.
- Byron's signature reproduced (smaller), but not commented on.

Dr. J.-Ch. GILLE-MAISANI, "The Planetary Types in Handwriting", *Graphology* no.15, pp.4-36, 1991 : see pp.24-25.
- An analysis of Byron's writing from the viewpoint of the mythological types : first Mars, then Sun, Mercury and Moon; deficiency of Venus.

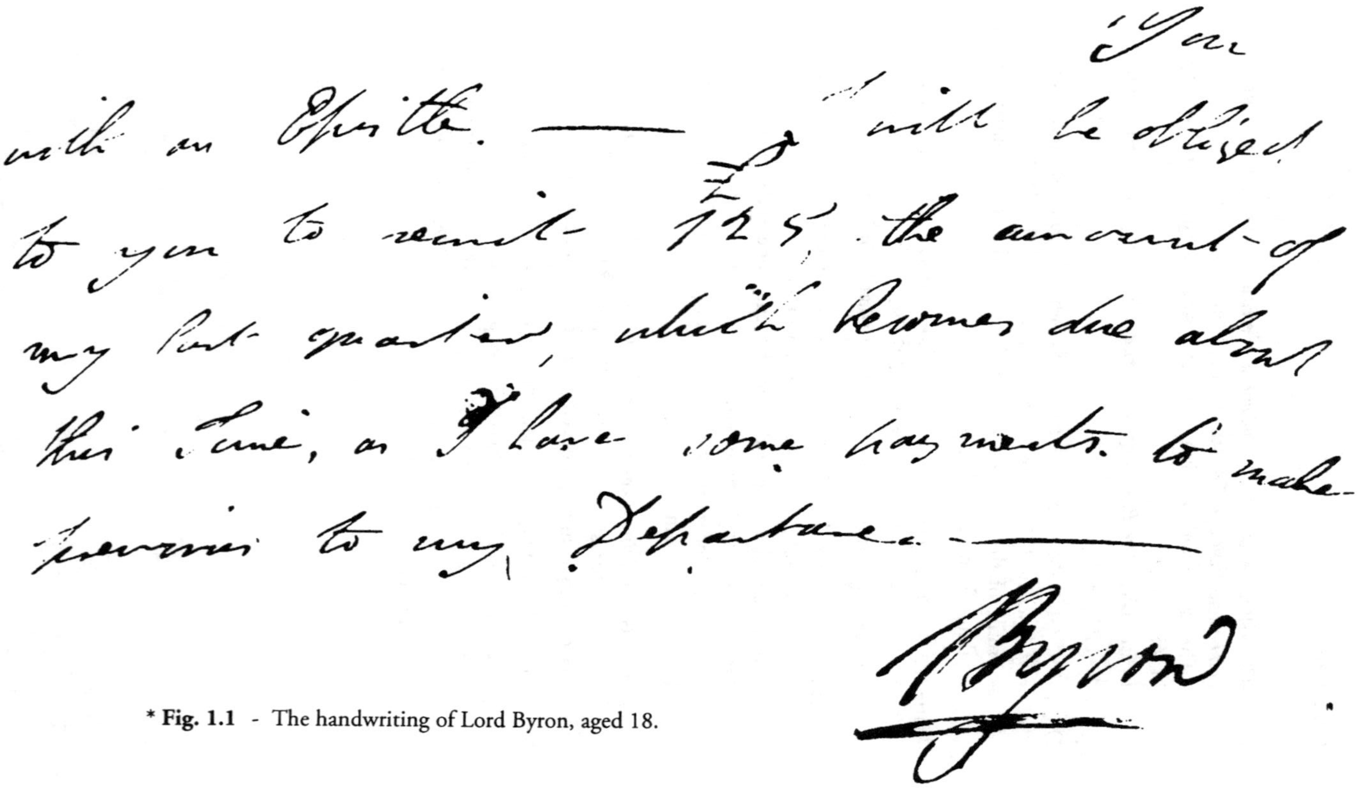

You

with an Epistle. —— I will be obliged to you to remit £125. the amount of my last quarter, which becomes due about this time, as I have some payments to make previous to my Departure. ——

Byron

* **Fig. 1.1** - The handwriting of Lord Byron, aged 18.

* **Fig. 1.2** - Byron, aged nearly 18 and 21 respectively.

to state that in the published copies there
are additions to the tune of 300 lines
or so towards the end — & if revised
it should not be from the previously
printed copy — So much for scribbling. —
I shall manage to see you somewhere

* **Fig. 1.3** - Byron, aged 25.

* **Fig. 1.4** - Byron, aged 29.

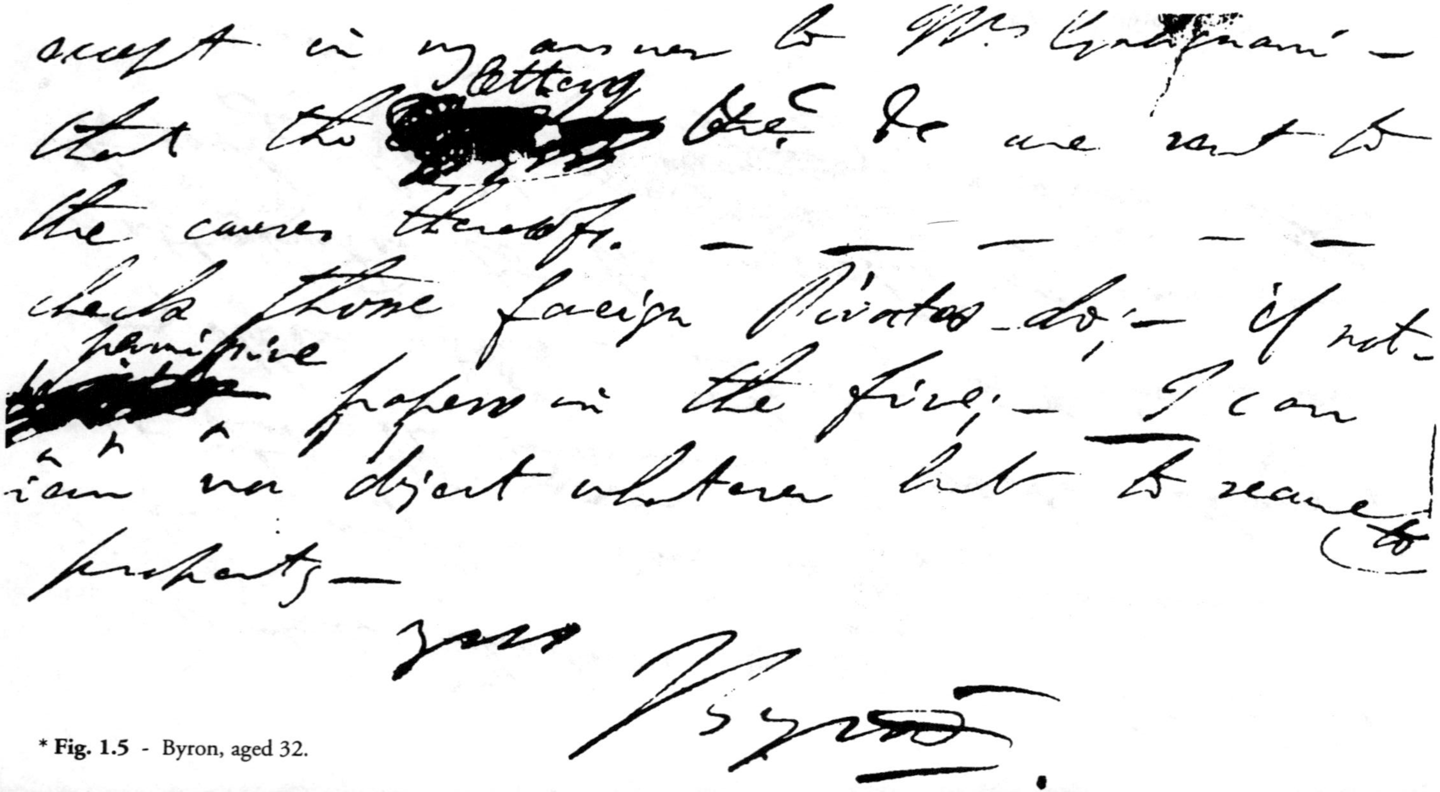

* **Fig. 1.5** - Byron, aged 32.

Officers buried — and Capt. Parry's Ar=
=tillery mutinied under pre=
=tence that their lives were in danger
and are for quitting the country —
they may. — On Saturday we had
the smartest shock of an earthquake
which I remember (and I have felt
thirty slight or smart at different periods
the are [illegible]

* **Fig. 1.6** - Byron, aged 36.

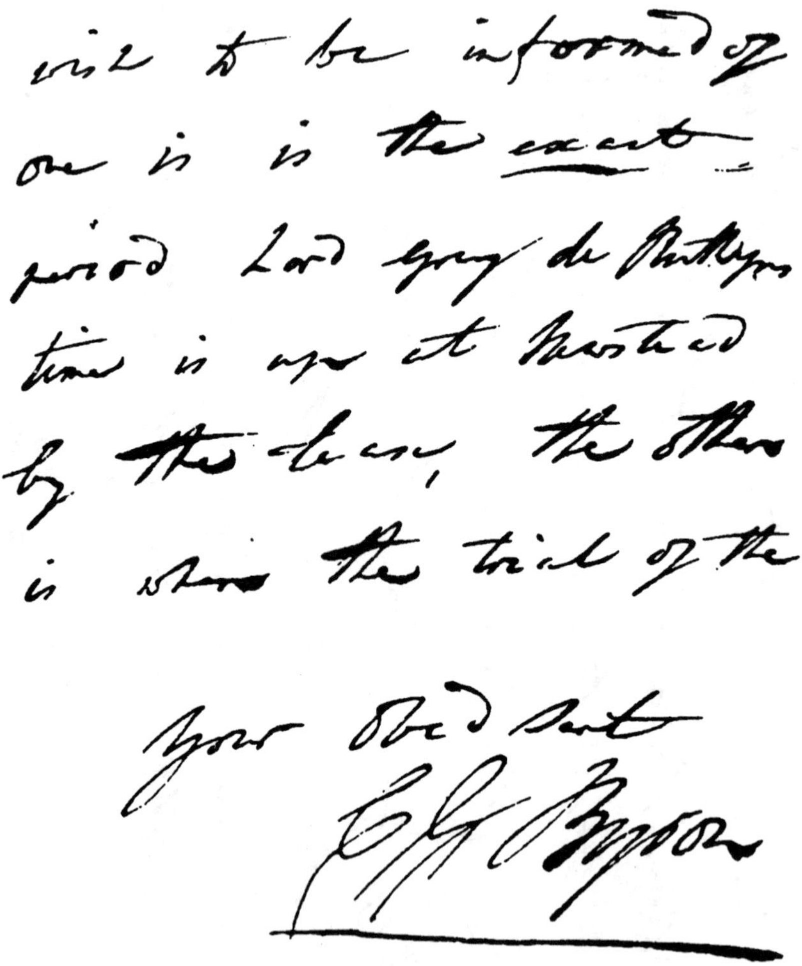

wish to be informed of
one is is the exact
period Lord Grey de Ruthyn's
time is up at Newstead
by the lease, the other
is when the trial of the

Your Obed Servt
C G Byron

* **Fig. 1.7** - Lady Byron, the poet's mother.

2

John KEATS
(1795 - 1821)

Keats is the most modern of the English Romantics.

Son of a stableman who married his employer's daughter, John was born prematurely. He was always small of stature. The eldest of four brothers, he was a normal, sane, combative child. His mother, widowed in 1804, remarried quickly and died in 1810, probably of consumption.

John began to study surgery, but gave up (1816) to devote himself to poetry.

From then on the story of his life is that of his poetical works (two long poems : *Endymion, Hyperion* and a great number of shorter pieces, notably his famous *Odes,* on his love for Fanny Brawne to whom he became engaged (January, 1819) - and of his tuberculosis which, after taking the life of his brother, Tom, in 1816, struck down John in his twenty-sixth year....

Keats, unlike most Romantics, was neither a lyricist, nor a teller of tales, nor a descriptive poet. In some way, he distils the present moment, savouring its resonance within him. Attracted by the temptation of death and melancholy, he escapes by projecting the here and now onto the background of eternity, looking for Beauty itself. The opening line of *Endymion* is well-known :

"A thing of beauty is a joy for ever",

as also is the end of the *Ode on a Grecian Urn* :

"Beauty is truth, truth beauty - that is all
Ye know on earth, and all ye need to know".

Like all innovators, he was judged varyingly by his contemporaries and he was "discovered" in the middle of the last century by the Pre-Raphaelites. In the twentieth century, he is by far the most read English Romantic poet and most studied by literary critics. Psychologists should read the book *The Nightingale and the Hawk. A psychological study of Keats's Ode* by Katherine M. Wilson (Allen and Unwin, 1964), which points out that "a fantastic correspondence exists between Keats and aspects of Jungian psychology. Jung can be elucidated in terms of Keats, and Keats in terms of Jung." The book studies the evolution of Keats between 1817 and 1820 from the angle of Jungian psychology.

*

It is moving to follow the variations in the handwriting of Keats, as seen in the abundant collection of letters preserved in the British Museum. Examples 2.1 to 2.5 date from each year between 1816 and 1820 inclusively. We will first look at the poet's "average" writing and then briefly comment on its evolution.

ORIENTATING SYNTHESES :

The writing is *evolved* with a few personal strokes (*g, yo, Jo, q*); *harmonious* (despite some exaggerated irregularities in direction and a few tangles) with quite a high Formlevel.

Tension is not very strong : III in examples 2.1 and 2.2, then later III-II; with some discreet IVb strokes (mistakes, a few distortions). It is the *relaxed* writing of Christiansen-Carnap (elastic, velvety stroke, rounded, regular, natural forms, tension II).

Movement creates the form; the rhythmic use of space is harmonious (notice the spacing, the exterior letters, the slant). The *rhythm*, never very strong, is sometimes slightly upset (irregularity of the slant in 1816; in all the examples there is narrowing in certain letters like *f, J, I*). The rhythm has become regular by 1820 (nearly static in figure 2.5).

First level of DEFINITION :

Notably it is *ample* and *compact* (some *tangling*).

Clear; *enriched* (figs. 2.1, 2.2), then *simple* (figs. 2.3 to 2.5).

Garlanded with *double curved* joins.

Velvety; some *blurred* strokes.

Direction is very *irregular* (now concave, now convex); so are the height (diminishing, some enlarging) and the width (some squeezing); the same with continuity and speed (*connected*, with logical breaks and finals held back and sometimes centripetal).

Graceful strokes (the "lyrical *d*", cup-like lower exten-sions), *superelevated* and *ornate* capitals.

FREE MOVEMENTS :

Dot over the *i* : placed very high and carefully.

T-bars : irregular in height, length and direction; usually long, starting before the letter, light, rising, sharp-pointed; sometimes neglected, missing.

Signature : simple, similar to the text (taller in figs.2.2 and 2.3), followed by a dash.

*

The stroke is most expressive. Rhythmic pressure, which masses the ink in certain downstrokes and horizontal strokes (without becoming spindled) and lightens it on the upstrokes, reveals the man who lives simultaneously on two levels, passing continually from a concern with reality to a state of meditation.

The strength of pressure bears witness to the intensity of emotion. The velvety quality of the stroke and its blurring correspond respectively to great sensorial receptivity and to a poor state of health.

The stroke confirms *receptivity* to sense impressions (garlands, cup shapes, velvety stroke), to imagination and to an interior life (fullness of the middle zone, certain upper extensions and capitals, regressive strokes). Keats is "naively" receptive to all this (spontaneous writing, tension II, overfilled layout) and it is there that he finds his guiding light (connected, slightly right-slanted writing, garlands) : the *t*-bars are not imperious; the simple forms are easy to read. A feel for nature and a passion for the beautiful is easily deduced (large, enriched writing and upper extensions, graceful strokes).

The value of this personality lies in its good balance (harmonious writing; fig. 2.5 almost calm). The intelligence, without being original (relatively, commonplace forms), is of a high quality, judgement is mature (simplification, a few combinations, clarity), more sentimental than critical (garlands, ample, tangling). Contact with the world is good (connected, garlanded, spontaneous writing), adequate outgoingness (right-slant, easy finals, open tops), with tact and tolerance (velvety strokes, double curves). In a word, the character is easygoing, predictable and reliable (connected, homogeneous writing : figs. 2.4 and 2.5 are simple).

A touch of anxiety is noticeable, with a frank, but thwarted, ambition (superelevated capitals, ornate and squeezed, and the signature sometimes higher than the text) and a temperament inclined to depressions (writing alternatively convex and concave, varying direction). Moreover, this contemplative man, governed by his interior experience, has a certain uneasiness in his relation with others (spaces between the words, irregular dimension). Finally, one wonders to what degree Keats was able to learn from experience (enlarged finals).

It must be admitted that the poet of genius does not shine through. Sometimes genius appears in handwriting (Beethoven, Berlioz); more often, the graphologist must confess that handwriting is only a part of activity, as G. P. Brabant [(1)] forcefully reminds us. Keats's writing is graphogenic, in the sense that

---

(1) G.P. BRABANT, *L'Ecriture considérée comme un secteur du comportement*, L'évolution graphologique, Paris, 1960, 63p.

the intensity of impressions can be read, as they control feeling without submerging it. One sees that Keats had plenty of heart and behaved like a well-balanced man, but the search for poetic genius is beyond the graphologist's competence.

*

From the TEMPERAMENTAL point of view, Keats is a model example of the *"moist Lymphatic"* (Lymphatic-Sanguine temperament), of which he has all the graphic characteristics (water and air writing; lively, velvety strokes, developed middle zone, clean, dancing curves, rounded, easy and flowing connections which are characterological (sensitive to natural vibrations with youthful freshness; refined, imaginative and contemplative; affectionate, sociable and considerate).

On the second level, a fairly complex element of the *Nervous* (a nuancée writing, irregular in dimension, direction and pressure) : sensitivity, but anxiety, seriousness, an interiorised life, and a proneness to fatigue.

The MYTHOLOGICAL TYPES Jupiter, Moon, Sun and Venus are dominant.

Moon appears typically in the light, blurred upstrokes (delicacy), and in the calm, but nuancée writing (sensitivity behind an apparent aloofness), in the high i-dots and the small imprecisions (reverie, suggestibility), in the soft or missing *t*-bars, and in the rounded connections (moderate activity, gentleness).

Sun is apparent in the tall writing (fervour, thirst for perfection, attraction towards the universal), in a few narrow letters (modesty of feeling). Sun and Moon are nearly always associated in poets' writings .

Venus can be seen in the expansion of the middle zone and in its ovals (importance of everyday emotions) and in the garlands (conciliatoriness, frankness). The letters with lower extensions and nearly all the capitals start in the middle zone.

Jupiter inspires the rounded width of the writing, which is broad without being spread-out (richness of feelings, zeal, spontaneity, desire to communicate), and its easy regularity (patience). The high *i*-dots denote Moon (reverie), Jupiter and Sun (enthusiasm for an ideal).

Saturn is there too (sobriety, sombreness), but the other types are hardly there at all. *Earth* is not there, in spite of the simple, ordered hand and the low connections (he does not stop at prosaic reality); nor *Mercury*, in spite of the nuancée writing and some sharpness (Keats is the opposite of the dry, critical intellectual), nor is *Mars* (double curve, imprecision, gentleness, frequent weakness in the stroke and the t-bars: receptivity, lack of drive).

*

From the SZONDIAN point of view the general look of the writing (fig. 2.3) is ruled by the reactions *k+/-* (forms that are idiosyncratic without dominating the movement, a middle zone noticeable for its well-shaped ovals, but which is irregular in height) *h+* (warm stroke, Anima writing) and *p+* (rhythm, width).

The Ego is therefore an "Ego in search of an ideal" B_2D (*Sch* = *k+/- p+*) : a mature, ardent Ego, but "overburdened" and anxious (rhythm, width).

In the *Paroxysmal* vector the reaction of factor *e* is obviously *e+* because of the stroke, which is well-nourished, clinging and pastose and because of the rhythm, which is sustained, personal and not too fast. The factor *hy* reaction is less easy to determine; there are traces of *hy+* (moiré or variegated stroke, flowing rhythm) on an *hy-* background (simplicity of forms, slight restraint in the rhythm, dominance of Lymphatic temperament). To sum up, the profile of vector *P* is *e+ hy+/-*, as so often with poets : intense feelings (*e+ hy+*) are socialised with simplicity (*hy-*) and goodness (*e+*).

The reactions of the *Sexual* vector are *h*+ and *s*+. The very intense *h*+ is expressed by the pastose, velvety stroke, by the rounded, supple rhythm of the writing, which is almost poised, by the Lymphatic-Sanguine temperament, by the oral components and the strength of the Anima. The resultant *s*+, less strong, is expressed by the slant, by the connections and by the uplift of the lower extensions. The resultant in this harmonious setting, with strikingly expressive strokes, is good sexual equilibrium, with a strong, differentiated sensoriality.

The *Contact* vector reactions are *d*0 and *m*+. The reaction *m*+ (very clear in the signature) is seen in the well-nourished, warm stroke, in the easy, rounded writing, in the garlands, in the spread-out ovals of the middle zone. The reaction *d*0 is probable in this script, the weak tension of which (III to II on the Pophal scale) expresses the liberating of anality. Well-resolved orality can be deduced from this : much openness (connected, slightly right-slanted writing with cup-like lower extensions), non-aggressive relationships (compact, rounded hand), team spirit (developed feeling, prominent middle zone, simplicity).

*

From the JUNGIAN point of view, the signs of extraversion (ease, considerable size) and of introversion (nearly vertical writing, narrow letters, leftward strokes, especially on *d* and lower extensions) cancel out. The predominance of the inner life is accompanied by successful exteriorisation. Keats is something of a relaxed extravert (ability to go along with others, humour, the present moment lived intensely, a feeling for the concrete) and of a relaxed introvert (interior life and reverie both demand expression, his character is conciliatory, rather shy and with a strong sense of modesty over intimate feelings; a love of books and of nature). According to Christiansen-Carnap, the extravert is the poet who tells stories, and the introvert the lyric poet who sings of his emotions.

Two functions, both developed and mature, can claim to be ranked first : *Sentiment* (wide writing, garlands, an emphasis on the middle zone, right slant - but the writing does not give an impression of warmth) and *Intuition* (rather light writing, nuancée and with intuitive simplifications and combinations - but the writing is not rhythmic). *Sensation* is rich, differentiated, but not in command (velvety stroke, uneven pressure, right-tending or light lower extensions, both blurred and static). *Thinking* is of a good quality, but neglected (forms generally commonplace). The hierarchy of the functions offers difficulties if Keats has to be reduced to a formula at all costs. Is he the Sentiment or the Intuitive type? Each of these two views recognises only a part of reality. As a working conclusion, we see a Sentiment type in the man and an Intuition type in the poet.

To see in Keats a *Sentiment* type, with Intuition as an auxiliary function and a high quality Sensation, conforms with his general equilibrium, with his clear and delicate feeling for people and human situations, with the tact that always accompanied his behaviour. His lack of interest in logical thought is typical of a weak Thinking function. In 1817 Keats wrote : "I have never yet been able to perceive how anything can be known for truth by consecutive reasoning". And in *Lamia* :

Do not all charms fly at the mere touch of cold philosophy?

To see in Keats an *Intuition* type explains the essential character of his poetry, which is based on sense impressions (Sensation) but which overtakes them by looking for what lies beyond (Intuition), towards a world of pure, legendary beauty. Sensation plays an essential part in the life and poetry of Keats : he always clings to the world and to present delights. "I scarcely remember counting upon any Happiness - I look not for it if it be not the present hour - nothing startles me beyond the Moment" (1817). His epithets condense surges of emotion, his verses combine the impressions of the different senses. But, unlike a Sensation type, Keats always perceives a halo of meaning; an impression only interests him because of its resonance within him.

This is how Keats states how different he is from Byron : he "describes what he sees", whereas "I describe what I imagine". The following reflection is surely that of an introverted Intuition and Sentiment type : "I am certain of nothing but of the holiness of the heart's affections and the truth of imagination - what the imagination seizes as beauty must be truth - whether it existed before or not". The interest Keats took in his dreams and the dreamlike atmosphere of several of his poems are certainly indicative of an introverted intuitive. Likewise his interest in mythology, with its archetypal themes, where he discovered the most adequate expression of his interior life.

The complexity of Keats explains why different judgements have been passed on him. In conformity with Jung's ideas, K.Wilson sees a character of inferior function in the fact that, with Keats, Sensation is "contaminated" by unconscious representations and unleashes intuitive activity. On the other hand, W.P.Witcutt believes that Keats is an extraverted Sensation type because he indulges in sensory impressions, not realising that the latter simply play the part of a stimulus for intuitive activity [(2)].

The handwriting of Keats is a good example of *Anima* writing: large, wide, rounded, velvety with Intuition and Sentiment predominant. It intensely expresses receptivity to what lies in the unconscious, and fascination with its eternal images.

Keats's Muse had for a long time no living rival to fear. In 1818 he wrote :

"The roaring of the wind is my wife and the stars through the window pane are my children. The mighty abstract idea I have of beauty in all things stifles the more divided and minute domestic happiness (....). I feel more and more every day, as my imagination strengthens, that I do not live in this world alone but in a thousand worlds". A few weeks later, he was engaged to Fanny Brawne.... The sonnet, *On a dream* (April, 1819), ends upon the union of the dreamer and the Anima, more explicitly still in his prose commentary : "The fifth canto of Dante pleases me more and more - it is that one in which he meets with Paulo and Francesca. I had passed many days in rather a low state of mind (....). The dream was one of the most delightful enjoyments I ever had in my life. I floated about the whirling atmosphere as it is described with a beautiful figure to whose lips mine were joined, as it seemed for an age".

---

(2) Appendix to BLAKE, *A psychological study*, Hollis and Carter, London, 1946. With Blake, the relationship of the two 'irrational' functions (perceptive functions) is quite the opposite. Blake starts from internal images that he elaborates, and then expresses in his pictures : the starting-point is in the area of introverted Intuition, and Sensation comes in with the final work. But, with Keats as with Blake, the intuitive function plays the leading role.

It would be interesting to study the pictures of the Anima and their evolution in the poetry of Keats, signposted by the mysterious Indian woman in *Endymion, La Belle Dame sans Merci* and *Lamia*, two poems full of the bipolarity of this archetype. At the same time, one would have to study, from this point of view, the biographical events and evolution of Keat's conception of Poetry.

The harmonious writing of Keats bears witness to a remarkable psychic balance and shows hardly any COMPLEXES.

Except for small signs of anxiety (what writing has none?) and of narcissism (ornate capitals, centripetal movement), the only real complex is a noticeable *inferiority complex* (tall writing, signature higher, initial reinforcement with super-elevated capitals, breaks in the rhythm caused by squeezing, noticeably in the personal pronoun *I* (it has always been thought that for the English, this pronoun is a symbol of the self). It is fitting to remember here that Keats was only five foot tall and suffered greatly because of this. The fact of his shortness cannot be deduced from his writing,[(3)] but his feeling of inferiority must, at the very least, be due to his height. Biographers and critics have not waited for Adler to bring out his theory of overcompensation to collect the allusions and reflections that show how much Keats suffered from being short and to suggest that it was not accident that in *Hyperion*, over which he spent much time, he praised the Titans... . J. H. Murry, one of the best modern commentators on Keats, went as far as to say that nineteenth century English literature would have been different if Keats had been three inches taller... . It is best to note that

---

(3) Certain early graphologists thought this could be done. In 1945 Father Girolamo MORETTI suggested a method of calculating the height of a writer from his script (*Grafologia Somatica*, Europa, Verona, pp. 91-96; pp.41-45 of the second edition, Ancona, 1960). I have not had the opportunity to apply this method. There is a more recent work, by Pedro José FOGLIA, *Grafología descriptiva. Obtención de la figura umana a través de la escritura*, from the author, Buenos Aires, 1988, 160p.

the graphologist should find out about the physical characteristics of the writer (especially height, for a man, and beauty, for a woman), which often generate feelings of inferiority.

*

During the years of his poetic career, cut short all too soon, the handwriting of Keats showed an EVOLUTION. Over and above the fluctuations in size and direction (reflecting his moods) and the varying blur, due to his state of health, this evolution expresses magnificently the maturing of the personality.

The writing of 1816 and 1817 still has adolescent signs, notably capitals that are ornate, in spirals or knotted. It lacks assurance (hesitant irregularity in direction, slant and height), and the signature is very enlarged.

The writing of 1818 (fig. 2.3) is larger and less hesitant, the capitals are simpler and the cup-like lower extensions more developed. The preceding year had seen the birth of *Endymion* whose more or less complex symbolism expresses an interior quest where K.Wilson sees, quite rightly, the first indication of the process of individuation described by Jung.

Fig. 2.4, dated May 1819, is concurrent with the Odes, *On Melancholy, To a Nightingale* and *On a Grecian Urn*. Keats, who had lost his brother, Tom, some months previously, decided to get engaged (after much struggle and hesitation), felt the temptation of death (*Why did I Laugh?*) and perhaps took drugs. A few weeks later he had fits of jealousy and temporarily ceased writing to Fanny. All these signs, according to Jung's concepts, are a phase of "going through the dark night of the soul (Nachtseefahrt)". The graphologist will guess this from the disturbance in the movement (congestions) and the layout (concave lines, vacillating slant) : a struggle against sensuality and against depression, interior distress.

By 1820 the writing has become homogeneous and calm, and has gained in width and harmony. Keats emerged from the crisis, at peace and clear in mind, able to confront serenely the death he knew was near.

*

BIBLIOGRAPHY

Josef RANALD, *Pens and Personalities. Handwriting as a Guide to your Personality,* Vision Press, London, 1958, 247p : see pp.162-163.

- The author analyses a piece of writing consisting of eight lines by Keats (fig. 2.6) and discovers in it the poet's character.

Unfortunately, these lines are not in the handwriting of Keats and that fact is immediately apparent to whoever knows his hand (the *British Museum* in London has a fine collection of the poet's writings) and it has been confirmed by two graphologists and two experts. The writing reproduced and analysed by Ranald is very different from that of the poet. Nevertheless, this graphologist has succeeded in "making it reveal" pretty well everything he knew about Keats.

In order to illustrate this fine example[4] of the influence of suggestion upon the graphologist's activity, the two principal paragraphs of Ranald's analysis are reproduced *in extenso.* The terms describing the writing are in *italics,* and my own comments on the words in SMALL CAPITALS, are in the footnotes.

"The ideality of John Keats, who walked in the light of the rich, manifold beauty of nature and who joyously gave himself to "the great end of poesy, that it should be a friend to soothe the cares and life of man", finds manifestation in the *inspirational* DISCONNECTED LETTERS [5] of his modest autograph, which denote a person guided largely by imagination, impressions and a psychical subconsciousness

---

(4) Not the only one by any means. At the end of chapter 7, there is a quotation from an analysis by G. E. MAGNAT of something written in the handwriting of Verlaine, which the graphologist thought had been done by Rimband. Because of this error Magnat deduced from the writing things he knew about Rimbaud (but which did not apply to Verlaine....).

(5) The writing of Keats is connected and grouped. The example studied by Ranald is connected, but with frequent interruptions between a capital and the following letter.

of mind. So, with the hopefulness of his ASCENDING LINES[(6)], the extreme ardour, alertness and sensitiveness of his SMALL[(7)], ANGULAR[(8)] script SLOPING TO THE RIGHT[(9)] in indication of a sympathetic, generous, emotional nature, he believed in the truth of beauty and the beauty of truth, and, for that faith, hoped to be led into a nobler life, numbered among the immortal bards. (...)

- Keats's lively interest in life is indicated by the aforementioned signs, emphasised by the *in-and-out left margin*, which, in turn, accentuates the happy-go-lucky carelessness of the *careless punctuation.* Impulse rings out of the RAPID[(10)] trading; love of pleasure, out of the LONG LOWER LOOPS[(11)]; vivid powers of fancy, out of the LONG FINALS[(12)]; extreme sensitiveness twice again, out of the *variable size of the letters* and the INCURVE OF THE CAPITAL 'M' [(13)]. Amiability and keen mental faculties are indicated by the *concave downstrokes*, *finals*

---

(6) In the examples by Keats that I know, the writing does not climb, but gradually presents an irregular direction (lines often concave, sometimes convex, and often the end of the line goes down).

(7) In Ranald's reproduction the average height of the middle zone is indeed 1 to 1.5mm (which makes it "small"), but the hand of Keats is 2mm and sometimes 3mm.

(8) On the contrary, the writing of Keats is *rounded* and extremely so.

(9) Ranald's example indeed starts between 25 and 45 degrees from the vertical, but the average slant of Keats is between 15 and 30 degrees.

(10) Keats's writing is not really rapid.

(11) With Keats the lower extensions are above all irregular in size and proteiform. Those in the example are long, but the majority (especially the *f*) are extremely narrow, to the point of producing "covered forms" instead of curls. Finally, some point downwards at the base (final *g* and *y*), instead of going back to the line. How does the graphologist make out a "love of pleasure"?

(12) After the age of twenty-two the finals in the handwriting of Keats are nearly always *short*, except for some formed easily with concave, *curves toward the top*, and generally *very small;* at twenty-one they were irregular in size and movement, now short, now developed, but in this last case, always curved. There is nothing in common with the finals in Ranald's example, which are centrifugal, noticeably rectilinear and near to the horizontal.

(13) The form of the *M* in the sixth line of the example has nothing in common with the *M* of Keats.

descending to the right and GOOD SPACING[14]. But over all is the restlessness of the QUICK[10], ANGULAR[8] hand; the *independence of the first stroke of the capital 'M'* : the mobility of feelings expressed by the *variable letters*".

Baruch LAZEWNIK, *Handwriting Analysis. A Guide to Understanding Personalities*, Whitford Press, West Chester (Pennsylvania), 1990, 208p. : see p.106.
- The autograph published by J. Ranald is reproduced (reduced by 13% in size) in a chapter devoted to angularity[15] : a sign of combativity, criticism, desire to dominate the environment, inability to be adaptable, analytical thinking (!). But in Keats's case "the shading in pressure in the middle and upper zone area (...), coupled with the right slant, speak of a sensitive temperament - notwithstanding (!) the angularity".

Nigel BRADLEY, "Places of graphological interest. 5 : Cambridge", *The Graphologist 7* (2) : 29-33, 1989 (pp.31-32).
- Reproduction of the beginning of the original manuscript of Keats's *Ode to a Nightingale.*

(14) The writing of Keats is rather *compact.*

(15) See footnote 8.

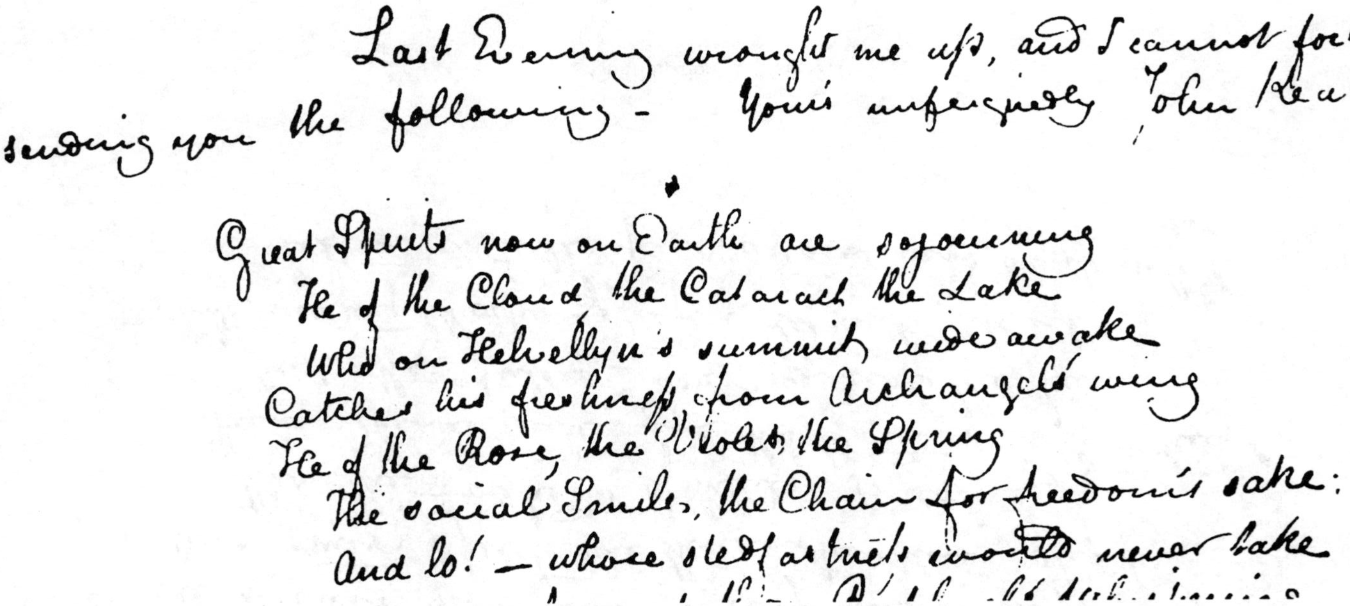

Last Evening wrought me up, and I cannot forbear sending you the following - Yours unfeignedly John Keats -

Great Spirits now on Earth are sojourning
He of the Cloud the Cataract the Lake
Who on Helvellyn's summit wide awake
Catches his freshness from Archangel's wing
He of the Rose, the Violet, the Spring
The social Smiles, the Chain for freedom's sake:
And lo! — whose stedfastness would never take

* **Fig. 2.1** - The handwriting of John Keats, aged 21 (1816). (Unavoidably reduced by 15%.)
(Sample continued overleaf)

A Meaner Sound than Raphael's Whispering
And other Spirits are there standing apart
Upon the Forehead of the Age to come;
These, These will give the World another heart
And other pulses _ hear ye not the hum
Of mighty Workings in a distant Mart?
Listen awhile ye Nations and be dumb.!

Continuation of * **Fig. 2.1**

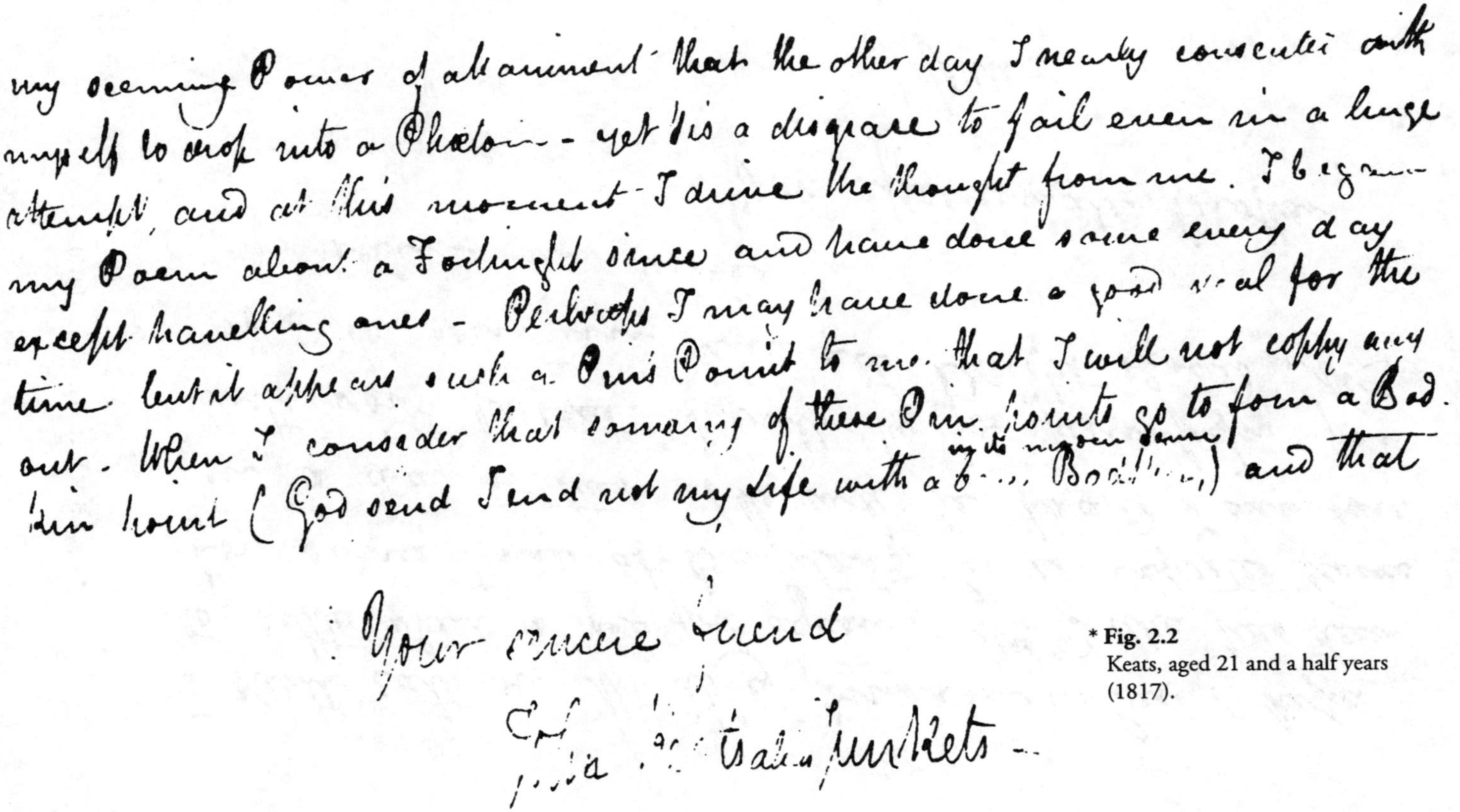

my seeming Power of attainment that the other day I nearly consented with myself to drop into a Phaeton - yet 'tis a disgrace to fail even in a huge attempt, and at this moment I drive the thought from me. I began my Poem about a Fortnight since and have done some every day except travelling ones - Perhaps I may have done a good deal for the time but it appears such a Pin's Point to me that I will not copy any out - When I consider that so many of these Pin points go to form a Bodkin point (God send I end not my life with a bare Bodkin, in its modern sense) and that

Your sincere friend

John keats alias Junkets -

* **Fig. 2.2**
Keats, aged 21 and a half years (1817).

I shall call on Mr. Abbey tomorrow: when I hope
to settle when to see you again. Mrs Dilke has been
for some time at Brighton. She is expected home
in a day or two. She will be pleased I am sure
with your present. I will try for permission for
you to remain here all Night should Mrs
D. return in time.

Your affectionate Brother

John –

* **Fig. 2.3** - Keats at nearly 23 (1818).

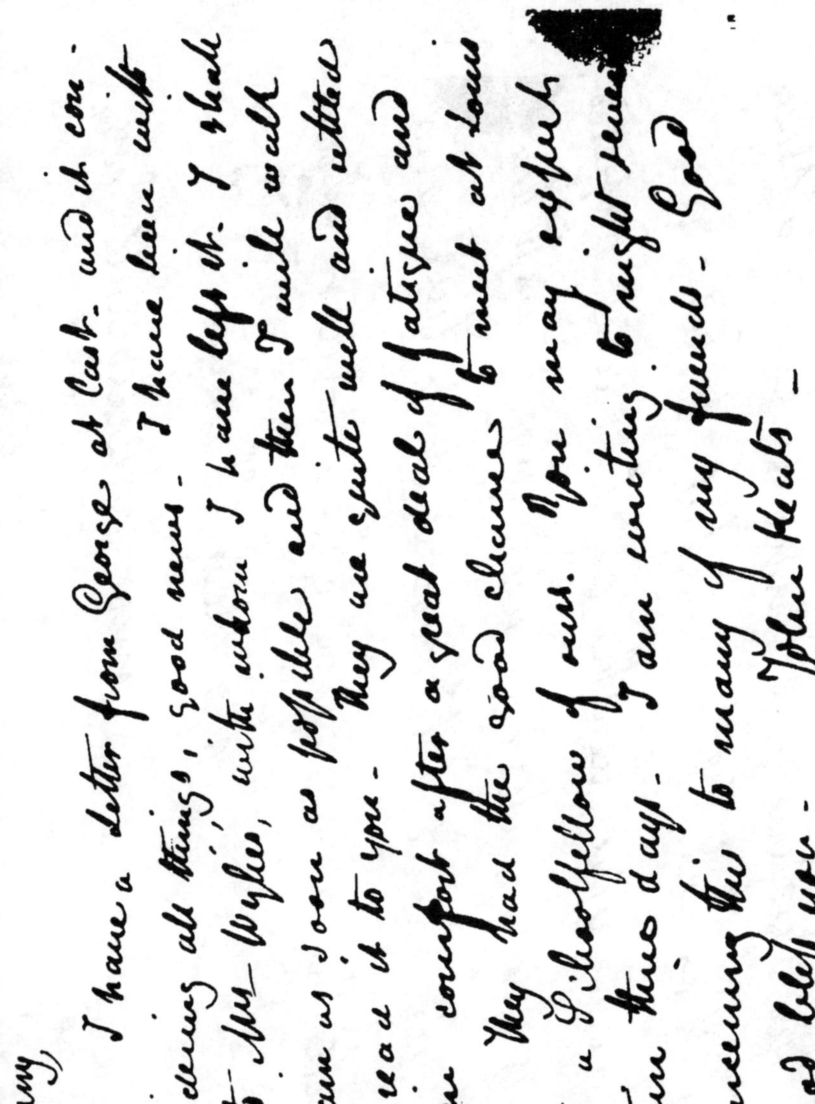

My dear Fanny,

I have a letter from George at last - and it contains, considering all things, good news - I have been with
it today to Mrs Wylie's, with whom I have left it. I shall
have it again as soon as possible and then I will walk
over and read it to you - They are quite well and settled
[illegible] in comfort after a great deal of fatigue and
harass. They had the good chance to meet at Louis
ville with a Schoolfellow of ours. You may expect
me within three days - I am writing tonight several
notes concerning this to many of my friends - Good
night! God bless you - John Keats -

* **Fig. 2.4** - Keats at 23 (1819).

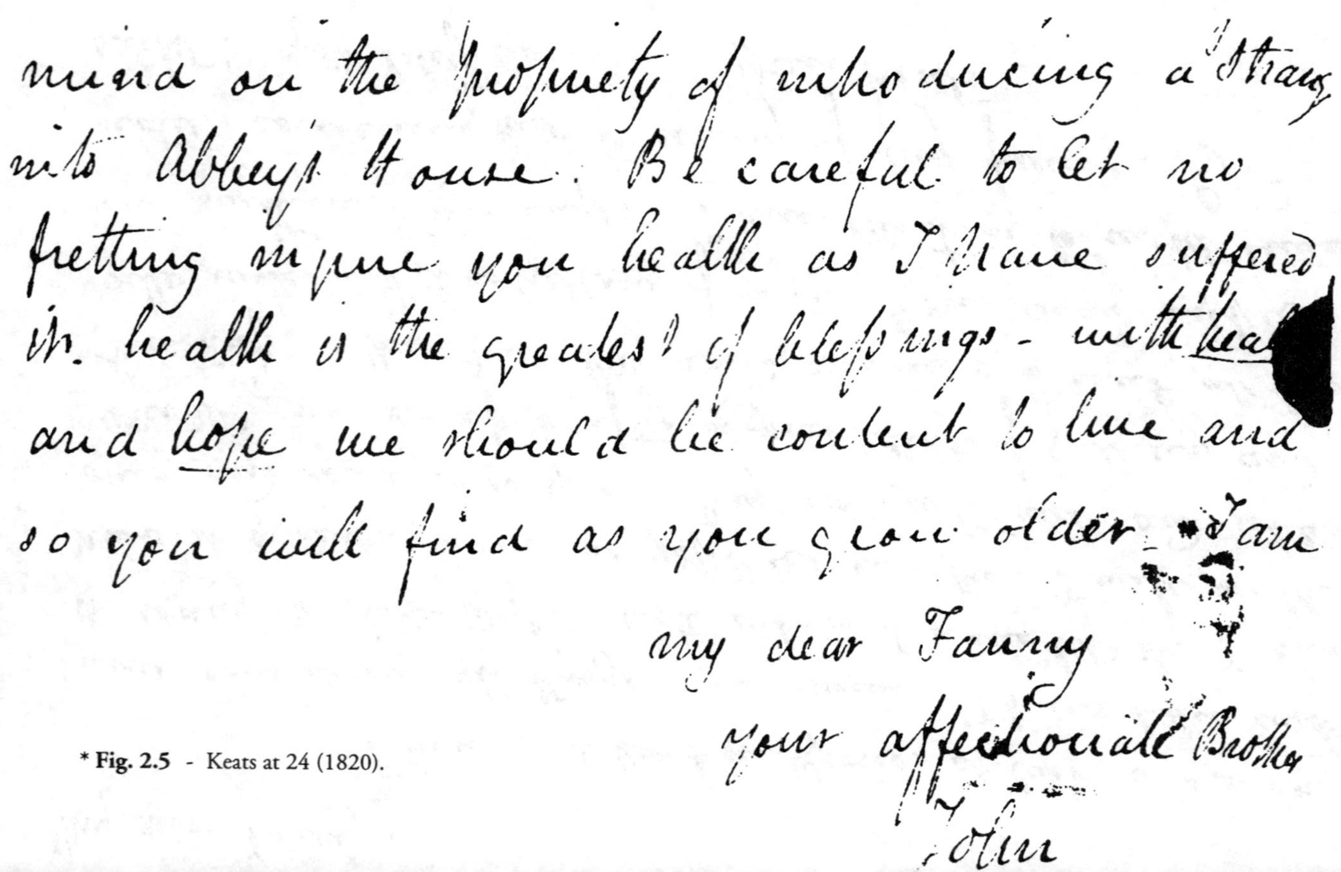

mind on the propriety of introducing a stranger into Abbey's House. Be careful to let no fretting injure your health as I have suffered it. health is the greatest of blessings – with health and hope we should be content to live and so you will find as you grow older – I am

my dear Fanny

your affectionate Brother

John

* **Fig. 2.5** - Keats at 24 (1820).

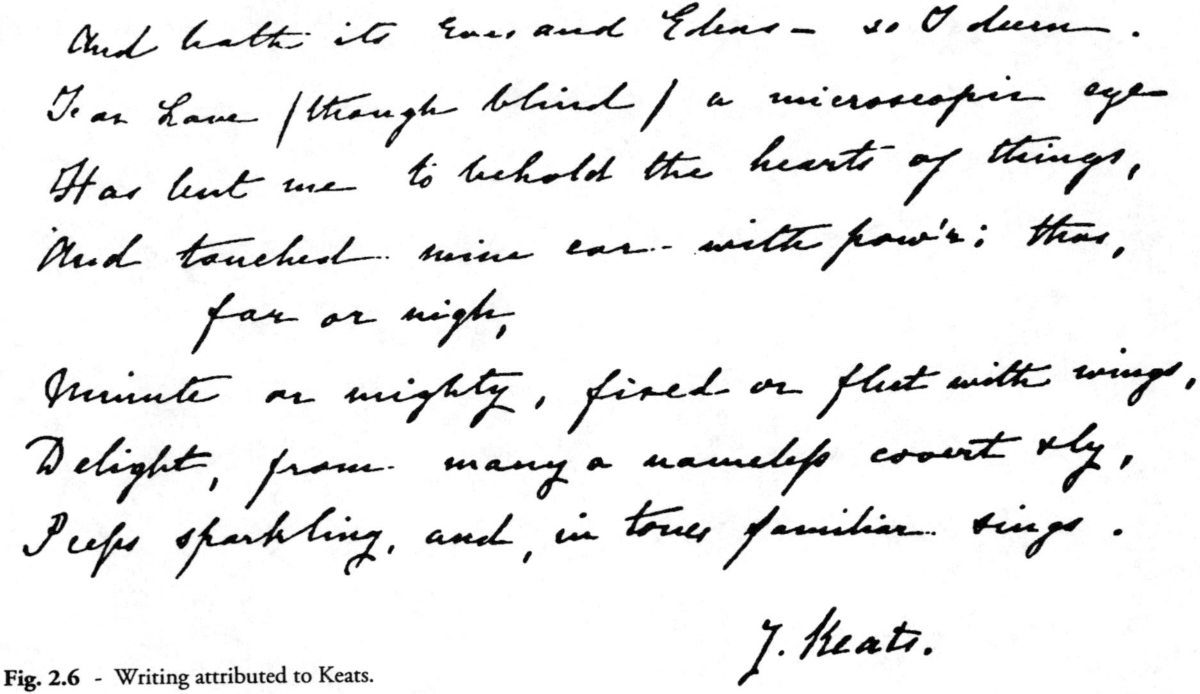

And hath its Eves and Edens — so I deem.
For Love (though blind) a microscopic eye
Has lent me to behold the hearts of things,
And touched mine ear with pow'r: thus,
far or nigh,
Minute or mighty, fixed or fleet with wings,
Delight, from many a nameless covert sly,
Peeps sparkling, and, in tones familiar sings.

J. Keats.

Fig. 2.6 - Writing attributed to Keats.

3

Victor-Alfred de VIGNY (1798 - 1863)

J'ai dit ce que je sais et ce que j'ai souffert[1]
(Last words in the *Diary* of A. de Vigny).

Alfred de Vigny came from a family belonging to the former nobility, ruined by the Revolution. He was an officer (like his father), but, disappointed, gave up a military career. He married an Englishwoman, and with Victor Hugo, became involved in the Romantic movement, wrote poems, novels, translations, a drama on the themes of the misfortunes of the nobility, of the distress of the soldier (*Servitude et Grandeur Militaires* is still popular) and of the poet (the novel *Stello*, and the drama *Chatterton*), all martyrs of society. After having tried in vain to play a role in politics, Vigny retired to the life of a country gentleman. His philosophical poems (gathered under the title of *Les Destinées*) date from the last period of his life and are today the most admired of his work.

(1) I have told you what I know and what I have suffered.

Vigny is today the least out-of-date of the Romantic generation. Several contemporary commentators see in the anguish and despair of his philosophical poems the first expression of twentieth century existentialism. Having lived half my life abroad, I can judge that Vigny is the French poet most highly thought of by those who study French literature. They easily grasp his clear thinking which he illustrates by precise symbols. His language is more accessible to the non-French speaker than the rich vocabulary of Hugo or the subtle music of the Symbolists. During the decades of the Communist domination, I often noticed how the people of the Socialist countries were particularly moved when reading Vigny. Deprived of liberty, especially that of self-expression, they understood in their tragic depth, both the stoicism of "performing with energy their long heavy task" and the greatness of the command "suffer and die without speaking", because they were living through both. (On the other hand, most French Canadians are unmoved by Vigny, being generally insensitive to the ideas of nobility and courage.)

Since the Second World War several books of psychology or criticism have shed light on Vigny's personality. A masterly description of Vigny, a Sentimental type with a narrow field of consciousness, appears prominently in René Le Senne's *Traité de caractérologie* (Presses universitaires de France, 1945). In 1960, Jean-Paul Weber studied the theme of Vigny and the clock, and endeavoured to prove that "all Vigny is here". This analysis is the best known part of his *Genèse de l'oeuvre poétique* (Gallimard, 1960). Lastly *l'Imagination d'Alfred de Vigny* by François Germain (Corti, 1961) is a deep, penetrating study of the poet's psychology.

Oddly, no graphologist has yet dealt with Vigny's handwriting, although a century ago, several numbers of *l'Autographe* reproduced plenty of examples of his hand. Except for a complete analysis by J. Brach, based only on a few lines of the poet's writing, French and other graphologists limit themselves to characterological or typological aspects. It is hoped that the following will fill in what is missing.

*

The handwriting of Alfred de Vigny, developed noticeably. Figure 3.1 is one of the oldest documents found, a request for an extension of leave, for health reasons, from Captain de Vigny, nearly twenty-eight years of age. The examples in 3.2 date respectively from about 1830 and 1835 (the years 1833-35 produced *Chatterton* and *Servitude et Grandeur militaires*). At forty (1837-38) Vigny lost his mother, broke with Marie Dorval and went through the most cruel crisis of his life. Figure 3.3 is a few famous lines from the *Mort du loup*. Figures 3.4a and 3.4b are part of drafts of letters written in 1843 and 1845. The personal notes 3.5 (the upper part is dated 1854) are very typical of the numerous writings of de Vigny in his maturity. Figure 3.6 comes from a letter written by the poet a few months before his death.

The following characteristics are pretty well stable :

Developed, homogeneous writing, with a *high Formlevel.*

Significant *tension* : IVa (rigid firmness, angles and arcades), sometimes even V (dented, twists, clubs).

Movement is powerful, but *the forms are predominant* by being solid and monomorphous (systematic). Movement, creativeness in the form and spatial layout are lively and rhythmic, the rhythm of form being the strongest.

Angular with a tendency to *arching, harsh.*

Concave, generally *right-slanted.*

Diminishing, restrained, some horizontal free strokes are *flying, jerky* and sometimes *needle-pointed.*

Numbers are *slow* and *hesitant.*

Signature: *angular, right-slanted* like the text, *stable, superelevated, thin, slowed-up* and *underlined* (the paraph is made of a straight stroke and a curved stroke).

The *stroke* is dark and usually precise, though not always. Relief is weak, but spasmodic movements affect the horizontal strokes. These *spasms* occur in every example, frequently in maturity, but disappear when the writing becomes disorganised (fig. 3.6).

Broadly speaking, the writing becomes more and more *tormented* and artificial. After the age of forty Vigny writes a very personal hand. From 1835, the ovals become *discordant* and *twisted* in shape, as a result of a tendency towards *narrowness, angles* and *arcades.*

As to continuity, the youthful examples are connected, but with static interruptions. In about 1830, the hand is *disconnected* and *constrained.* Then the degree of *joining increases* : the writing is grouped, even connected.

*

A powerful personality is at once apparent because of the very personal monomorphous shapes, the firmness of the writing, and the tension of its strong, but hindered spring forward. Formlevel is high because of originality, intensity and strong rhythm, held down by a regular rhythm.

Here we have a writing which is constructed and artificial, because of its constraint and a few exaggerations. The manner of the connection brings us to the heart of Vigny's personality. Figure 3.1 has angles and some angular garlands. Arcades appear in 1830. The examples after that are angular, with a strong tendency to arcades which is less evident in the last example. *Angular firmness,* the effort towards monomorphism in the strokes of the middle zone, uniform before diminishing at word endings, are signs of will power, one which constructs (regular monomorphous shapes) but also holds the reins (slowed down, held back, narrow, sober hand) albeit painfully (tormented, twisted writing).

It is easy to see here, firmly anchored in the personality, the devotion to Duty which is one of the leading themes in Vigny's work :

> Fais énergiquement ta longue et lourde tâche
> Dans la voie où le sort a voulu t'appeler [(2)].

Vigny has Admiral Collingwood say : "The sense of Duty ends by so taking over the mind that it enters into the character and becomes one of its principal features, just as healthy food, constantly supplied, can change all one's blood and become one of the principles of our constitution [...] But one cannot divest a man of everything, and there are things which grip the heart more strongly than one would like".

Arcades and *superelevations* point to an aristocratic pride (distinguished writing) which refuses to "do things like everybody else", a pride which impregnates all Vigny's thought. This is best summed up perhaps in the notes for a poem "The lion walks in the desert alone". Cowardly animals herd together. May the poet always walk alone. There is arrogance and much self admiration here. Although Vigny once wrote that no one has the right to despise others, his scorn sometimes breaks out as in this laconic note: "I have never managed to be interested in fools".

Graphologists to whom the writing of Vigny in his prime has been shown, have exclaimed: "You would say that this is an old lady's writing, the sort learnt in her convent school!" In truth, the *individually artificial* handwriting of Vigny shares characteristics with the conventional (collectively artificial) Sacré-Coeur writing, created in 1853. The aristocratic height and the constraint produce a script which is angular, uniformly right-slanted (except for certain rough notes), connected and with pointed narrow ovals.

The similarity has a psychological interest. When sketching the history of conventional handwriting in France, M. Delamain

---

(2) With energy perform your long and heavy task
Along the path which fate allotted you.

reminds us[3] that it came into being in the seventeenth century, bearing witness to the "high point at which the personality renounces the self in favour of positive values". After the eighteenth century, the Revolution and Romanticism had passed away, "it (conventional handwriting) reappeared in a different, caricatured form which was mechanical and scarcely legitimate, in the manner learnt in convents, particularly the one named the Sacred Heart. This was not the expression of a lofty, self-assured society, but was rather a *reaction*, a *closing of ranks* of the aristocratic society which the Revolution has diminished to the point of threatening its very existence". This reaction was basic to Vigny. This gentleman was proud of his family, calling himself "Count" and claiming a long noble line. Because of the ravages of the Revolution, Vigny had to live the life of an ordinary citizen and deplored this. The novel *Cinq-Mars* expresses his nostalgia for the France of feudal times. In politics, Vigny was a reactionary royalist. During his active life (an officer in the National Guard, a candidate at elections, in favour of the Empire), "he was less attracted by a desire to act than by a concern to reduce disorder [....]. To maintain or to re-establish order is not an action, but a reaction".

It is not surprising that such a traditional and even reactionary state of mind should show itself in a personal and indeed a whole style of writing. Vigny himself described this state of mind. The following lines, written about French-Canadians, express the psychology of these somewhat stilted writings :

---

(3) "Réponse sur l'écriture artificielle collective (ou conventionnelle)", *La Graphologie,* no.20 : 25-34, 1945. See also J. Depoin, *Les écritures à la mode et l'évolution de l'écriture en France,* Société de Graphologie, 1920, 66p. *Sur l'écriture du Sacré-Coeur* : J.-H. Michon, *L'écriture des élèves du Sacré Coeur, La Graphologie 4*(15): 113-115, 1875 and J. Depoin, "L'écriture du Sacré-Coeur", *La Graphologie, 23*(3): 336-338, 1893, *30*(12) : 288-289, 1900 and *31*(1): 6-8, 1901.

"If they love their old laws, it is because they are contrary to English customs. If they defend them, it is in order to disobey and remain French [....]. But this feeling, which causes them to resist, also freezes their activity so that they stay still in a progressive world which finds them a nuisance in its midst. This feeling was meant to be a fortress, but it imprisons them".

Nowadays, when the sense of dignity is disappearing, let us not consider this constraint to be a limitation. We ought rather to admire the true nobility of a man, who two months before his death dared to write, in reference to the Nordic superstition that we rejoin our ancestors after death: "More than once I have acted or refrained from acting at the sudden thought of the judgement of that supreme council [....] and I have often said to myself : I must live in such a way that I shall deserve that at my entrance they shall rise to greet me".

Vigny must have been a difficult man to live with. His writing expresses distant and disdainful reserve. He was a grumpy critic (harsh writing), authoritarian (superelevated, spasmodic writing with triangles) and capable of behaving with unreasonable arrogance (whip-like *t* made like final Gothic *s* in his mature years). But he was a man of upright principle (angular, simple, very homogeneous and with form predominant).

His interior life was rich, but painful (concave, tormented hand). There are many interior conflicts: the affirmative surge of the large right-slanting writing is blocked by inhibitions (constrained, interrupted, narrowed writing with held-back finals). The rightward flying, free strokes, which were full of ease in 1824-25, have from 1835 the marks of over-compensation (spindles, sharpness). It is easy to see here the partial expression of a strong sensuality (*Eloa*), and how reason is struggling with feeling ("my feeling is concealed by a mask of bronze"). One sees how a critical, analytical mind reduces ruthlessly both the desire for action and enthusiasm. Basically, we have the opposition between Stello and the Docteur-Noir, as Vigny himself wrote at the end of *Stello* and in his *Diary* in

1832. The end product is a solitary, sad and unexpanded personality. Vigny often wondered whether his sadness was natural or due to his early experiences, and he was well-nigh obsessed by the problem of Fate. We can see how much Vigny suffered, how authentic his sadness was and to what extent he saw himself in other sufferers. Vigny's handwriting is a tragic writing.

Vigny's intelligence was high by reason of its great imagination, concentration and depth. His firm, careful, simplified writing points to a widely-cultured hard worker. Vigny's scripts show meticulous, scrupulous care. He dated everything, frequently re-copied his work and kept the rough draft of his letters (see the top example in fig.4.4). Nevertheless, in spite of his love of reasoned criticism, Vigny was subjective and his judgements were often faulty (artificial writing with discordances of form). Sainte Beuve notes this with ruthless clarity.

From the point of view of psychopathic constitutions, Vigny offers an example of a paranoid person with *schizoid* features. This disorder is evident in the discordance between the richness of the interior life and the difficulty of manifesting it, in the aloof reserve which hides a vulnerable sensitivity. The paranoid syndrome is complete : pride, a mistrustful solitude, false judgement and inadaptability. As early as 1823 Vigny's Moses calls himself "powerful and alone".

This paranoid syndrome explains the importance, in Vigny's work, of the theme of persecution. The nobleman is persecuted by the powers that be (*Cinq-Mars*) and by the common people. The soldier is also a victim (*Servitude et Grandeur militaires*) and the poet has "a curse upon his life" (*Stello, Chatterton* : a clear prediction of the theme of the poet accursed). Those who are persecuted usually find something or someone to blame. Vigny accuses nature, woman, the lumpen crowd, power wherever it may be, Fate and God Himself because of the absurdity of the world, as Lautréamont and Sartre were to do. This blaming of God is not just in the *Mont des Oliviers*, but all through Vigny's works, from *La Fille de Jephté* (1822) up to the *Diary* of 1862-3), when the poet was suffering atrociously from illness.

The syndrome has another consequence, the propensity to generalise his personal problems beyond bounds. There are many examples. Marie Dorval is unfaithful to him and lacks discretion. So *la Colère de Samson* claims the war of the sexes to be endless and universal: "It is between the goodness of Man and the wiles of Woman". Vigny hoped, by his pen, to become more famous than his forebears : the *Esprit pur* professing faith in this superiority of the "Universal written word, the Visible Holy Spirit". It has often been noticed how all Vigny's characters resemble him, and that the incoherent parts of his philosophy are the mirror image of his interior conflicts.

The term "paranoia", now that it has entered everyday speech, has acquired a pejorative meaning, so it is well to recall that it simply describes a constitution which can belong to very intelligent men with a high moral code as well as to unintelligent or delinquent people. To mention only poets, several authentic Romantic geniuses such as Byron, Leopardi and Mickiewicz were paranoid. As for our present subject, Vigny's writing, with its discordances in pressure and form, remains homogeneous and noble with evidence of great superiority of intellect, moral sense and will. The strong points of the writing (height, slant, firmness) display not only the aristocratic ideal, in the true sense of the term, to which Vigny was always faithful (pride, moral purity and an acute sense of duty), but also an effort to transcend his pessimistic critical sense. Vigny, as is well known, had faith in the influence of ideas (*La Bouteille à la mer, L'Esprit pur*); in spite of his reserve and taste for meditation he worked directly for others and was concerned with many problems of his time. He discreetly helped many Chattertons, drew up precise suggestions for the conduct of the army and for laws relating to literary copyright.

*

Faced with Vigny's writing, the graphologist will certainly see the man of noble mentality and intellect, but less probably the poet. Given that he knows that this is the writing of a poet what could he "guess" about this poetry? He could, it seems, discern:

1) The intellectual poet who likes to deal in ideas rather than in pictures or form (sober, monomorphous shapes);
2) Intense work and great self-discipline (voluntary inhibitions, precision);
3) Perhaps a talent that is more visual than auditory (precise forms which are more important than movement), more of a draughtsman than a colourist (abstract mind, dry cutting strokes);
4) Perhaps, finally, the stability of the hand with its rigid and sometimes monotonous rhythm (the clock dear to Jean-Paul Weber?) is all of a piece with the heavy rigid alexandrine of Vigny, who hardly made use of any other metre.

*

The basic TEMPERAMENT of Alfred de Vigny is that of a Bilious type desiring to impose himself (angularity, slant, spasmodic movements, signature underlined) proudly and even exclusively (arcades, narrowings).

A *warm Bilious* type, haughty and removed from reality, by the height of the middle zone and the superelevation of the signature. Moreover, the type is *dry Bilious,* a temperament of which he presents all the characteristics : a sense of responsibility, moral rectitude and a proclivity to moralise (rigid, connected, arched writing), anxious tension (restrained hand with flying strokes, jerks), reserve (restrained, narrow, regressive strokes) and criticism (harsh, needle-pointed writing).

The *Nervous* component is important : darkly depressed

nervosity, with interiorised sensitivity (concave, simple, rigid, tormented hand); the Sanguine element (wide, exaggerated strokes) is less so. The Lymphatic element is practically non-existent.

The MYTHOLOGICAL TYPES confirm this. Vigny is a Mars-Sun with a touch of Saturn and Mercury : Earth and Venus are deficient. His writing is dry Fire.

The combativity of *Mars* is strong (angularity, spasms, numerous crosses, right slant). The types' "formula" suggests that this combativity manifests itself above all in the area of ideas, with an overwhelming, even ruthless judgement (sober forms, rather dry strokes, needle-points) which displays itself courageously, uncompromisingly and with intolerance (stiffness, connectedness and full layout).

Vigny has the noble, haughty ambition of Sun (high, simple writing) and its reserve (restraint, regressive movements, juxtaposed letters). Pride and haughtiness are evident (arched, superelevated handwriting with final *t* as a Gothic *s*). There is no question of a pose, this mental attitude being so deeply rooted in the personality (personal forms, homogeneous writing). One would expect that such marked *Sun* characteristics would be supported by a stronger relief, the sign of a spontaneous personal authority, but this power was not developed with Vigny.

Saturn brings deep reflective gravity, a systematically synthesizing mind (sober, regular letters, precise punctuation), and also sadness and the pessimism of the lonely man (black, rather precise, concave, narrowed and restrained writing) who is mistrustful and bitter. There is a tendency to hypochondria and meanness. *Mercury* appears in the frequent needle-points. There are also the secondary signs of *Jupiter* (a straining after effect, a desire to be influential) and of *Moon* (imagination).

The *Venus deficiency* is seen in the stroke and the rigid angularity (refusal to adapt or make concessions, lack of pliability), *Earth deficiency* is apparent in the height of the writing and in the artificial forms, notably the ovals pointed at the base (lack of a practical sense, neglect of everyday events).

The resultants are obvious. Mars and Sun give ambition in the realm of ideas and pugnacity in the service of an ideal. Mars and Saturn show the painful refusal to compromise. Very intellectual (Saturn, Mercury), Vigny is a thinker (Sun-Saturn) rather than a poet (Moon is in the background). Vigny's behaviour was that of an aloof and impractical aristocrat (Sun, Saturn, deficiency of Earth); he could probably be most unpleasant on occasions (Mars-Saturn, with Venus deficient).

*

From the PSYCHOANALYTICAL point of view, the *libido* is intense (homogeneous, firm, right-slanted and consistent), but with some blocking (sudden stops, restrained finals, twists) and a barrier between a powerful interior life and difficulty in giving it external expression. The theme of silence inspired the most famous lines of the *Mort du loup.*

Seul le silence est grand tout le reste est faiblesse [...] .
Puis après, comme moi, souffre et meurs sans parler[(4)],

and of the *Mont des Oliviers* :

Le Juste [....] ne répondra plus que par un froid silence
Au silence éternel de la Divinité[(5)].

Introversion overcomes extraversion, but not without a struggle (sober, arched handwriting with narrow capitals and restrained finals). We have a tense introvert in the meaning given by Christiansen and Carnap (angles and arcades, monomorphous forms, dryish stroke).

---

(4) Silence alone is great. All else is weakness [...]
So then, like me, without speaking, suffer and die.

(5) The Just One [...] henceforth answers only with a cold silence
The eternal silence of the Godhead.

Vigny is an accentuated *Thinking* type - his triumph is the philosophic poem. His writing typically expresses the strong conflict between Thinking (simple, monomorphous, angular, connected and sober) and *Sentiment* (width, prominent middle zone, slant, "pathos"); the conflict is undifferentiated and undeveloped. Comparison between figures 3.1 and 3.5 shows the progress of the repression of feeling : it is the Docteur-Noir rather than Stello.

Sensation is strong, but undifferentiated and largely repressed (Vigny struggled against the power of his senses: his *Journal* (1839) suggested that Beethoven might have been a lesser composer if he had been distracted by the ability to hear). Intuition is weak - Vigny had little interest in religion and despised the occult.

There are signs of a predominantly *obsessional* neurosis (constrained hand with a certain monotonous movement; the very connected stroke of his later writing has something obsessive about it), with considerable *anxiety* (inhibitions, narrowings, twisted and tortured hand), and numerous complexes, of which the principal are the Persona (artificial writing, tall middle zone, signature) and anality (dark stroke with spasmodic and sharp points, angles, a tendency to fill the page, precision).

The *Persona* corresponds to Vigny's aristocratic pride and aloof dignity. There is a certain *narcissism* with an *overcompensated* inferiority complex (arcades, superelevations).

Anality brings together the already noted traits of harshness, inadaptability, solitude, mistrustfulness and meticulosity. One might presume that Vigny lacked generosity (but in fact he attached little importance to money). There is also indisputable cruelty and considerable masochism, of which Vigny's work is full. He admitted that the line :

J'aime la majesté des souffrances humaines[(6)]

(6) I love the majesty of the sufferings of mankind.

holds the meaning of all his philosophical poems. The paranoid syndrome studied already, is connected with anality.

Lastly, the thin lower extensions, the spasms and twists betray strong *sexual complexes* with a largely unsatisfied sensuality. The result of undeveloped emotion and of the struggle against sentiment and sensuality, is that the *Anima* is not integrated. This sort of man usually projects it upon ideal and angelic images (*Eloa* and the plans for poems which were intended to follow, show clearly this aspect and the lack of contact between the Ego and the Anima). These images have in some way as unhappy rivals, Delphine Gay, Lydia Bunbury and Marie Dorval.

The play between his functions and his complexes helps us to reconstitute Vigny's personality easily. There we find his character traits and his "problems". One sees that his faithfulness to high ideals (a soldier's honour, the pride of a nobleman and the mission of a poet) makes of them an organised and sublimated synthesis.

From the SZONDIAN point of view, the overall appearance of the hand is ruled by the reactions *k+* (structured and closed forms which dominate movement), p+ (animated, superelevated writing) and *d-* (signs of anality).

Vigny's writing is one of the best existing examples of the *Ego in peril* (*Sch* = *k+p+*) : the forms take precedence over movement, they are personal and have an impressive middle zone which is drawn with effort, the lower extensions are sketchy and the capitals simple. Rhythm is strong and tense, inhibitions are noticeable, temperament is Bilious with a strong Saturn element.

Truly the psychology of the Ego in peril corresponds perfectly with that of Vigny. Madame Lefebure and I have summed up the psychology as follows :

"Such a subject would want to become affectively involved, make contact in the realm of ideas, communicate verbally, search for a collective goal (*p*+), but at the same time feels the need to stand aloof from these aspirations, watching himself as if from outside himself, and finally holding back [....]. The conflict then takes on the classic state of the opposition between thought and emotion, the subject wanting to "put things in order" and yet stand at a distance (k+). Now, his emotions and the irrational side of his personality (*p*+) upset these tactics. Whence there is considerable tension, the subject being a spectator of this conscious or preconscious conflict (*p*+) which he watches as if from outside. (*k*+). For example, in his intellectual or artistic production (....) too many ideas flood in upon him (*p*+) and all hold his attention (*k*+). Using the expression of S. Deri, he will feel "both inspired and held back" (7).

Each of these traits applies to Vigny. The internal opposition between the appetites *p*+ and the concerted mastery of *k*+ is put into words in the dialogues between Stello and the Docteur-Noir who draws up a plan of life for his disciple and warns him, at the start of his second consultation (*Daphné*) "that ardour must be kept closed in the depth of the soul, as if it were a bad thought, in the times in which we live". Vigny really felt that he was "both inspired and held back" : his *Journal,* so full of plans that come to nothing, says in 1840 : "My list will be most amusing for my friends when they see the number of books I have begun and abandoned".

The following passage shows how typically the Ego in peril feels and puts into words (p+) his internal conflicts, watches them like an outside observer and rationalises them (*k*+) in order to neutralise their emotional content :

"I believed I could perceive two separate beings inside myself; *my dramatic self* that lives with violent activity, feels with drunken pain, acts with persistent energy and my *philosophical self* which daily stands aside from the other self, scorns and criticises it, watching it go by and laughing or crying over its mistakes, like a guardian angel would".

The behaviour of people who are *k*+ *p*+ is that of "oddities, eccentrics who have great schemes at heart, are alone in their

---

(7) The article appeared in *La Graphologie* in 1973 (no.130, p.37). It was reprinted in *Graphologie et Test de Szondi: Tome I: Le Moi* (1976), p.86 of the third edition, Masson, Paris, 1990.

ivory tower, and are noticeable for their scorn for rules and for their verbal pugnacity". These traits belong to Vigny : he had a lofty idea of the poet's mission and aimed at "bringing men to everyday goodness by the route of the poetically Beautiful". But in his *Journal* and his *Memories* , he spoke with little esteem, not only for the common man and politicians, but even for great writers like Pascal, Chateaubriand and Larmartine. As for the expression "ivory tower", it was to Vigny that it was first applied.

The factor *e* is negatively charged in the *Paroxysmal* pulsion; trenchant stroke, spasmodic movements; rhythm of movement is tense, jerky with angles, crosses, thrown; compactness, "inferior" Bilious temperament, Mars and Saturn types. The deduction is frustrated emotion, aggressivity, intolerance, moodiness. The factor *hy* is ambivalent. On the one hand the simplicity of closed forms and the restrained rhythm point to the reaction *hy-*. One deduces that the writer is possessed of the modesty of his sensitivity and interior imaginings. On the other hand, the "pathos" and the exaggerations of movement (superelevations, spasms, *t*-bars) would point to *hy+*: the desire to attract attention and to prove one's worth.

In this *e- hy+/-* profile we see perhaps another Cain (*e-hy+*) who represses his aggression because of moral or social disapproval (*hy-*); or perhaps an anxiety-ridden person, because of the blockage (*hy-*)of his brutal side (*e-*), who tries to overcome his anguish by presenting a worthy picture of himself (*hy+*).

The *Sexual* vector is typically *S* = *h-s+*. The reaction *h-* (dry stroke, strong tension, angles) expresses a rejection of tenderness. The reaction *s+* can be seen in the well-nourished, spasmodic and sharp stroke, in the great vitality of the hand (tension IVa, connectedness, right slant, height), in the predomi-nance of the Bilious element and the Mars type : combativity, forth-rightness and intolerance in passing judgement. To sum up : a hard man who represses his erotic tendencies and concentrates his energy, a self-centred and difficult character (connected with the tendency *e-*).

The *Contact* vector gives the profile C = *d-m-*. The reaction *d-* is seen in the connected angular hand, in the compact layout, in the black, congested stroke, in the frequent dashes : exclusive, rigid attachment, anxiety when faced with change, mistrust. The reaction m- is seen in the dry stroke, the stiff rhythm of movement (angles, arcades), and in the narrowing of the ovals: rejection of everyday sociability, frustration.

The rejection of orality, rationalised and weighed up, is one of the themes of Vigny's poetic work. It is enough to recall once more the most famous of the lines in *La Mort du loup* :

> Seul le silence est grand, tout le reste est faiblesse.
> [...] souffre et meurs sans parler[(8)].

and the lines the poet added to the end of *Mont des Oliviers*:

> Le Juste opposera le dédain à l'absence,
> Et ne répondra plus que par un froid silence
> Au silence éternel de la Divinité[(9)].

in which the rejection of orality *m* is stated masochistically[(10)] and projected onto God!

The profile *d- m-* is one of the most difficult to live through[(11)]. Together with Mme Fanchette Lefebure, I have written on this topic [(12)].

---

(8) Silence alone is great, all the rest is weakness.
[...] suffer and die without speaking.

(9) The Just one will meet absence with disdain,
And henceforth answers only with a cold silence.
The eternal silence of the Godhead.

(10) This is not a literary attitude, but a drama lived by Vigny. In a personal letter written by him in the year of the publication of *La Mort du loup* and *Le Mont des Oliviers,* we read : "I am oppressed by so many things that I never speak of! Writing something like *La Mort du loup* is enough to drain me!"

(11) and (12) see overleaf

"*There is no security here* : neither that given by orality, nor that given by anality.

d- : intense and exclusive attachment to the object

m- : at the same time there is a doubt that the object can give happiness, or that it even exists.

There is a terrible internal contradiction, which provokes a feeling of *detachment from reality.* This is why this formula stands for the kind of contact that is most difficult to live through.

These deeply *unrealistic* people, who have no tangible bond with daily life, are nevertheless always very *rational* intellectually. They obey the laws of life, while rejecting them from their scale of values. In extreme cases, they are *non-conformist* and, above all, deeply autistic, unconsciously refusing any opportunity to calm their initial frustration.

This way of denying the importance of pleasure, this lack of interest in things and in people does not allow the reaching of a level of abstraction that would permit sublimation. A strong but negative narcissism supplies the power of the sacrifice. But what a useless and painful sacrifice it is!"

All these traits apply tragically to Vigny. They are at the root of his personal problems and supply the theme of his literary work. In his handwriting they are expressed by the extreme predominance of form over movement and by the intensely tormented writing.

*

One last point remains to be commented on : Vigny's *mother complex.* This complex rarely has direct graphic signs, but in his case its existence can be suspected because of the poor contact between the Ego and the Anima, and the strong but repressed and undeveloped feelings.

In fact, Vigny's mother complex is of great importance. The *Journal d'un poète* and the *Mémoires inédits* tell us how, as the only son (his parents had, before his arrival, lost three

(11) This profile exists among other pessimistic poets whose writing I have studied : Leopardi, Leconte de Lisle, Lautréamont and Laforgue (partially for the latter, who has *d- m+/-*).

(12) *Graphologie et Test de Szondi. Tome 2: Dynamique des Pulsions* (1980), pp.46-47, from the second edition, Masson, Paris, 1990

infant sons), he received a careful and strictly directed education from his mother, whom he both admired and feared. Alfred felt that she was hard and overpowering, and repressed his sensibility (his own words).

The mother can be found in many parts of Vigny's work. She is first of all present behind the symbol of nature: psychoanalysis, the theory of the continuity of psychic life, reminds us that the mother was the first external influence for the child and shows how the way a man loves nature reflects his personal mother complex. While Lamartine, who had a loving and gentle mother, saw in Nature the great consoler, Vigny thought of nature as hard and indifferent to a man's sufferings. There is surely an echo of these feelings towards his mother in these famous lines from *La Maison du Berger* :

> "Je n'entends ni vos cris ni vos soupirs: à peine
> Je sens passer sur moi la comédie humaine
> Qui cherche en vain au ciel ses muets spectateurs [...]
>
> On me dit une mère et je suis une tombe [....]"
> C'est la ce que me dit sa voix triste et superbe,
> Et dans mon coeur alors je la hais [....] (13)

Madame de Vigny watched jealously over her son and when he left for the army handed him an *Imitation of Christ* with the dedication, "To Alfred, from his only friend", and gave him moral advice, and in particular, to beware of actresses. She forced him to give up Delphine Gay, whom he loved. Under these conditions his affair with the actress Marie Dorval is significant, as is also his great feeling of guilt after his mother's death.

François Germain has skilfully detected the presence of the mother behind Alfred's dreams of tenderness, his search for a refuge and his conception of authority and also how the analytic mind of the Docteur-Noir is all of a piece with traits of Madame de Vigny which the child received and put into the imagined character.

Vigny, who was always meditating about himself, saw clearly the indelible importance of the mother's imprint upon a man's emotional life. *La Colère de Samson* expresses the idea that in woman man is seeking the

---

(13) Neither your calling nor your grieving do I hear,
Scarcely do I feel the passing by me of the human comedy
Which vainly calls upon the silent watchers in the sky [...]

It calls me mother, but I am a tomb [...]
That is what its sad, proud voice says to me,
And it is then that I hate it with all my heart [...]

delight experienced at his mother's breast. The psychic umbilical cord is clearly described in the following reflection (to which there are several parallels in the poems *Destinées* and in the *Journal d'un poète*) : "Every man believes that he will be able to follow the promptings of his soul and his will throughout his life, but he feels something that holds him back and turns him aside. It is a link. When he looks at it he sees that the link is part of a chain which goes back to the day of his birth". These words are heavy with philosophic and emotional meaning for a man haunted all his life by the problem of Destiny! They allow us to see the picture of the mother behind Vigny's questions about what we call nowadays the problem of heredity and environment, and behind his acute awareness of the limits of human freedom (in 1835, he wrote: "Independence was always my desire, and dependence was my destiny").

The library of the Academy and the Archives de la Defense Nationale have specimens of Madame de Vigny's writing. Figure 3.7 is a few lines written in the margin of the first volume of poems published by Alfred. The graphologist will easily conclude that this is a woman of superior intelligence, activity and culture, with a strong and rather intrusive will. The temperament is Bilious-Nervous and the Jungian type Sensation-Thinking (14).

One could study in detail the relationship between the writings of the mother and the son. (it would be even more interesting if we had the writing of Vigny as a child). But the influences which conditioned young Alfred were not only those of his mother: we must also consider his innate tendencies - a field too neglected by the psychology and medicine of the twentieth century - and the influence of his father, and through him, of various ideal images of the masculine Ego.

Vigny's handwriting tells us what he became and his life and work confirm this. Wanting to depend "upon man and man alone" he was doomed to failure. But he remains great because of the power of his lucid mind, his courage in suffering and his moral purity.

---

(14) I have studied a lengthier example in figure 27.1 in the *Psychologie de l'écriture, Suite à L'ABC de la graphologie* (Payot, 1978, 4th edition 1988).

BIBLIOGRAPHY

Jean-Hippolyte MICHON, *Système de graphologie. L'art de connaître les hommes d'après leur écriture* (1875) 4th edition, *La Graphologie*, 1878, 323p. Numbers in brackets refer to the edition of 1944, Payot, 234p, 1875 : see p.160 (123).

- Connected writing with some breaks : powers of deduction with a little intuition.

Matilde RAS, *Grafología, las grandes revelaciones de la escritura* (1929), 3rd edition, Labor, Barcelona, 1942, 192p : see pp.101-102.

- Signs of pride in Vigny's hand - large, non-diminishing letters, large signature, verticality.

Jacques BRACH, *Les douze facteurs du caractère. Leur influence sur la physionomie et sur l'écriture.* L'Arche, 1953, 222p : see pp.180-181.

- A complete graphological and physiognomic study, in the form of a chart presenting thirteen signs (writing that is narrow, irregular except for form, with spindles, angles, some slackening, slow, with lines often descending, encircling paraph, t-bars clubbed, then sharp-pointed, letters shaped like numbers, large, varied in form) with their interpretations and finally, the following summary : "An inactive temperament, touchy, not objective or analytical, easily offended, often dissatisfied, but very aware of his own feelings, with a sense for what is great, noble and worthy. Capable of powerful expression".

Emile CAILLE, Caractères et Ecritures. (Presses universitaires de France, 1957, 290p : see p.122.

- Writing typical of the Heymans-Le Senne Sentimental type: "inhibition, uneasiness in the graphic movement, poor forms (except for some typically imaginative capitals)" with a strong awareness of self (enlarged signature), contrasting with weakness of character. Narrow field of consciousness (affected stiffness), Mars polarity (sharp, clublike, centrifugal endings) : "a painful contrast of the destiny of a man, torn in spite of his genius, between his lively combativity and the powerlessness of his inaction".

Dr. J. RIVÈRE, *Le monde de l'éctriture*, Gonon, Neuilly-sur-Seine, 1958, 294p : see p.33.

- "The "A" of Alfred de Vigny, a cold-hearted Sentimental type (of Le Senne)".

Dr. J-Ch. GILLE-MAISANI, *Psychologie de l'écriture. Etudes de graphologie.* Payot, 1969, 270p : see pp.33-34.
- Vigny's harsh writing (constrained, angular, almost dry).

Dr. J-Ch. GILLE-MAISANI, "L'écriture d'Alfred de Vigny", *La Graphologie* no.138 : 8-22, April 1975
- First version of the present chapter.

Dr. J-Ch. GILLE-MAISANI, "L'écriture systematisée". *La Graphologie,* no.142, 59-60, 1976. Reprinted in *Psychologie de l'écriture,* chapter 30, 1977
- Vigny's handwriting, monomorphous, with angular arcades.

Madame F. LEFEBURE and Dr. J-Ch. GILLE-MAISANI, *Introduction à la Psychologie du Moi. Les Seize profils du Moi de Szondi et leur expression dans l'écriture.* Mont-Blanc, Geneva, 1976, 159p : 3rd edition. *Graphologie et Test de Szondi Tome 2: Le Moi,* Masson, Paris, 1990, 182p: pp.91-92
- Vigny's handwriting, typical of the Ego in peril.

J-Ch. GILLE-MAISANI, *Psychologie de l'écriture*, 2nd edition, Payot, Paris,1978, p.149; p.199 of the English edition *The Psychology of Handwriting,* Scriptor Books, London, 1992.
- Straight-lined writing of an intelligent, self-willed and authoritarian woman.

Dr. Claude VILLARD, "Diagnostic sur courrier. Comment les maladies peuvent se déceler dans l'écriture", *Le Crapouillot,* new series, no.54, *Les Secrets de la graphologie,* pp.24-37, 1980, see p.35.
- Typical handwriting of a paranoiac. Very angular signature, clubbed finals: vigorous assertiveness, inadaptability.

J-Ch. GILLE-MAISANI, "Il test di Szondi", *Il gesto creativo. Studi grafologici,* no. 1/2, pp.11-26, 1985-1986 : see pp.15, 18, 25.
- Profile of the Ego k+p+ (dominant middle zone, constructed rhythmic shapes), very paranoiac.

Luc UYTTEHNOVE, *Connaissez-vous par votre signature,* Marabout, Verviers (Belgium), 1982, 253p. - Spanish translation : *Cómo conocer a una persona por su firma,* Deusto, Bilbao, 1987, 211p, see pp.78, 175, 198; pp.70, 147-148, 166-167 of the Spanish translation.
- Rigid signature : earnest, but narrow mind. Tangled and clubbed paraph : touchiness, contentiousness, dignity. Lofty, needle-pointed signature, spindle-shaped, larger than the text : assertive pride, aloofness, fastidious speech, pessimism, passion.

Anne-Marie SIMOND, *La Graphologie planétaire. Une typologie de l'écriture et de la personnalité,* Albin Michel, 1990, 239p : see pp.222-223.
- Mars-Saturn-Sun handwriting verging on Uranus (resolved tension, spasms, rising lines, drooping accents), which corresponds to the character of Vigny.

J-Ch. GILLE-MAISANI, "The Planetary types in Handwriting", *Graphology,* no.15; 4-36, 1991 : pp.25-26.
- An analysis of Vigny's handwriting from the viewpoint of the planetary types : primarily Mars and Sun, then Saturn and Mercury, deficiency of Venus.

P. d'HUST, *Les Signatures célèbres, miroirs de la personnalité,* Hermé, 1991, 221p : see p.109.
- Shark-toothed *A* - violent aggression through lack of self-control. (pp.132-133) : signature sometime pale: "occupies the world of the mind for fear of been plunged into that of the earth and the senses". (pp.107-108) : Curved paraph, jarring with the angular signature; lack of harmony in the masculine and feminine pulsions : inflexible, ruthless character with dreams of comfortable happiness. (pp.176-177) signature occasionally reared; masochism. Discordance between the curved paraph and the angular signature.

* **Fig. 3.1** - The handwriting of Alfred de Vigny at nearly 28 years of age.

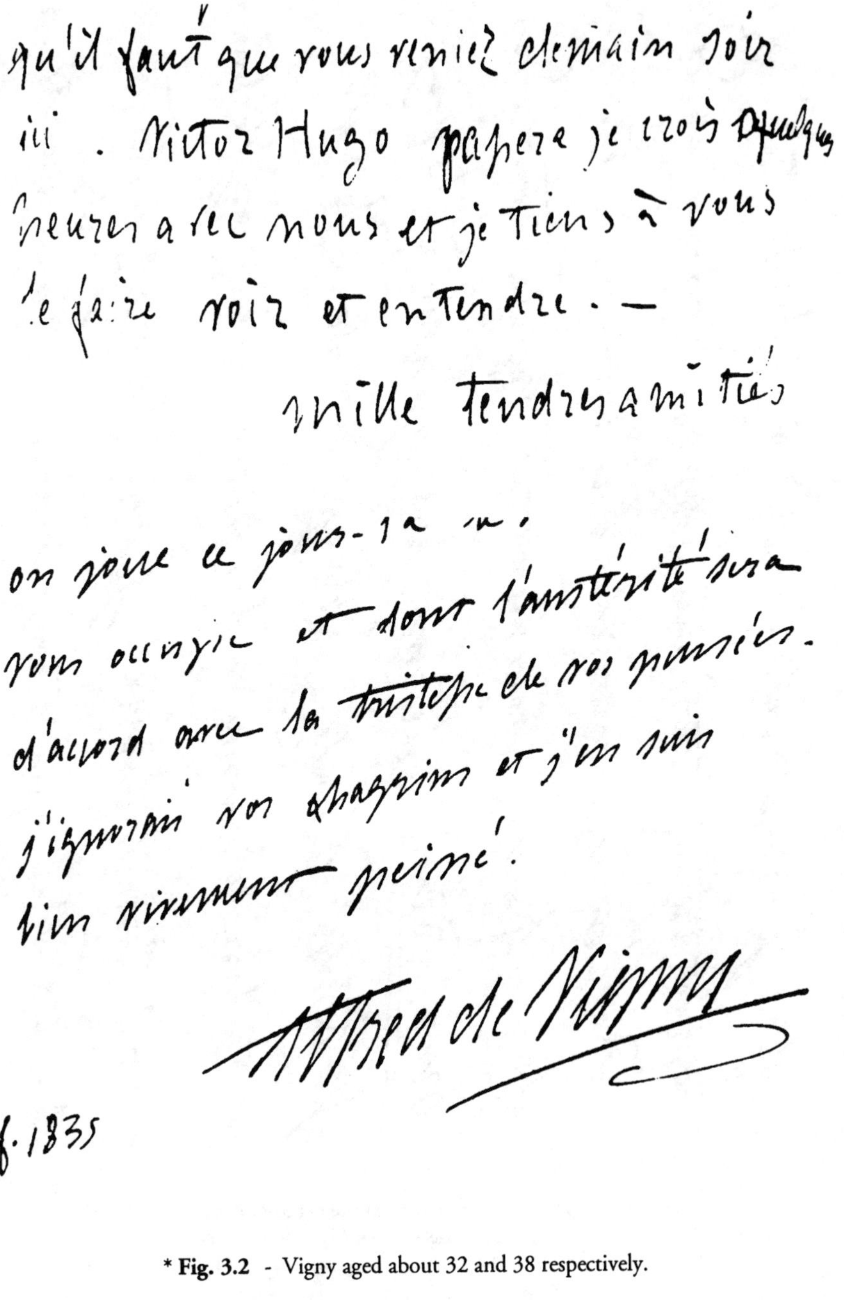

qu'il faut que vous veniez demain soir
ici. Victor Hugo passera je crois quelques
heures avec nous et je tiens à vous
le faire voir et entendre. —

mille tendres amitiés

on joue ce jour-là …
vous occupe et dont l'austérité sera
d'accord avec la ~~tristesse~~ de vos pensées.
j'ignorais vos chagrins et j'en suis
bien vivement peiné.

Alfred de Vigny

f. 1835

* **Fig. 3.2** - Vigny aged about 32 and 38 respectively.

Jésus, se rappelant ce qu'il avait souffert
depuis trente-trois ans, devint homme et la crainte
Serra son cœur mortel d'une invincible étreinte.
Il eut froid. Vainement il appela trois fois :
Mon Père ! — Le vent seul répondit à sa voix.
Il tomba sur le sable assis et, dans la peine
eut sur le monde et l'homme une pensée humaine.
— Et la terre trembla, sentant la pesanteur
du Sauveur qui tombait aux pieds du créateur.

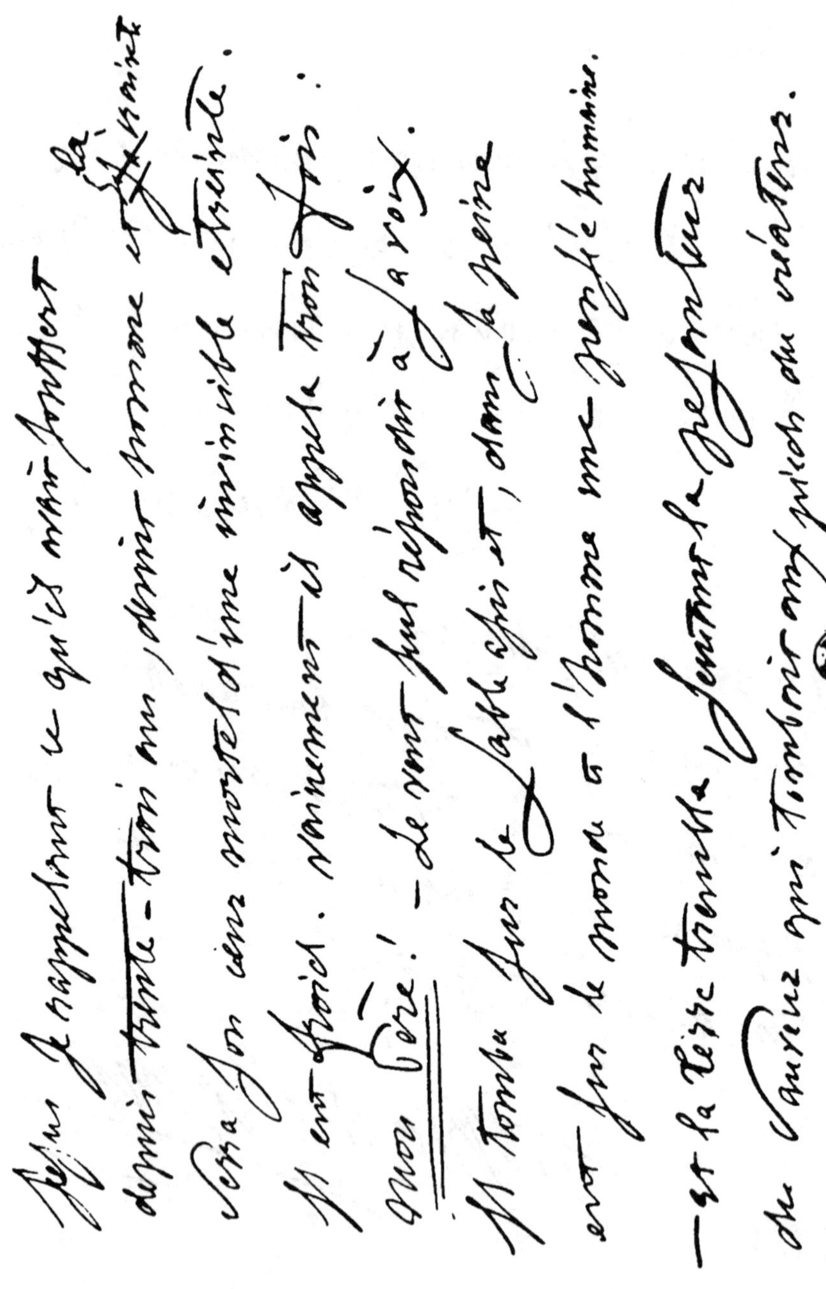

* **Fig. 3.3** - A fragment from the manuscript of Alfred de Vigny's *Mont des Oliviers*.

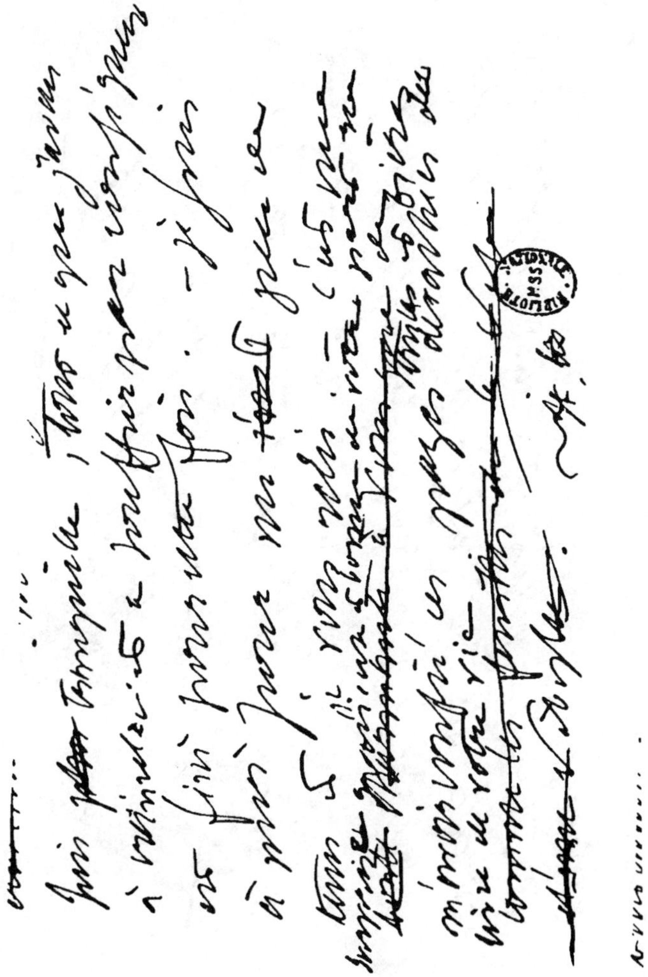

* **Fig. 3.4a** - Vigny aged 46.

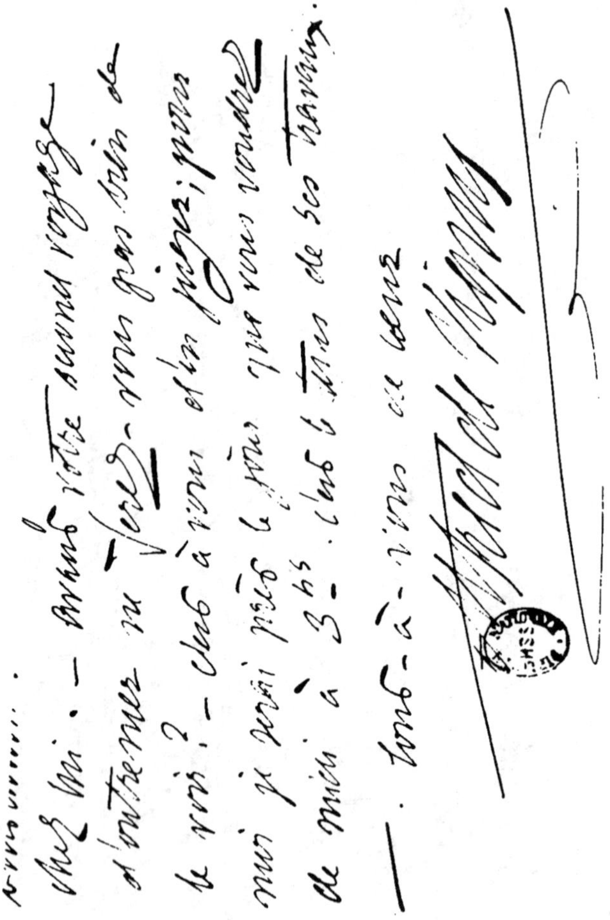

* **Fig. 3.4b** - Vigny aged 47.

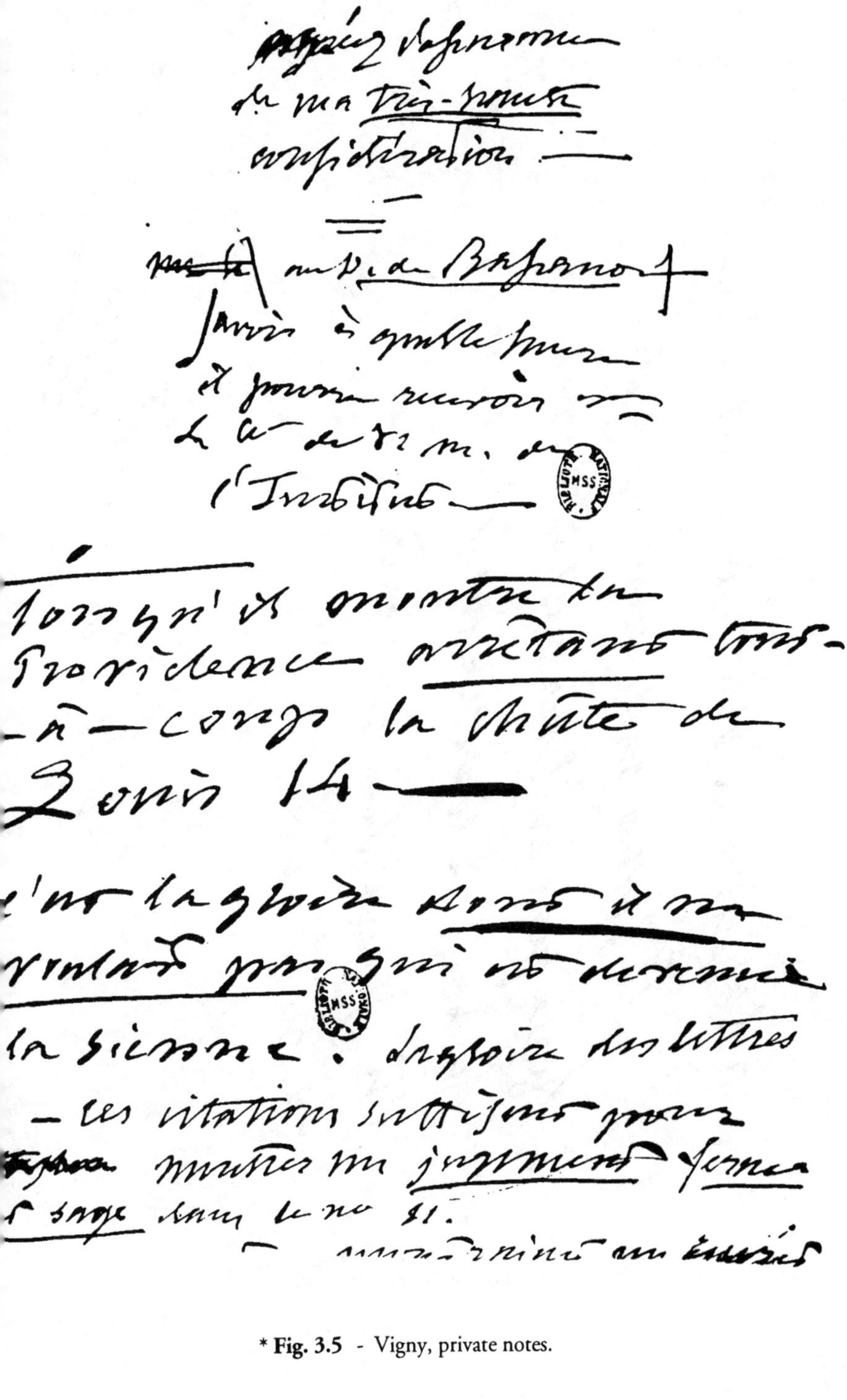

* **Fig. 3.5** - Vigny, private notes.

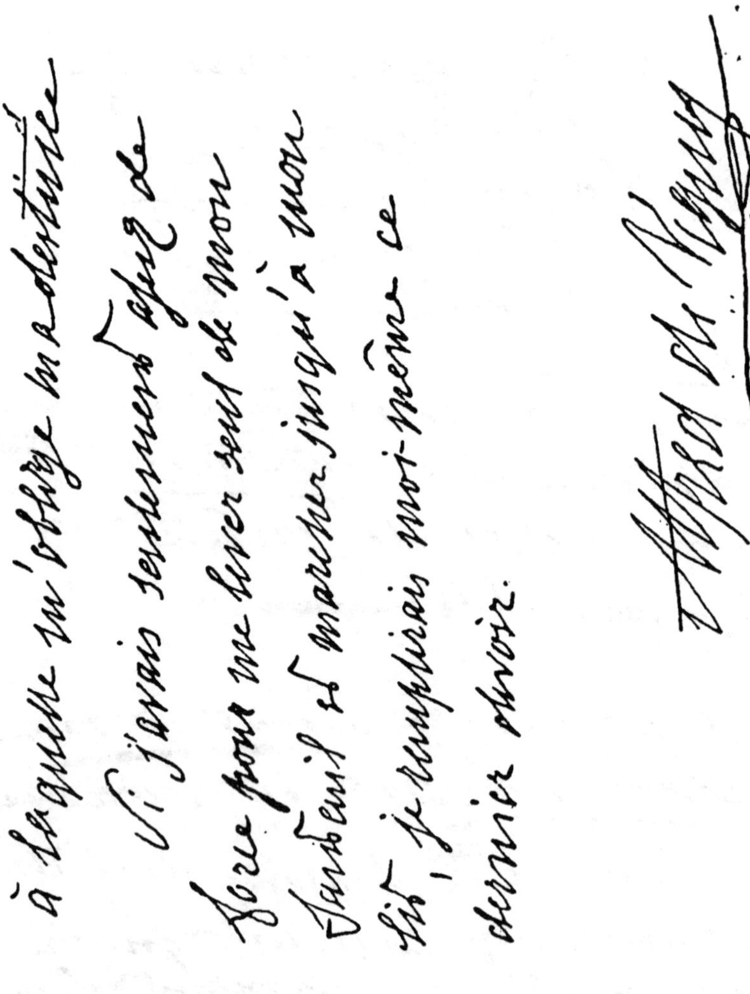

à laquelle m'oblige ma destinée
Si j'avais seulement assez de
force pour me lever seul de mon
fauteuil et marcher jusqu'à mon
lit, je remplirais moi-même ce
dernier devoir.

Alfred de Vigny

Fig. 3.6 - Vigny at 65.

CHANT III. 65

Que pourra sa pitié? Ce que toujours on vit,
Plaindre, non l'être mort, mais l'être qui survit;
Moi-même j'ai bien cru que la mort d'une amante
Était le plus grand mal dont l'enfer nous tourmente.
Ah! que ne puis-je en paix savourer ce malheur!
Il serait peu de chose auprès de ma douleur.
Dans son temps virginal que ne l'ai-je perdue!
A se la rappeler ma tristesse assidue
La pleurerait sans tache, et distillant mon fiel,
Je n'aurais qu'à gémir et maudire le Ciel.
Je dirais : Héléna! que n'es-tu sur la terre?
Tu laisses après toi ton ami solitaire,
Renais! Que ta beauté, belle de ta vertu,
Vienne au jour, et le rende à mon cœur abattu.
Mais de pareils regrets la douceur m'est ravie,
« Il faut pleurer sa mort sans regretter sa vie;
« Et si ces restes froids cédaient à mon amour,
« J'hésiterais peut-être à lui rendre le jour.
« Malheur! je ne puis rien vouloir en assurance,
« Et dédaigne le bien qui fut mon espérance!
« Héléna! nous n'aurions qu'un amour sans honneur :
« Vas, j'aime mieux ta cendre encor qu'un tel bonheur.

* Je vous dit tout, il faudrait parler a ~~descendre~~ je supprimerais toute cette tirade parce qu'elle renferme un sentiment factice qui ne peut être que le fruit de la réflexion mais dans l'instant où cette malheureuse helena se punit d'un crime dont elle est innocente un amant bien passionné, bien tendre ne doit que gémir et regretter. toute cette réflexion dont d'une injustice et d'un égoïsme bien masculin.

* **Fig. 3.7** - Madame de Vigny, the poet's mother.

4

Alexander Sergeyevich PUSHKIN (1799 - 1837)

Alexander Sergeyevich Pushkin is the greatest Russian poet.

He belonged to a noble family and had a touch of African blood (responsible probably for his fleshy lips and his curly hair): his mother was the granddaughter of an Ethiopian whom Peter the Great had brought young from Constantinople to St. Petersburg.

A gifted, but capricious child, Alexander was entrusted to tutors, then became one of the first set of the Imperial High School, which he left in 1817 to become an official. Exiled in the south of Russia because of his epigrams and then in his father's village because of his Voltairian ideas, Pushkin lived mainly in St. Petersburg from 1826. He was married in 1831 and served the Tsar as a "gentleman of the court".

Spied upon by the police and by censorship, falling more and more into debt because his wife and life at Court obliged him to live beyond his means, and further, being unable, though married, to give up his dissolute life and driven to the point of mad jealousy by his wife's successful flirtations, Pushkin was the victim of a social cabal and was mortally wounded in a duel.

Pushkin was the main founder of the Russian literary tongue. His work consists of poems of all kinds, the novel *Eugene Onegin,* the drama *Boris*

Godounov and some "little tragedies". In prose he tried the historic novel and wrote many novels of varied lengths. A great part of his work was composed, not in the whirl of city life, but in the course of two autumnal periods he was obliged to spend in the country.

While still alive, Pushkin's fame was immense in Russia, where his name is the greatest in literature. Unfortunately, the interest of his work lies for the most part in its Racinian perfection of expression, its powerful soberness and its musicality, qualities that translation cannot reproduce. Thus, his work is hardly known abroad, except when a composer adds to it the prestige of music, as did Glinka (*Russlan and Ludmila*), Tchaikovsky (*Eugene Onegin, The Queen of Spades*), Rimsky-Korsakov (*The Golden Cockerel*) and above all Moussorgski, thanks to whom *Boris Godunov* is world famous.

*

Figure 4.1 shows two youthful scripts that deal with the poems that Pushkin was already thinking of publishing. The first (reduced in size) is a list of them. The second is a sort of title page of the future collection "Verses of Alexander Pushkin 1817".

Figure 4.2 is a typical specimen of Pushkin's rough drafts, a passage from *The Demon* (1825).

Figure 4.3 consists of four relatively carefully penned lines, with a signature.

Figures 4.4a and 4.4b are two extracts from rough work dating respectively from 1833 (*Autumn*) and 1835 (*I have seen again this piece of land ...*).

Figure 4.5 has two slightly reduced examples written in 1835 and 1834 in French, a language that, like all cultivated Russians of the nineteenth century, Pushkin spoke perfectly. (His parents spoke it at home, and Alexander, at the age of ten, wrote a comic heroic poem of six cantos in French verse ...).

The differences in these documents are obvious even to the untrained eye. Figure 4.1 is full of an energetic, juvenile self-assurance. The rough work has the fire of inspiration and its crossings out show the labouring after perfection. As a contrast, the harmony of figure 4.3 gives an idea of the perfection of the finished work. The writing in 4.4b looks disintegrated (other scripts of about the same time or later, confirm this observation) and shows how deeply unsettled Pushkin's state of mind was during his last years.

Although the reader may be unfamiliar with the Cyrillic hand, it is nevertheless better to look at the pieces in Russian, paying attention less to the form than to the layout and above all to the movement.

The examples in French (fig. 4.5) are of a lesser graphological interest. One can apply to the handwriting the words of a critic who compared Pushkin's French and Russian: "The French verses are those of a master! In his own tongue he was a Titan!".

The scripts in figures 4.2 and 4.3 will be taken as the basis of our study.

Pushkin's HANDWRITING is *combined, harmonious enough* in spite of some exaggerations, and has a *high Formlevel.* By its speed and continuity, it is of above-average vitality, but not by its pressure or size, which are irregular.

The *tension* is III with, above all in the rough work, elements of II (flowing speed, supple with consistent garlands, imprecise forms and certain rounded flying strokes) and IVa (pressure on the vertical of the lower extensions).

The *forms* are *carried along by the movement.* The *rhythm* of the movement is intense; it is based on the relief, the differences in height and the throbbing ebb and flow of the middle zone that ends either with a sudden stop or a flying stroke. The latter is integral to the rhythm, but not the congestions. The rhythm of the spatial layout is quite strong. The Russian letters, though less familiar to us, do not appear to have a strong rhythmic form.

To define the writing I suggest :

Easy, rapid, dynamic and *regularly right-slanted.*

Connected (1), sometimes *over-connected.*

Constant but with strong jerky *irregularities* in height (*superelevations* and *prolonged downwards*), a tendency to *diminishing because of speed* in the rough work; height often varies (*spread-out* and *squeezed*).

In *relief* or *pastose,* depending on the particular example(2), *spasmodic* or *congested* in several examples.

Sudden *centrifugal flying strokes* (while other finals are *restrained,* almost "*suspended*" and *centripetal*).

Horizontal, straight-lined and with a few *"foxtails".*

The signature is like the text, *wide, over-connected* and with a *lasso.*

The youthful hand is above all *easy, connected, rapid* and *soaring;* the title and signature of 1817 have many *inflated arabesques.*

Pressure tends to be displaced onto the horizontal strokes between 1822 and 1825, and then after 1835.

The writing in 1835 is strikingly *low in vitality* (small, vague irregularities). *Movement is disturbed* and there are signs of tension IVb.

*

If a Russian reader should see this book, he would no doubt expect that a beginning should be made by explaining how the genius of Pushkin is seen in his handwriting. Creative intelligence certainly appears in the combined, rapid, rhythmic

---

(1) I have made some statistical calculations about the breaks in Pushkin's hand. In the rough work they allow the proper forming of the next letter, and much more rarely aim at clarity or the isolation of a capital. In texts designed to be read, clarity and logic motivate the breaks.

(2) I have not been able to work with the original scripts.

and spread-out hand. But, graphologically speaking, the dominant in Pushkin's hand lies elsewhere, namely in the *extreme intensity of temperament and drives.*

Pushkin loved life (writing garlanded and right-slanted, well-developed lower extensions, intense movement), wished to fulfil his ambitions and took them to heart (rather strong pressure, great difference between the middle zone and the exterior zones). He wanted to make his mark, to conquer and attract attention (superelevations, spasmodic signs, left-tending strokes). An appetite for conquest must have weighed as much as sensuality in his womanising.

How was this energy regulated? The rapid, right-slanting, flying, irregular writing speaks of impatience and impulsiveness. Subjectivity results from the signs of exaltation, (flying strokes, exaggerations[(3)]) and of imagination (width) and brings a lack of critical sense in such a proud man.

Pushkin always wanted to be in the right (superelevations, spasmodic, tension IVa), was very touchy and ready to blame others (superelevated, right-slanting, narrow writing) and, moreover, practically incorrigible (over-connected, straight-lined hand with emphasised enlarging finals). Perhaps this can be related to the after-taste of dissatisfaction expressed by the irregularities and the jerks (irritability, nervosity). Moreover, impulsiveness and sensuality (right-slanted, garlanded writing, with large lower extensions, spasms and congestion), added to imprecise forms and the unusual association of tensions II and IVa, point to the probability of a dissolute life.

However, one must not exaggerate. There is satisfactory control in the spatial layout, which is balanced and rhythmic;

(3) Pushkin, like all enthusiasts, frequently used capitals instead of lower case letters. Let us note apropos of this, a peculiarity of the collected edition of his works in 1924, one highly revealing of the moral climate of the Communist countries: the capitals were left in, except in the case of the word God (Bog), in which the Soviet censor ordered the letter B to be set in lower case.

the baseline is stable and the direction regularly right-slanted So, on the whole, Pushkin was well-integrated socially. When necessary, he knew how to be effectively charming, in a masterly way (combinations, with emphasised initial letters and graceful strokes). His critical intellect and his skill led him to understand the need to adapt himself to others, at least on the surface, as is seen in figure 4.3 where there is care, good layout and relative clarity. His impulsive, narcissistic and rebellious nature can, however, be glimpsed in the superelevations and in the flying strokes, which are now curved and graceful, now pointing more eastwards.

*

Pushkin's TEMPERAMENT was firstly warmly Sanguine (or Sanguine-Bilious : Air and Fire writing), then Nervous, with Lymphatic traces.

The *Sanguine* element appears in the dynamic hand, with its great wild movements, its irregular pressure and form. Warm Sanguine is in the *Bilious* element (superelevated, right-slanted, straight-lined, in relief with spasms). This warmly Sanguine man is emotional, quick to react, always busy, impatient. He is also jealous, possessive, subjective, vain and easily offended.

The *Nervous* element is above all that of a "sensitive Nervous" (rapid, simplified, nuancée, combined and in relief) a hypersensitive person, lacking in prudence and somewhat unstable, yet not excluding, all the same, in the background, a "cerebral Nervous" (dark, sober writing with a regular slant) reflective, pessimistic and sometimes bizarre character.

The *Lymphatic* element is not absent. It can be seen in the unfinished elements, the lack of precision of the rough work and in the significant blank spaces. But it does not appear in documents meant to be read. Inspiration is well under control.

From the point of view of the MYTHOLOGICAL TYPES, Pushkin's handwriting is remarkable, because all eight types are present. In this graphic context it is the sign of a personality that is extremely rich, but therefore difficult to pin down.

The writing of 1816-1817 is naively *Jupiterian* (inflations) with considerable *Venus* elements (curves) and *Mars* (regular slant) : ambition aiming at succeeding by sheer charm.

Pushkin's adult hand is that of a pronounced *Mars* type (straightlined, right-slanted, cruciform signs), with passionate desires, irresistible impulses excluding all prudence and economy. *Sun* (superelevations, high arcades, relief and combinations) is also in the foreground, and channels the energy of Mars towards a high ideal. The springing finals show the spirit of Mars and also the generous flow of inspiration. *Jupiter* (semi-rounded ease, wide and constant writing) is not less important : display of talents, panache, desire to be in one's rightful place, vanity.

All the other mythological types are present in this uncommon writing. Intellect is of the *Mercury* type (rapid and nuancée writing) : mind lively, inquisitive and critical - but without excluding *Saturn* (blackness, sobriety): severity when working. *Moon* appears in the imprecise forms, in words left unfinished and in the frequent blank spaces which are sometimes rhythmic, sometimes discordant. In this solar graphic context, one can feel poetic inspiration and an auditive aesthetic sense. *Earth* (simple forms, rather constant and connected middle zone) brings in a natural note whose sincerity is the happy counterpart of Sun and permits creativity. Finally, *Venus* (constant, semi-rounded and pasty) corresponds to a feeling that has a strong admixture of sensuality.

From the JUNGIAN point of view, extraversion (right-slanting, dynamic, thrown writing with a large signature) is stronger than introversion, but the latter is of a good quality and is not inferior in Janet's sense of the word (writing sometimes small and vertical). The four functions are strong, appearing in turn in the different documents. The combinations and the connected writing point to the development of *Thinking*; and the speed and rhythm to *Intuition. Sentiment* (width, pathos) and *Sensation* (weight, constant rhythm, pastosity and lower extensions) are strong, but less differentiated (occasional hard angles, congestions) and linked together. It would be rash to come to a definite conclusion. Pushkin could have been an Intuition type or an extraverted Thinking type, but it seems pointless to want to identify the main function in such an excessively rich nature.

*

From the SZONDIAN viewpoint the overall appearance of Pushkin's writing is dominated by the reactions *p-* (straight-lined, soaring and narrowed letters) but also *p+* (animated, rhythmic and superelevated writing) and *s+* (above average vitality, right-slanting, stroke having tension IVa).

In the *Ego* vector the reaction of factor *k* is ambivalent (a prominent, but irregular middle zone; individualistic, but not always precise forms). The type of Ego is questionable. In rough notes, the movement is carried along by the tide of inspiration, to the point of almost dissolving form. One is reminded of the *possessed Ego* E_{p1} (*Sch* = *k*0 *p+*). In the other documents the writing appears to evoke the *ideal-seeking Ego* (*Sch* = *k+/- p+*), rather than the *fugitive Ego Sch* = *k+/- p-*. Now, it seems that this last judgement would correspond better to the poet's personality (as it does to that of Byron, whom Pushkin admired, to the point that critics speak of a "Byronic phase" in his literary production). There is a distinct immaturity in the contrast between his desire for independence from the social world with its constraints, and his leaning (urged on by his ruling avidity) towards the creation of social bonds, as if

Pushkin had himself woven the spider's web in which he struggled. Typical also of the fugitive Ego is his inability to put up with stable situations, like the service of the Tsar or the bond of marriage[4]. Now, in spite of the signs *p-* (straightness of the lines, some narrowness, soaring, northeastward movements) the writing appears rather to be that of a *p+* [5] subject. I submit this problem to future graphologists, especially to those familiar with the Russian handwriting of the period.

The *Paroxysmal* vector seems to present the most ambivalence. On the one hand the well-nourished stroke, the sustained, constant rhythm of movement and the regular slant are signs of the reaction *e+*; on the other hand, the spasmodic, often sharp-pointed, flying strokes, the firm baseline and the Mars element associated with the signs of *p-*, indicate *e-*. As for the factor *hy* : the rapid and easy rhythm of movement, the balance between movement and form, the exaggerations, the arabesques and the Sanguine-Nervous temperament are signs of the reaction *hy+*. However, the simple shapes and the regularity of lines and slant show a trace of hy-. From this can be deduced an accessibility to every emotional behaviour (feelings of revolt and belief in the usefulness of an interior law, an urge to histrionics and the desire to 'fit in' socially), a state which is very hard to control by the reason and the will.

---

(4) The circumstances of the marriages of Byron and Pushkin were very similar. Both poets entered into marriage without conviction, but just to possess a young girl who had refused their first advances. During the weeks preceding the official ceremony, both felt the falsity of their situations. Their attitude during the ceremony was equally characteristic. "During the exchange of rings, says H.Troyat, one of the rings fell on the ground. Bending forward to pick it up, Pushkin bumped into the lectern and, said a witness, the cross and the Gospels slipped to the floor with a crash. Pushkin's candle went out. The poet straightened himself up and, very pale, murmured simply : All the ill omens".

(5) It needs to be pointed out that the reactions *p+* and *p-* are, in a certain sense, close to each other. The very great intensity of the first (strong awareness of desires) obviously encourages the vindictiveness of p-.

In a word, a rich nature, but "tormented", a complex temperament in the meaning given by Léone Bourdel (Harmonic-Melodic-Rhythmic).

The *Sexual* vector, it would seem, presents, the profile *S* = *h*+*s*+/-. The reaction *h*+ results from the well-nourished, pastose stroke, from the Pophalian elements of tension II, from the mainly Sanguine temperament: dependence on the senses, subjectivity. As to factor *s*, *s*+ comes from the prominence of the upper and lower zones and a writing that has strong vitality, connected, well-nourished, right-slanted and soaring : activity, desire to be in charge. From the weak relief, the irregular height and the relatively careless shapes, *s*- can be deduced. There is an attenuated *s*+ rather than a masochistic inturning or a sublimation. This profile, frequent in adolescence, is associated with a normal, but invasive sexuality that can become erotomania. In Pushkin's case there is a strong *m*+ reaction (cf. below); comforting affection is looked for (*h*+) either by gentle friendliness (*s*-) or, when frustration appears, by insistently demanding claims (*s*+, going with *p*-).

The *Contact* vector offers the accentuated profile *C* = *d*+*m*+. The reaction *m*+ follows from the ease of movement, garlands, comfortable finals and the prominence of the middle zone: sociability and a demand for communication and contact. The reaction *d*+ appears in the connected, rapid writing, form and relief being sacrificed to speed: the avidity is unsleeping. This profile (Szondi's "reality principle") means a great love of life, wit, the desire to make conquests, and this completes the picture of Pushkin's complex temperament. In this graphic context, characterised by an exalted state of mind (flying strokes, exaggerations), imagination (ampleness) and pride (superelevations) one can read dissipated activity, a ceaseless chase after new pleasures, coloured by a touch of competitiveness which finally leads to dissatisfaction.

*

The study of COMPLEXES is relatively easy. There is a strong over-compensated *inferiority complex* (superelevation) with narcissism and a *histrionic complex* (forms either fine or neglected, lassos, arabesques in the youthful writing samples). The pastose, congested stroke, the proteiform lower extensions show an over-developed sexuality. The very strong *Anima* (semi-rounded wide strokes, graceful soaring strokes, rhythm) is discovered under the wild sensuality : desire for amorous conquests and control. There are a few *anal* elements (pugnacity in some soaring strokes, heavy crossings-out).

Lastly, it is possibly to imagine a *paranoid* constitution, because of the signs of pride (prolonged up and down), of making demands (flying strokes) and an inability to conform (superelevations, straight-lined and with "foxtails") and because of the resultants that can be deduced from them. It seems easy to look for the manifestation of this constitution in Pushkin's life - noticing among other traits the poet's extreme susceptibility and his morbid jealousy, which ruined his stability during his last years and caused the final drama, but the circle he lived in must be reckoned with, as also the stifling atmosphere of permanent suspicion and police harassment.

Regretfully, we will not take any further the study of Pushkin's handwriting. It is impossible for us to go any deeper with the Russian hand, for fear of making dangerous extrapolations based on experience of Western writing, or of relying too much upon what is already known of the poet's life and work. Instead, this chapter will close with some reflections on Pushkin's drawings.

*

Pushkin's manuscripts are full of numerous DRAWINGS executed with rare talent: heads of men (some of them self-portraits) and women, human figures, horses, scenery, devils and witches, politicians, hanging corpses, etc. About four hundred of these have been listed and studied in relation to their context, in a book by Abraham Efros[6], published in 1933. A few examples will give an idea of the interest of these drawings.

The one in figure 4.6 is from the end of the manuscript of the unfinished novel *Dubrovski.* The text relates that a letter has just been brought to the hero giving bad news of his father's health. "He is very poorly and his mind sometimes wanders. From morning till night he stays motionless in his armchair, like an unreasoning infant". So the hero decides to go to him. "When daylight came he dispatched urgent business and was able to set out after forty-eight hours. He travelled by carriage in the company of his faithful Gricha". The drawing shows the doddering father and the carriage. There is a face, on the right. Specialists on Pushkin say that it is the profile of Napoleon. It is possible that Pushkin was thinking of introducing the historic scenes of the French invasion of 1812 into the rest of his novel.

The first drawing in figure 4.7 is a doodle in the form of a bird and was often made by Pushkin. The second, from 1830, illustrates the comic poem *La petite Maison de Kolomna (The little House at Kolumna).* These two drawings are of interest for another reason, namely, to study Pushkin's psychobiologic temperament (Léone Bourdel). The first drawing is strongly *Rhythmic* (the outline of the bird being formed by a repetition of the same movement). The second has a strong Rhythmic element (dominant straight lines with a few points, background covered with conventional parallels endlessly repeating the same sequence), but with some *Harmonic* elements (overall composition) and some *Melodic* (encircling ovals). The whole gives an impression of cramming and of fudging, which is typically HMR (Harmonic-Melodic-Rhythmic, i.e. *Complex*).

(6) *Risunki Poeta* (The poet's drawings), Academia, Leningrad, 1933, 472p. (This book is in the Turgenev library in Paris, section P167).

Most of Pushkin's drawings, like this second one, are HMR with a very strong Rhythmic component.

The notion of the Complex temperament helps in the understanding of several traits in Pushkin's personality, in particular his greediness - a common feature with all HMR subjects - his masochistic taste for danger and being provocative, and lastly, the great richness of his personality, so difficult to picture. In this Complex scene, the Rhythmic element is the most arresting: a lack of inhibition in public (Pushkin had the effrontery to reply to the Tsar that if he had been in St. Petersburg in 1825, he would have joined the insurgents), incorrigible obstinacy in repeating the same imprudent actions (perseveration), a critical Voltairian mind closed to spiritual questions, pointed ironic behaviour (objective causticity), a way of life emotionally unlike that in several of his novels (such as in *Snow Storm*), the sober precision of his style. But the Harmonic elements (belief in Art) and the Melodic (communication, desire to be sociable) are not absent, the personality being too rich, too polymorphous to be purely Rhythmic. Pushkin understood the complexity of his nature when he described himself as being "unbalanced, jealous, touchy, violent and weak all at the same time".

Pushkin's art is also HMR. Note especially the importance, in his work, of the theme of defiance of destiny, of the love of macabre comedy, of pessimism, and finally of the breaks in rhythm which cause an abrupt passage from one level to another, for example, from tenderness to irony. The complexity of Pushkin is projected onto the doubling of the hero of *Eugene Onegin* by the Harmonic artist, Vladimir, and the Rhythmic skeptic, Eugene, and by the duel in which the latter kills the former.

Figure 4.8 brings together some of the numerous drawings of feet (nearly always women's feet) which are found throughout Pushkin's manuscripts. These come from the rough drafts of

Eugene Onegin, Autumn and the *Gabrielade.* They are unrealistically pointed. The extremely frequent appearance of feet and their abnormal shape is explained if one remembers that Pushkin had a fetish for feminine feet. In the first canto of *Eugene Onegin* the following lines are explicit :

> I love the furore of youth, the crowd, the splendour and the joy - and the dresses women wear : I adore their little feet. But, really can you find three perfect little pairs of feet in all Russia? Ah! There are two little feet I have long been unable to forget! ..... saddened, grown cold, I think of them all the time, and they come back to trouble my heart in my dreams. Where, when, in what desert, fool, will you forget them? Ah! Little feet, little feet, where are you today? [...] The bosom of Diana, the cheeks of Fiona are delightful, dear friends! But the little foot of Terpsichore somehow delights me more. It promises the eye a priceless reward and by its cunning beauty awakens a mad swarm of desire. [...] Sometimes, in my secret dreams I hold the happy stirrup and I feel the little foot between my hands, and my imagination throbs afresh, again its touch fires the blood in my withered heart, again comes nostalgia, again love ...

Simply literary imagination? All doubts disappear in the intimate details of the drawing in 4-9 sketched by Pushkin for himself in 1833 : feet of a woman dressed for a ball, upon a cushion in front of an armchair. At the time Pushkin was very concerned about the dissipated life of his wife, who was always at parties. ("You only work when you are dancing with your little feet, and you help your husbands to spend their money", he wrote to her a little later). Her flirtatiousness persisted until the final disaster.

*

BIBLIOGRAPHY

Adrien VARINARD, "Pouchkine, Poëte russe", *La Graphologie 14*(17) : see pp.129-132, 1st Sept, 1884. (10 lines in Russian with signature).
– Detailed analysis of Pushkin's writing according to the Abbé Michon's system. Impossible to sum up. Can be found in the Bibliothèque Nationale, Paris, section 4° V.326.

Arsene ARUSS, *La graphologie simplifiée. Art de connaître le caractère par l'écriture*, Kolb, 1891, 286p : see p.211.
– Capital *P* reversed : extravagance.

I. F. MORGENSHTERN, *Zhurnal psikho-grafologii,* (St. Petersburg), *1*(2) : see p.20, 1903 (under "The Laws of Graphology". Illustrated by the lines in this book, figure 7.3).
– In the handwritings of poets and writers the letters are generally connected, right-slanted, sometimes unfinished, but simple and always original, with finesse and affectation.

I. F. MORGENSHTERN, *Zhurnal psikho-grafologii,* (St. Petersburg), *1*(3) : see pp.33-34 (under the same heading as above. Illustrated by the signature in our figure 4.3).
– Men with the gift of abstract thought (Tolstoy, Pushkin) usually sign without a paraph. Letters are simple, connected and flowing. These thinkers are concerned with analysis and synthesis and ignore the beauty of form.

I. F. MORGENSTIERN, *Psikho-Grafologia ili nauka ob opredelenii vnutrenniago mira chelovieka po iego pocherku* (Psychographology, or the science of determining the inner world of a man from his handwriting), Neierman, St. Petersburg, 1903, 693p : see pp.295-296. (Illustrated by our figure 4.3). Here follows the complete translation of Morgenstiern's analysis :
– "Straight, precise, diminishing, connected, unfinished and barred letters with no adornment. They are simple, but each has the sign of individual beauty. Some extensive movements, rounded in an original way, seem executed as a joke : astonishing emotional caprice. The deep perspicacity of thought causes unexpectedly grandiose effects. The writing shows the variety of emotions and the power of happy creation. Also visible is the whole gamut of feelings deeply experienced, that Pushkin only expresses in his epigrams, or allusively. The feelings in the higher areas of the brain are clear; they awaken suffering and agitation, without which he would never have reached genius. He was not a practical man in daily life and he was prone to waste money. A fine, generous Slavonic nature. Jealous, with a sickly self-love, but faithful and trusting. - Dark hair, handsome long face, large dark eyes".

*D. M. ZUEV-INSAROV, *Pocherk i licznost. Sposob opredelenia kharaktera po pocherku, grafologicheskii metod izuchania lichnosti* (Handwriting and Personality. How to determine the character from the handwriting. Graphological method of personality analysis) (1929), 2nd ed., self-published work, Moscow, 1930, 124p : see pp.95-99.
– A detailed analysis that I have translated and published in its entirety in *Ecritures de poètes de Byron à Baudelaire* (Dervy-Livres, Paris, 1977, see pp.119-121). Here is a summary.

Pushkin's handwriting is as artistic as his drawings, the latter being commented on by A. Efros: not "pretty" writing, but impetuous, connected and creative of symbols and of sounds. An unstable hand, now calm, now explosive : capable of anger and cruelty. Speed, combinations. Pressure irregular : changes in mood and activity. Open vowels, diminishing word endings: a trusting nature. Pronounced margins and interword spaces : generous, with no practical sense. Flying strokes : sickly self-love, capable of extravagance. Conclusion : a lack of prudence. Writing illustrated by drawings : visual imagination. Unstable direction, varying pressure and layout : sensibility overcomes the will. In his last writings there are spasmodic and thrown movements with sudden stops, and closed vowels: morbid self-love, surliness and suspicion. In short, a passionate but sane nature: "He was, as it were, hunted down by the life he led and by his surroundings, for he was incapable of bearing that another should have any hold over his personality, but he had not the strength to free himself".

J.-Ch. GILLE-MAISANI, *Psychologie de l'écriture*, 2nd ed., Payot, Paris, 1977, 310p : see pp.94-95 and 149. In the English translation, *The Psychology of Handwriting*, Scriptor Books, London, 1992, 347p : see pp.126-127 and 199.
– Commentary on two drawings by Pushkin (start and end of the manuscript of *Autumn*), in relation to their context. Pushkin's writing is straight-lined, but irregular : character both intractable and emotional.

Arcadio BACQUERO, "Pushkin, un escritor rebelde con una firma alucinante", *Escritura y grafología,* no.39, pp.29-31, 1991.
– (Concerning three lines of text with a signature, dating from 1823). The lines of the text are correct, balanced, horizontal, but with some leftward-turning strokes (self-centredness). However, the creative genius and the rebellious, aggressive non-conformist can be seen in the paraph.

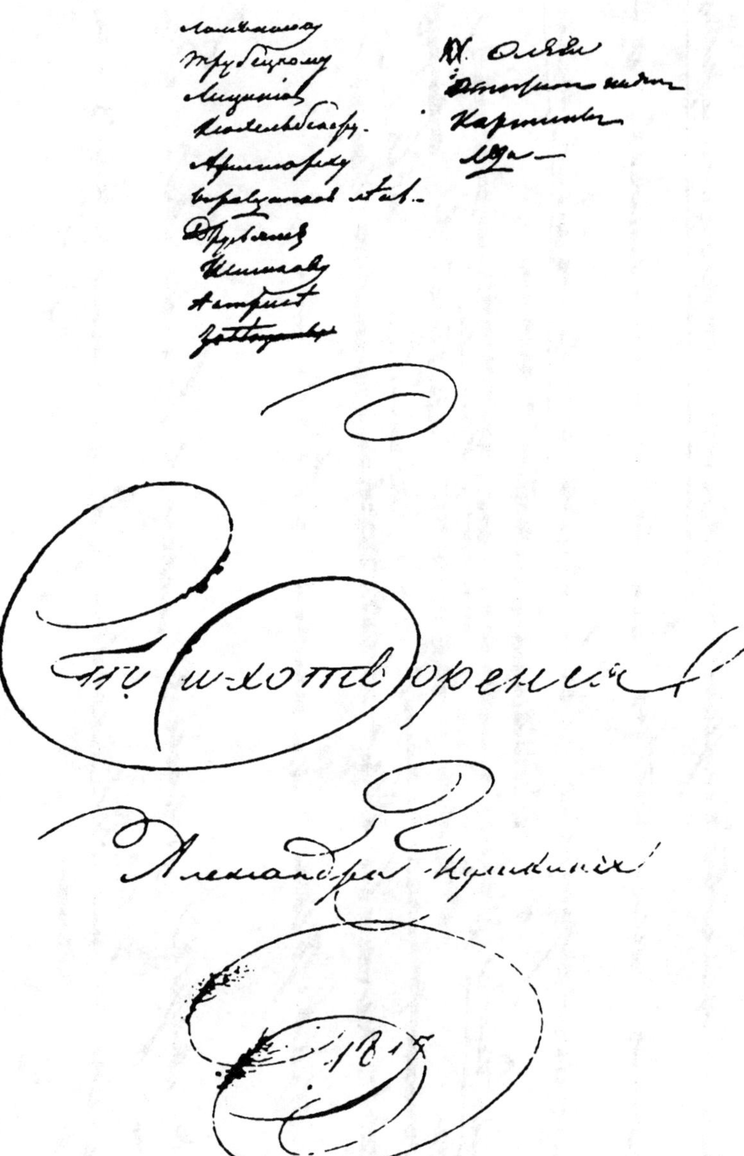

Fig. 4.1 - The handwriting of A.S. Pushkin, aged 16 and 18 respectively. (The upper lines are certainly reduced).

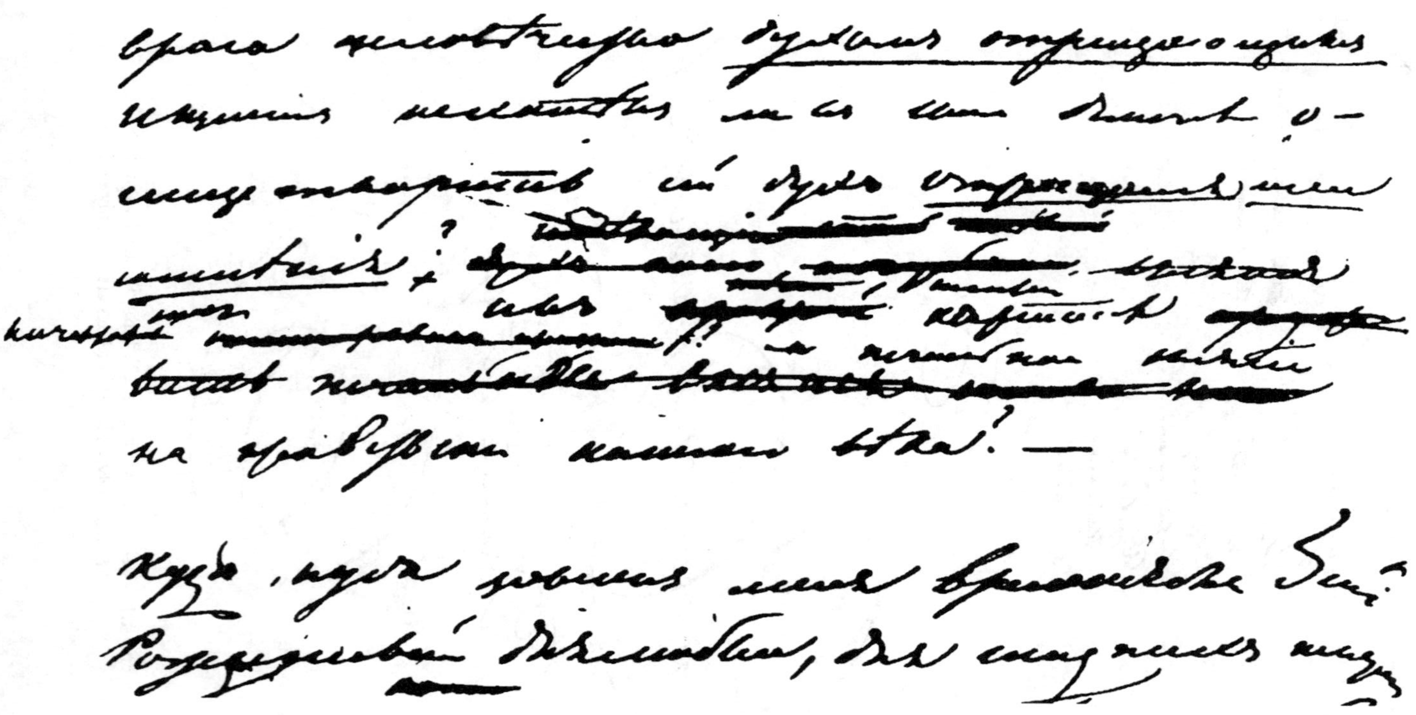

Fig. 4.2 - Sketches of Pushkin's poems at the age of 26.

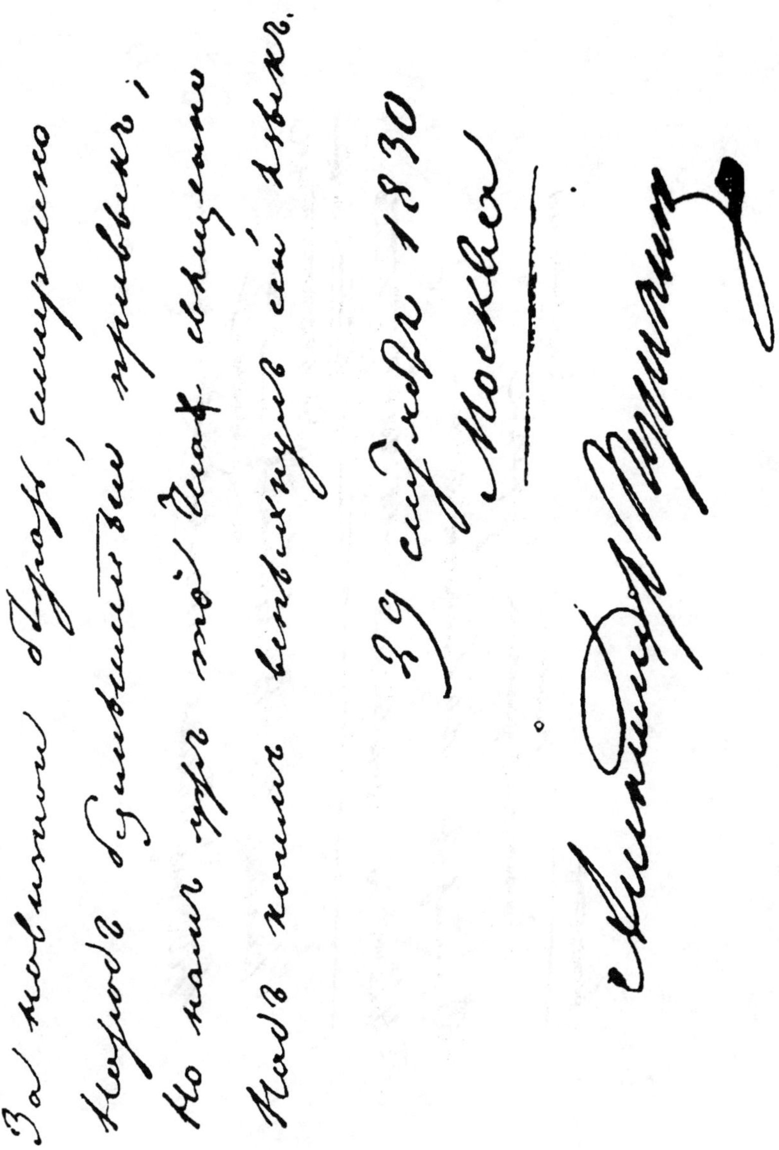

Fig. 4.3 - Pushkin at 31.

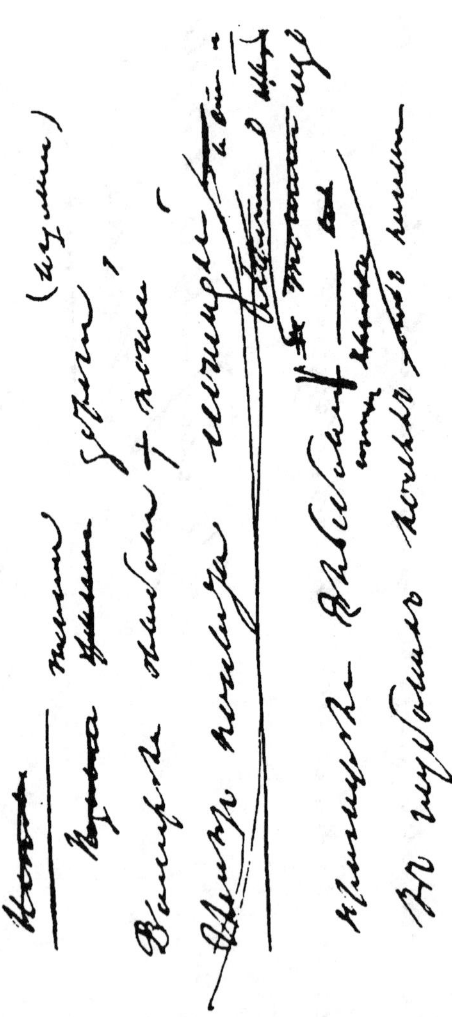

Fig. 4.4a - Sketches of Pushkin's poems at 34 years of age.

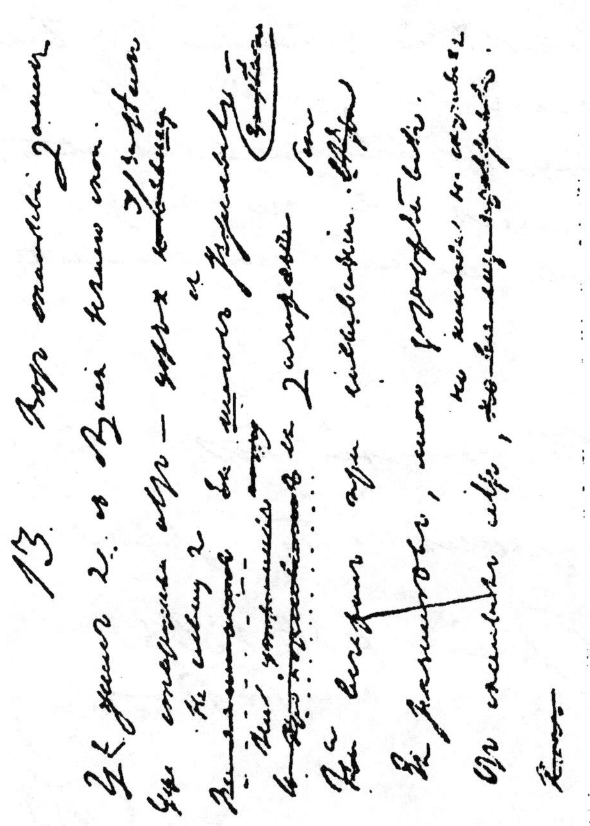

Fig. 4.4b - Sketches of Pushkin's poems at 36 years of age.

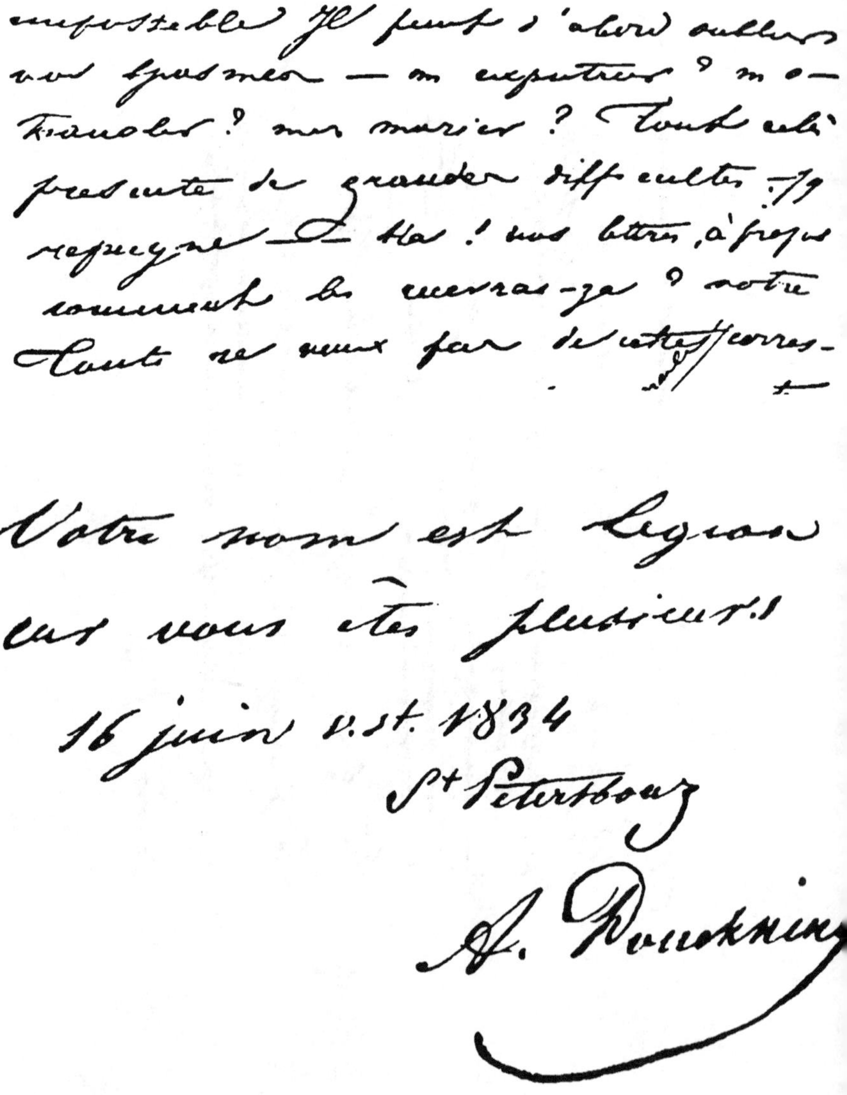

Votre nom est Legion car vous êtes plusieurs.

16 juin v. st. 1834
St Petersbourg

A. Pouchkin

Fig. 4.5 - Pushkin's writing in French.

Fig. 4.6 - Drawings by Pushkin.

Fig. 4.7 - More drawings by Pushkin (reduced).

Fig. 4.8 - Pushkin's drawings of female feet (slightly reduced).

Fig. 4.9 - Pushkin the female foot fetichist.

5

Charles BAUDELAIRE (1821 - 1867)

Into this *ruthless* book (*Les Fleurs du mal*) I have put all *my heart*, all *my tenderness*, all *my religion* (disguise) and all *my hatred*. It is true that I shall write the opposite, and I shall swear to high Heaven that it is a book of *pure art*, of *caricature* and *entertainment*, and I shall be lying through my teeth. (Letter to Ancelle, 16 February, 1866)

Ah! Seigneur! donnez moi la force et le courage
De contempler mon coeur et mon corps sans dégoût![1]
(*Un voyage à Cythère.*)

Charles Baudelaire's elderly father died when the boy was six. His mother then married commander Aupick (who later became a general and a senator). After good secondary school studies and a youth spent in the Bohemian literary world of Paris, Baudelaire acquired notoriety through his articles of literary, artistic and musical criticism and his translation of his admired Edgar Allan Poe in whom he recognised a kindred spirit. His

(1) Sustain my courage, Lord, and make me strong
To see my heart and flesh without disgust!

volume of poems, *Les Fleurs du mal* (1857), the expression of his neurosis, is today considered as marking a great date in the history of French poetry to which he brought, like Victor Hugo, a new 'frisson", but at the time it caused a scandal, a lawsuit for offending public morality, a fine and the suppression of some items. Baudelaire, worn out too soon by syphilis and drug-taking, died ill and paralysed at the age of forty-six.

His handwriting and drawings are reproduced in abundance in several editions of his works and handbooks of literature. Figures 5.1 to 5.8 are extracts from letters covering the period 1841 to 1860. Figure 5.9 is from his notebook.

Baudelaire's handwriting from the viewpoint of the ORIENTATING SYNTHESES :

Combined, with a *harmony* that is lessened by discordant height and exaggerated irregularity.

Formlevel high, but lessened by much irregularity.

As for *tension* : the inhibitions of IVb superimposed on a guiding image of III (tensing, reduced size, spasms and amendments).

Movement creates form, over which it predominates.

The handwriting is *rhythmic*, with a rapid and irregular pulse with which the thrusting strokes are well integrated. The three rhythms of movement, the creation of form and spatial layout go well together, but the stroke is *disturbed*.

The writing is remarkably *unstable*. The main dominant common to every example is extreme *irregularity in all the categories* :-

in speed : *rapid, thrown* but *amended* writing;

in continuity : *hyperconnected*, but with some *breaks*, "holes" in the words;

in height : *superelevation* to the point of cramping;

in direction, spaced out;

in pressure : *relief* is inconstant and there are *congestions* and *spasms*.

The *t*-bars are *inconsistent, long*, often *light* and *hesitant*.

The signature is a little *larger* and *firmer* than the text and is followed by a full stop.

Each document could be examined carefully on its own. Figures 5.3 and 5.4, because of their long finals and exaggeratedly wide spacing are typical of prodigality as Abbé Michon had already discovered. (At this time Baudelaire was leading a dissipated life, and in 1844 he had to be legally prevented from using up his inheritance).

The two documents from 1848 differ from each other. The writing in 5.5 is : *agitated, fine, simplified, imprecise, light, convex,* then *rising.* The writing in 5.6 is : *rising, spontaneous, wide, free, semi-rounded,* uncertain in direction, *galloping* : it has *exaggeratedly centrifugal* finals. Figure 5.7, similar to the preceding, is pretty well the usual hand of Baudelaire when he wrote in order to be read, but not in figure 5.8 in which movement is inhibited (*small, fragmented* hand) and form is sacrificed (*imprecise* writing).

Figure 5.9, on the contrary, is an example of Baudelaire writing for himself. *Irregularity* in continuity and direction are *extreme,* as are the flying strokes. There is much congestion and crossings-out (there are three in this example) are extremely violent as they are on other pages of the notebook.

*

There are four essential features to be noted in this rich, but complex hand : the ability of the writer, the poor quality of the stroke, the insufficient building up of the writing line and the good spatial layout.

1) The liveliness and subtlety of intelligence (rapid, connected and combined hand), fine and critical (writing which is nuancée and sharp-pointed), appear notably in figure 5.5. Figures 5.6 and 5.7 especially show the sense of form and the love of beauty (wide, graceful writing moving in curves).

2) The stroke is rapid and curved, generally weak in pressure and with edges that are usually blurred. This expresses receptivity of the senses and a thirst for impressions: "the imagination and the perceptions mutually influence and excite each other", engendering fantasy and mythomania (W. Hegar, type XIV). The stroke is also very disturbed. There are amendments, spasms and congestion which suggest poor physiological equilibrium, together with alarming overexcitability and a poorly integrated sensuality.

   These imperfections in the stroke are all the more interesting, because the movement of the writing trail, the form and the distribution of space are rhythmic and go well together. Baudelaire's handwriting is one of those that justify H. Pfanne in his advice to graphologists to treat the stroke as a special aspect of the handwriting, related to the three aspects of Gross and to be considered like them.

3) The study of the stroke, with its exaggerations and irregularity is easy. Baudelaire is sincerity personified : his very spontaneous handwriting excludes the calculated deceit perceived in his poetry by some critics of the nineteenth century. He is led by sentiment, sensation and imagination (garlands, prolonged, wide writing), he reacts immediately (right-slanted, rapid, thrown writing) with intensity and impatience, but without having any deep-rooted resistance (initial emphasis, irregular direction and continuity, light, hesitant *t*-bars : a weak will).

   His moods, extremely variable (unstable writing, very irregular in direction), go from euphoric and imprudent affirmation (large, wide, right-tending writing) to mistrust (small writing, decreasing left margin, signature ending in a full stop): nervous equilibrium is bad (agitated, jerky writing), and health appears affected (the cramped writing trail brings us back to the disturbances in the strokes). Baudelaire's intelligence and his desire to stand back and look at himself (frequently delicate upstrokes) only reinforce his anxiety.

4) Nevertheless, the writing is homogeneous; a sensible layout with rhythmic spacing makes up for the irregularity of the movement : the poet's ordinary behaviour was scarcely different from that of a respectable man concerned about fitting into society. (Biographers note how well he respected the conventions).

*

Before looking at the typologies, here is a GRAPHOMETRIC STUDY of example 5.7: cf. charts 5.1 and 5.2, kindly made for this book by Mme M.-T. Prénat.

The *instinctual component* I is abnormal in a twenty-seven year old man. The exposure of the variables 1 (stroke picture) and 2 (pressure) shows rich and diverse sensorial and pictorial perception and an enduring, energetic tension. Pastosity and congestion (shifting of the variable 3 towards expansion) reveal infusion by the prevailing surroundings and an invasion through sensorial permeability. The quality of the stroke (variable 4) and the clogging (variable 5) betray physiological wear and tear and the difficulty of having to make efforts.

As for the *rational* component (histogram II), the main thing is the dissociation of variable 8 : the simultaneous presence of angle and thread in "intermediary letters" betrays extreme ambivalence towards moral and social rules : abandonment to the instincts (-3), but an inflexible conscience (+2, +3). This creates on the histogram a "peak" in +2 and "trough" in +1 (inability to reconcile deep tendencies with everyday behaviour), in spite of the normal display of variables 9 and 10 (socially adapted attitude, a delicate analytico-synthetic approach).

"A quick inspection of this curve", writes Mme M.-T. Prénat, (the *Ego*: histogram III), "reveals the major problem of an Ego constantly in search of itself, because it successively lacked the initial assertion of self and identification with a

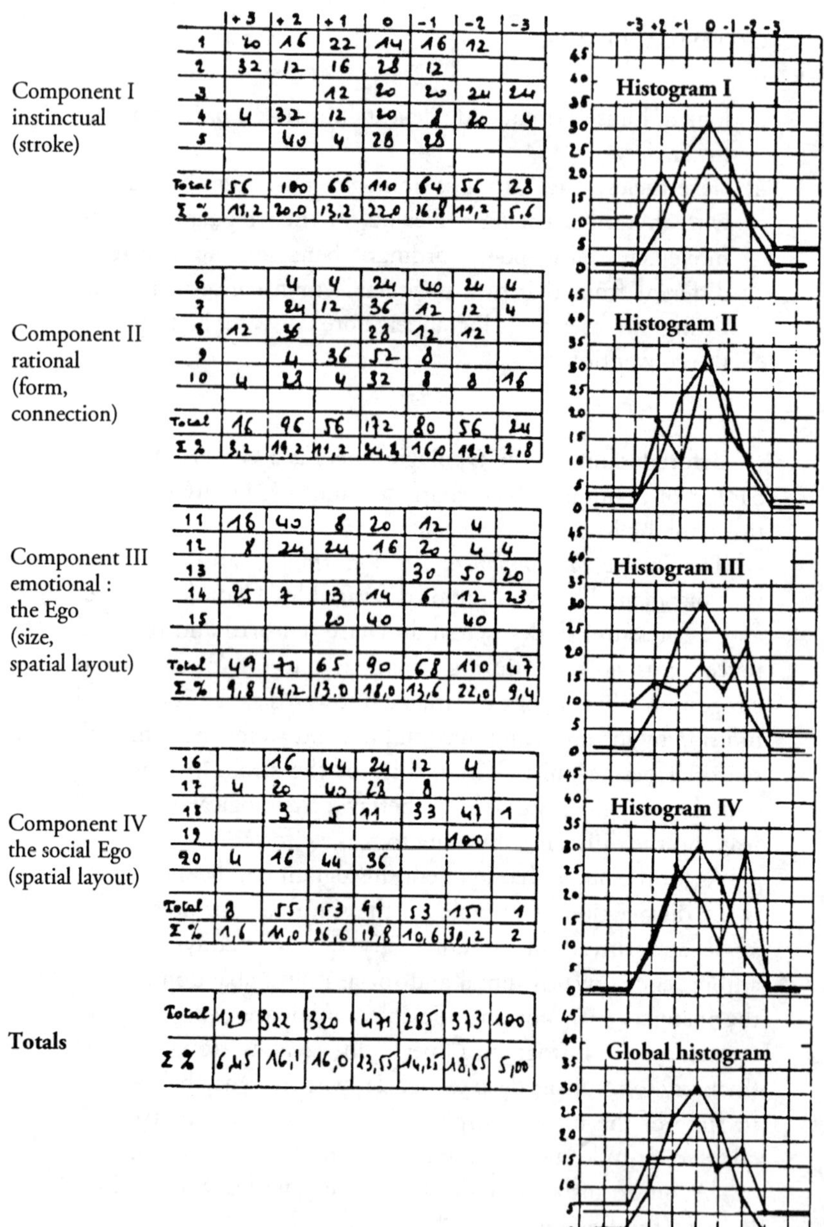

Component		+3	+2	+1	0	-1	-2	-3
Component I instinctual (stroke)	1	20	16	22	14	16	12	
	2	32	12	16	28	12		
	3			12	20	20	24	24
	4	4	32	12	20	8	20	4
	5		40	4	28	28		
	Total	56	100	66	110	84	56	28
	Σ %	11,2	20,0	13,2	22,0	16,8	11,2	5,6
Component II rational (form, connection)	6		4	4	24	40	24	4
	7		24	12	36	12	12	4
	8	12	36		28	12	12	
	9		4	36	52	8		
	10	4	28	4	32	8	8	16
	Total	16	96	56	172	80	56	24
	Σ %	3,2	19,2	11,2	34,4	16,0	11,2	4,8
Component III emotional : the Ego (size, spatial layout)	11	16	40	8	20	12	4	
	12	8	24	24	16	20	4	4
	13					30	50	20
	14	25	7	13	14	6	12	23
	15			20	40		40	
	Total	49	71	65	90	68	110	47
	Σ %	9,8	14,2	13.0	18,0	13,6	22,0	9,4
Component IV the social Ego (spatial layout)	16		16	44	24	12	4	
	17	4	20	40	28	8		
	18		3	5	11	33	47	1
	19						100	
	20	4	16	44	36			
	Total	8	55	153	99	53	151	1
	Σ %	1,6	11,0	30,6	19,8	10,6	30,2	2
Totals	Total	129	322	320	471	285	373	100
	Σ %	6,45	16,1	16,0	23,55	14,25	18,65	5,00

Chart 5.1 - Graphometrical analysis of Fig. 5.7 (Baudelaire)

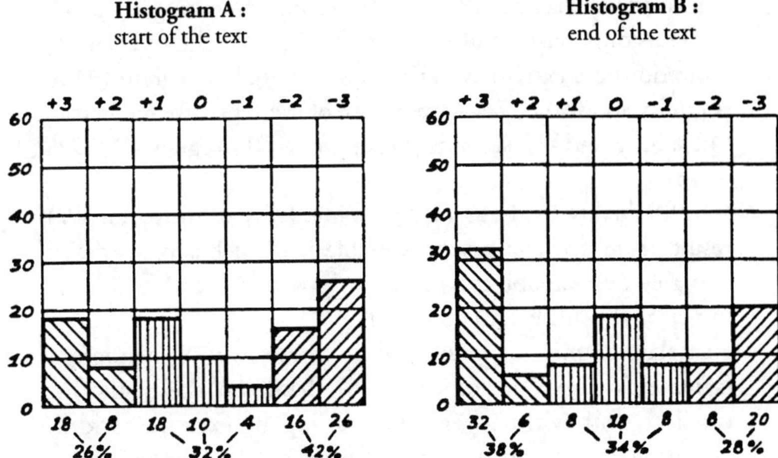

Global Histogram

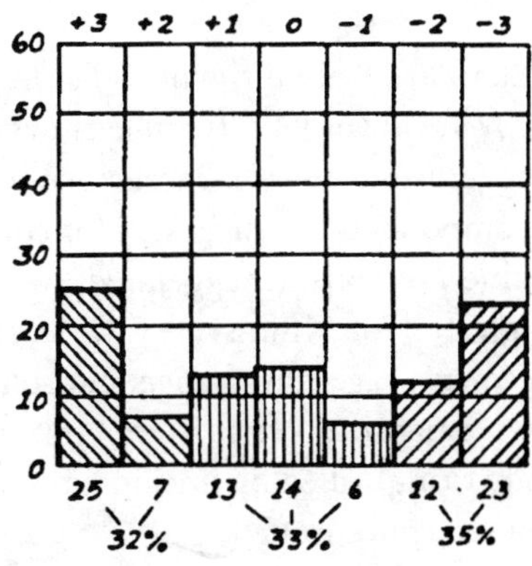

Chart 5.2 - Graphometrical analysis of Fig. 5.7 (Baudelaire) : sinuosity histograms

father serving as a support and model. The particularly strong unconscious (10 up to +3) entails, by its compensating impulses, a disorderly behaviour (9, 4 to -3), having something suicidal".

The consciousness of self (variable 11) and the intensity of aspirations are extremely variable. The initial histogram (A) of sinuosity shows the great importance of the expansive tendencies (42% in -2 and -3), secondarily suppressed (histogram B) (32% in +3).

The duality of the *social Ego* (bimodality of histogram IV) results from the strong slant (variable 18) which is very uneven (variable 19): variability in relationships (variables 16, 20) and in personal confidence (variable 17).

Relative unity is preserved in the *global* V histogram (symmetric curve, maximum in 0) thanks to the quality of intellect, but with a pendulum swing of excessive width, favouring extreme attitudes (a "plateau" at +1, a strong lift in -2). The index of operational intelligence (31%) is at the limit of morbidity.

*

The TEMPERAMENTS are difficult to list in an orderly way. First come the *Nervous* (instability, unevenness, jerks) and the *Sanguine* (exaggeration in the larger movements). Three differentiated components are suggested for consideration :

a) a Sanguine-Nervous (exaggerated, very spontaneous, thrown writing), full of whimsy, easily worked-up, with a subjective judgement, eager for change, but solitary;

b) a "moist Sanguine" (effortless, rounded, wide and connected handwriting) ruled by imagination, enthusiasm, but weak and unable to concentrate;

c) lastly, a "dry Nervous" or Nervous-Bilious (noticeable particularly in figures 5.5 and 5.8, small simplified, nuancée, hopping), anxious, fragile, sceptical with "more intelligence than heart, more nerve than muscle" (H. Saint-Morand).

*

Of the MYTHOLOGICAL TYPES *Sun* is in the foreground, because of the fine, simplified shapes (sense of the beautiful, clarity of thought) and of the high letters (taste for great things, ideal) with *Mars* because of the spring of the rapid, right-slanting handwriting, the cruciform signs and the enormous aggression that appears in certain pages of the notebook (negative Mars).

In the middle ground *Moon* brings a touch of the whimsical with the somewhat imprecise rounded shapes, the considerable white spaces and, above all, the accents in figure 5.3, and a varying signature. In the signatures in 5.3 and 5.8 *Mercury* brings a subtlety of mind capable of deception (small, sensitive, dryish, sharp-pointed writing) and *Saturn* dark moods (dark, fragmented writing).

Jupiter and *Earth* are present (width, good layout, downward strokes), but there is a deficiency of Venus (inability to adapt).

*

From the JUNGIAN angle, Baudelaire is a *Thinking* type (writing simplified, combined, progressive, sometimes small, sharp-pointed and with a simple signature). There is auxiliary *Intuition* (rhythmic, combined, wide and simplified, irregular writing) and strong *Sensation* (pastose writing). (It is important to remember that *Les Fleurs du mal* was not Baudelaire's only work. His contemporaries knew him above all as a literary critic). He is an *introvert* (simplified hand with centripetal strokes), but with many extraverted movements (slanted, progressive writing, flying strokes).

From the SZONDIAN angle, the overall appearance of the script is ruled by ambivalent reactions, namely *s+/-* (uneven hand, with elongated upper and lower extensions), *m+/-* (warm stroke, writing trail rounded, but direction is irregular, regressive movements) and *k+/-* (well-formed, but irregular middle zone).

In the *Ego* vector, the paranoid factor is also somewhat ambivalent: movement is rhythmic, strokes wide, the superelevations denote *p*+ and the narrow letters *p*-. We are therefore dealing with the most ambivalent Ego profile, that of the "integrating Ego" F_1 (*Sch* = *k*+/- *p*+/-). Probably the best way of describing the complexity of such personalities is to compare the partial Egos that live in them: autism (narcissistic Ego A_2 = *k*+*p*-) co-existing with auto-limitation (inhibited Ego B_2 = *k*-*p*+); the subject wants to be everything and have everything, whatever the external conditions, and to rationalise his appetites (Ego in peril *D* = *k*+*p*+), but he submits to generally accepted rules (disciplined Ego *C*= *k*-*p*-); he consciously chooses the compromises to be agreed upon for his own requirements and those of others (the ideal-seeking Ego B_2D = *k*+/-*p*+), but his dissatisfaction drives him to increase the number of his contacts (the evasive Ego A_2C= *k*+/-*p*-).

In such cases, the achievement of unity is only possible at the cost of a conscious and constant "balancing out" of which Baudelaire was incapable, despite the riches afforded by his ambivalence in other respects, and having zero reaction to factor *e*.

One can understand that these interior contradictions affected Baudelaire's behaviour in ways that were both diachronic (he oscillated between faith and doubt, between debauchery and the desire for purity) and synchronic (the author of *Les Fleurs du mal*, a book of shattering nonconformity, was extremely respectful of the rules of everyday life; he carried on a scandalous relationship while remaining strongly attached to his mother).

In the *Paroxysmal* vector factor *e* gives no reaction: the stroke is ink-filled, but has little pressure; it has no elasticity or internal density; the rhythm of movement is not sustained. Direction and margins are irregular. The reaction of factor *hy* is positive, but varying in strength from example to example. This is very evident in figure 5.5: movement stronger than form, rhythm of movement rapid, supple and mobile, pressure is uneven, width and exaggeration, initial reinforcement, volutes, Nervous-Sanguine temperament. This points to strong histrionic tendencies (*hy+*) and their translation into action (*e*0)[2].

Noticeable in the *Sexual* vector are : *h+* because of the consistent stroke with no real relief, the rounded strokes and the supple rhythm (intense search for comforting affection); *s+/-* because of uneven speed, pressure and height, elongated upper and lower extensions (ambivalence in connection with the body : a complex feeling over the adoption of a fully masculine stance). This association, common enough, suggests the possibility of homosexuality and the danger of drug addiction.

The *Contact* vector has the strongly ambivalent *m+/-* : *m+* because of the warm consistent stroke, the rounded writing, the garlands and the upper extensions often concave towards the right; *m-* because of unevenness in direction and in the left hand margin and because of regressive strokes.

From the PSYCHOPATHOLOGICAL viewpoint, it has become commonplace to see in Baudelaire the syphilitic drug-addict and just about all the complexes that psychoanalysis has described. In a note in the first volume of the *Zentralblatt für Psychoanalyse* (p.275), Rank had already identified his incestuous complex. In French, *L'Echec de Baudelaire* by Dr. René Laforgue (Denoël and Steele, 1931) and the end of Marie Bonaparte's book, *Edgar Poe, Sa Vie, Son Oeuvre,* (re-edited in the Presses universitaires de France, 1958) are classics of psychoanalysis. *Le Sadisme de Baudelaire* by Georges Blin (Corti, 1948) is a classic of literary criticism.

The graphologist who has some knowledge of Freud and Adler will easily find in Baudelaire elements of orality (signs of weakness) and of anality (signs of inadaptability and of

(2) The profile *e*0 *hy+* is usually that of exhibitionists.

aggression), sexual complexes (spasms, congestion, proteiform lower extensions), an overcompensated inferiority complex (superelevation) with narcissism and histrionic complex (fine, rounded shapes), an insufficiently structured Ego (instability, exaggerated irregularity). There will be no difficulty in deducing as a resultant, a neurosis that is mainly hysterical, considerable sado-masochism, the suspicion of a mother fixation and a homosexual component. (There is no fear of being contradicted over all this, provided the precaution is taken of qualifying each perversion as "latent"...).

Baudelaire's dream imaginings have built up this picture, better than anyone else can, in the character in a dream the poet recounted in a letter to his friend, Asselineau, in 1856 : a monster, the son of a prostitute, "who is always perched on a pedestal. [...] He is not ugly. His face is even handsome, very tanned, and oriental in colour. There is a lot of pink and green about him. He sits crouched, but in an odd, twisted way. There is something black that wraps round him several times and over his limbs like a great snake. I asked him what it was and he told me that it was a monstrous appendage which grew out of his head, something elastic like rubber and so dreadfully long that if he rolled it up on his head like hair it would be much too heavy and quite impossible to carry. So he is obliged to wrap it round him which incidentally, looks impressive. I talked with the monster for a long time. He has been obliged to stay in this hall for several years, perched on the pedestal, on show to the general public, but his main annoyance is supper time. Being a living being he is obliged to eat with the girls of the establishment and to stagger along, as far as the dining-room with his rubber appendage wrapped around him or placed on a chair like a coil of rope, because if he let it fall to the ground it would pull his head back. [...] I didn't dare touch him, but I found him interesting". The following detail shows how the monster is a part of Baudelaire : "I awoke tired and broken, my back, legs, and hips aching. I suppose I must have been sleeping in the twisted position of the monster".

This pathological "museum" certainly has interest that goes beyond the domain of medicine, because it sustains Baudelarian poetics. The "new frisson" that *Les Fleurs du mal* brought to art consisted, from the psychoanalytical viewpoint, in introducing into poetry the "regressive" aspects of the libido and expressing them in an irrational pregenital language[3].

Footnote (3) - see opposite page

Nevertheless, these considerations do not throw any light upon other aspects of Baudelaire which are, humanly speaking, as important as his neurosis: his artistic genius, his longing for security and spirituality, his indecision between remorse and repentance, his wavering between faith and doubt. About these subjects we can learn nothing from psychoanalysis or from nearly all the modern schools of psychology, because all are founded upon partial conceptions of man.

*

Ever since modern psychology has entered the field of literary criticism, it has become commonplace to quote as an example of the Oedipian situation, young Charles in love with his mother and hating his stepfather, General Aupick; or, according to more orthodox psychoanalysis, the opposition to the stepfather is a re-animation of the feelings the child had for his real father (who died when Charles was six). This has been repeated endlessly as evidence, although historians, using documental sources, have modified this summary vision.

I have discovered scripts written by Baudelaire's parents and stepfather, in order to put them at the disposal of graphologists who might desire to consider this question. This has been possible thanks to the kindness of Claude Pichois, professor at the Sorbonne, of Jean Ziegler and of the librarians of the Army History Service (Armée de Terre), the Archives for Foreign Affairs and the Senate.

Figure 5.10 is the handwriting of the poet's father, Joseph-François Baudelaire (1759-1827), a priest unfrocked during the revolution, who became a librarian at the Senate. Letters

(3) Until that time, the fundamental literary theme was love in its genital phase in a subject with a mature Ego, words keeping their rational meaning. This was well shown by O. Kucera (*International Journal of Psychoanalysis*, *31*: 98-102, 1950). Marie Bonaparte (*op. cit.* pp.799-833) reduced the famous "frisson" to a single component : sado-masochism.

5.11 and 5.12 are from the hand of his mother, Caroline-Archentaut Defayis (or Dufays) (1793-1871). Finally, figures 5.13 to 5.15 follow the career of Jacques Aupick (1789-1857) from the moment he offered his services to Louis XVIII after Waterloo, to the period when he was ambassador in Constantinople.

*

BIBLIOGRAPHY

Louis BOUVERY, *Le graphologue, Méthode par laquelle on peut, sans maître, connaître l'état moral, les aptitudes et les dispositions de sociabilité d'une personne, par la forme de lettres et des traits de son écriture.* Veuve Chanoine, Lyon, 1874, 54p : see p.51.
- Graphological study of three lines with signature: deductive mind; obstinately strong will, strong personality with great self-confidence, a mixture of greatness and a bourgeois mentality; "diplomatic skill and frankness, unbridled passion, an original style of poetry. Baudelaire has the most unusual signs of originality, oddness and speed of thought".

Ad. DESBARROLLES, *Mystères de la main. Révélations complètes. Suite et fin.* From the author, 1879, or 4th ed., Vigot, 1905, 1048p : see p.577.
– Exaggerated shape of letter *d* : the writer's exuberance and impetuosity of production.

Arsène ARUSS, *La graphologie simplifiée. Art de connaître le caractère par l'écriture.* Kolb, 1891, 286p : see p.180.
– Originality and grace of the *B*.

Marius DECRESPE, *Manuel de graphologie appliquée,* vol. 1, Guyot, 1895, 184p : see pp.103-104.
– "Typographic *B* of a charming originality."

Magdalene THUMM-KINTZEL, *Der psychologische und pathologische Wert der Handschrift,* Paul List, Leipzig, 1904, 208p.
– Aesthetic double curve (*C* p. 64): aesthetic sense. Personal form of the aesthetic curve in the signature (p.75): gift for poetry.

M. KINTZEL-THUMM (IVANOVIC), *Psychology and Pathology of Handwriting,* Fowler and Wells, New York, 1905, 149p, (By, Leo, Ba): see pp.48, 59.
– Characteristic curve of the artistic gift; types of abbreviations made by poets.

**E. de ROUGEMONT, *Commentaîres graphologiques sur Charles Baudelaire,* Société de Graphologie, 1923, 65p.
– Complete study of twelve examples ranging from 1841 to 1866. The author maps out the main lines of the personality (sincerity, great cerebral activity, abandonment to sensation and emotion, a lack of proportion, weak will) and of its evolution : at first simple, the writing becomes mannered (leftward-turning, complications : spiralling arabesques) from 1851; after 1858 sensitivity, exacerbated by suffering, leads to extremely caustic bitterness and to selfish scheming. De Rougemont shows how, in a letter dated 1854, Baudelaire has become impulsive, but ineffective (he "decides" to slap Ancelle : the large writing, underlined five times gets calmer five lines lower!) and, in a letter from 1858, there are the first symptoms of general paralysis (a lack of attention with a confusion of visual images.)

*K. H. BROEKHOFF, "Baudelaire en zijn Handschrift" (Baudelaire and his handwriting), *Tijdschrift voor wetenschapelijke Graphologie 1*: 17-29, 1929: see pp. 22-27.
– A study according to the principles of Klages of Baudelaire's hand from three letters in 1841, 1854 and 1861 (two are borrowed from the preceding reference which Broekhoff quotes). Original hand with quite high Formlevel. Excellent controlled layout, but disturbances in rhythm (amendments and congestion) in the stroke : contrast between mental finesse and an uncontrolled sensitivity. Extreme unevenness shows strong emotion, but the poor connections mean a weak character. With age, letters were disconnected (pathological phenomenon), became muddy (indulgence in coarse sensuality) and lost their simplicity (complication in the affective life). At the age of twenty, words were already sloping downwards, *t*-bars were weak, though hooked : a man full of nerves, with a weak character, but stubborn. In 1861, there was a serious breakdown in the mental faculties (one letter for another, or omitted). Signs of introversion and of sexual disorders (twisted lower extensions). In conformity with the theories of Freud and Stekel, Baudelaire projected his suppressed desires into his poetry.

ENIGMA, *Les secrets de l'écriture,* new ed., Paris, 1929, 239p; see pp.83-84.
– Signature followed by a full stop : discretion, precaution.

E. de ROUGEMONT, "La graphologie et la critique littéraire", *La Graphologie Scientifique* no. 64/65 : 17-21, February-March 1933 (p.20).
– Baudelaire's writing reveals his sincerity and his illness and helps to understand his work, which Brunetière misjudged.

G. E. MAGNAT, *Poésie de l'écriture,* Sack, Geneva, 1944, 108p : see pp.44-45.
– A fine commentary which underlines Baudelaire's complete honesty, a goldsmith rather than a poet, intoxicated by the joy of creating and by the religion of beauty. His genius lies in a vision of the world of which his work is the mirror.

G. E. MAGNAT, *Die Sprache der Handschrift,* Räber, Lucerne, 1948: see pp.47-48. Translation of the above.

G. E. MAGNAT, L'écriture du poète," *La Graphologie* no.47: 5-13, 3rd quarter 1952 : see pp.9-10.
– "[...] the flowering of a sensitivity, delicate in the extreme, supported, but not channelled, by a rigour of thought and a taste so exquisite that even illness could not entirely destroy it." "This hand, while being romantic because of its dynamic thrust, is quite classic in its strange sobriety, and the refined elegance of its forms. It is a world in which the lightning flashes of inspiration and the extraordinary "honesty" of purpose project the very picture of poetry by a sometimes overdone respect for form."

Philipp MILLER, *Einführung in die Graphologie,* Ullstein, Frankfurt am Main, 1958, 214p : see pp.96-97.
– (Concerning three lines and the signature) : Small writing, with letters prettily formed and with a strong basic rhythm : the writer stands well back from the world.

Dr. V. RIVÈRE, *Le monde de l'écriture,* Gonon, Neuilly-sur-Seine, 1958, 294p : see pp.34, 74, 122.
– The *B* : intimate complications. The importance of the monumental *S*, underlined in the word *Satan.* Careless letter shapes.

Madame M.-T. DELAMAIN, "Perspectives et relativité de la vitesse", *La Graphologie* no.94 : 3-12, book 2, 1964 : see pp.9-10.
– Homogeneous writing, varying very greatly in speed : "he vibrates like a violin under the bow".

Frank VICTOR (GRUENFELD), Letter to *La Graphologie* about the preceding article, no.96 : 29-30, book 4, 1964.
– The variation in speed is due to Baudelaire's tendency to escape from the middle zone (zone of daily life) by running for refuge in the upper zone (examine the letters that generally fly upwards); sometimes also the lower zone (that of the material) holds him back. The spasms in the middle and lower zones (slowing up, upsets in the deep rhythm) point to bad health.

Paul de SAINTE-COLOMBE, *Grapho-Therapeutics. Pen and Pencil Theory,* Laurinda Books, Hollywood, 1966, 340p : see pp.232, 233.
– Mysticism (centrifugal finals), sensuality (pressure), liveliness (i-dots), high intelligence (speed, movements towards the upper zone). "His contemporaries were scandalised that he should use poetry to speak of morbid pleasure and vices; but his work contains a moral : vice engenders anguish".

Claude PICHOIS, *Baudelaire. Études et témoignages,* La Baconnière, Neuchâtel, 1967, 272p : see pp.234-238.
– Several doctors have denied that Baudelaire had a general paralysis[4] (as is often said), an illness that Edouard de Rougemont[5] believed caused the deterioration in the writing from 1858, onwards. At the request of C. Pichois, the graphologist, Madelaine HASLER, examined nine letters of Baudelaire, written between 1852 and 1866. She observed, like Rougemont, a gradual break-up of the writing, with psycho-motor trouble from 1858. The latter, less dramatic than in the case of manifested general paralysis, could have been the forerunner of the stroke of 1866.

Augusto VELS, *La selección de personal y el problema humano en las empresas,* Luis Miracle, Barcelona, 1970, 564p. Translated into French: *La Sélection du personnel et le problème humain dans les entreprises,* ed. Mont-Blanc, Geneva, 1973, 444p : see pp.134, 155, 315 (1970).
– Ornate writing (ostentation, desire to be admired - compensated inferiority complex); much irregularity in size, slant, speed (irregular behaviour) and pressure (irritability); low moral level.

Suzanne BRESARD, *L'écriture empreinte de l'homme. La graphologie, méthode d'exploration psychologique,* Privat, Toulouse, 1976, 191p : see pp.58, 153.
– Baudelaire's crushed handwriting (sensuality) enlivened with "step-like" lines (fluctuations in strength, causing dramatic tension).
This book has been translated : *A grafologia, método de exploração psicologica,* Europe-America, Mira Sintra Lisbon, 1978, 191p : see p.64.

Curtis CASEWIT, *Graphology Handbook*: Para Research, Rockport (Massachusetts), 1980, 155p.
– Charles Baudelaire's signature reproduced as a frontispiece, without commentary.

(4) Tertiary syphilis localised in the brain and the meninges.

(5) Of his study in 1923, summarised above.

Roseline CRÉPY, *L'interprétation des signes dans l'écriture. III. La ponctuation, les chiffres et quelques ajouts singuliers. Deux analyses.* Delachaux et Niestlé, Neuchâtel, 1980, 402p : see p.293.
– (Concerning the 1859 letter in our figure 5.8). "The fourth digit of the year is smaller (fear of the future). Moreover it slopes downwards and is placed to the left of the page. His letter is a series of complaints [...]".

Luc UYTTEHNOVE, *Connaissez-vous par votre signature,* Marabout, Verviers (Belgium), 1982, 253p. - Spanish translation : *Cómo conocer a una persona por su firma,* Deusto, Bilbao, 1987, 211p : see p.191 (pp. 160-161 of the Spanish translation).
– The signature is just like the text. It is uneven, jerky and ink-filled, underlined and followed by a full-stop : a thirst for sensations and pleasure; a man in revolt and in poor health, longing for contentment.

Silvie BORIE, *Graphologie. Typologie planétaire : Uranus - Neptune - Pluton,* from the author, 1983, 90p : see p.54.
– "An inspired mixture of Uranus, Mars and Mercury : writing both "burning" and liquid. Pluto (dark strokes, descents to the lower zone, twists, crossings-out) : breaks because of contradictory vectors. Moon (liquid strokes, large blank spaces, evasive curves) : poetry and imaginative power. Mars : dynamic tension (flying strokes, rhythm, slant) and agitation (discordance in size and pressure, pointed strokes). Without Mars the lunary dreaming would be sterile. Mercury gives diversity and taste, gives sharpness of mind, but tends to break up (of the letters in pieces) [...]. If Moon gave the poet, Mercury made the art critic".

Suzanne BRESARD, *La Graphologie, méthode d'exploration psychologique,* Scarabée, 1984, 304p : see p.66.
– "What exuberance in this script from Baudelaire! Frequent crushing together of the strokes reveals strong sensuality". (P.163:) *crushed* writing. "*Ladder-like* lines reveal breaks in energy"; alternate depression and action, whence comes "dramatic tension from which *lightning flashes* appear".

Suzanne BRESARD, "Les différentes formes d'intelligence. Synthèses grapho-psychologiques", *La Graphologie* no.173 : 8-35, 1984 : see pp.15-17.
– Handwriting of "a sensorial intuitive, who, while writing, seems to want to offer a surface of contact ready for impressions that are agreeable, pleasurable, new and enriching, and whose intensity calls upon the personal expression which is that of the artist - provided that the strength of expressive talent is enough to give shape to what moves it".

Christian GOTH, *Écrivains. Écritures. Manuel de graphologie appliqué à l'écriture des gens de lettres*, Bordas, 1990, 256p : see pp.30-31.
– "The author has difficulty in controlling the reality of his thoughts. Alternately depressed and exuberant, Charles Baudelaire is an intuitive, representing the model of a perfect creative intelligence. Ideas unfold and link up in a quite subjective, but deeply evocative cohesion".

Sylvie CHERMET-CARROY, *La Graphologie autrement*, Jacques Grancher, 1994, 275p : see p.102
– Alternation of exaltation and discouragement revealed by the letter *a* sometimes inflated and sometimes hesitating or crossed.

José M. ESCOLA, "Baudelaire, el poeta maldito", *Boletin de la Agrupacion de grafoanalistas consultivos de España* no.12 : see pp.89-97.
– [Handwriting samples from 13 to 38 years]. Ambivalence between instinct-intelligence. At 13 years, enlarged upper zone (sensuality), right slant, superelevated *s*, angular and narrow (exalted arrogance), "exuberant" finals (boasting), left-tending *g* (nostalgia). At 38 years, typically *Plutonian* writing : black, tension in the rhythm of movement discharging itself in the finals and *t*-bars, typical movement in the *s* (aggression, virile pride, rapacity). Literary talent, thanks to his critical sense (Mercury). Consistently over-developed lower zone and left-tending *s* (unsatisfied avidity).

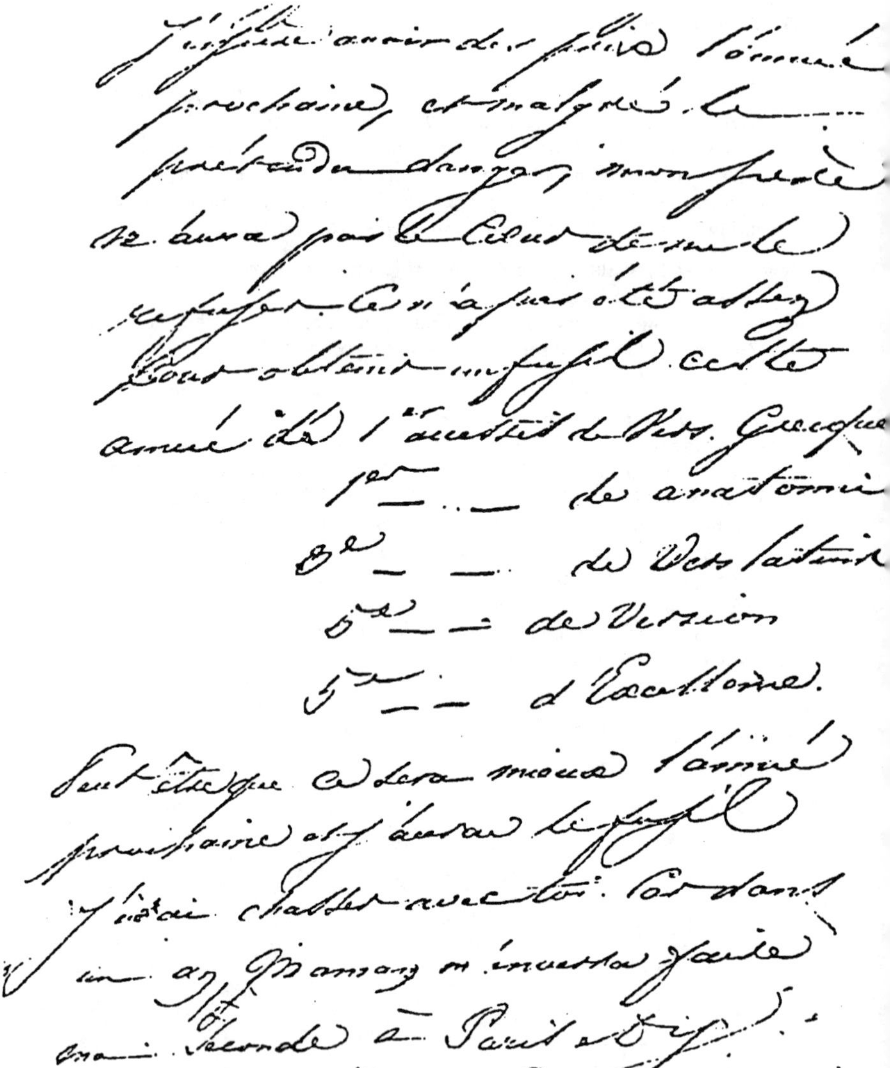

J'espère avoir des prix l'année
prochaine, et malgré le
prétendu danger, mon frère
ne aura pas le cœur de me le
refuser. Je n'ai pas été assez
bon pour obtenir un fusil. Cette
année j'ai 1er accessit de vers grecs
1er — de anatomie
3e — de vers latins
5e — de version
5e — d'excellence.
Peut-être que ce sera mieux l'année
prochaine et j'aurai le fusil
j'irai chasser avec toi. Cependant
un an. Maman m'a écrit de faire
mon retour à Paris et d'y
finir mes études. Écris-moi
souvent ton frère
Charles

Fig. 5.1 - Handwriting of Charles Baudelaire at 13.

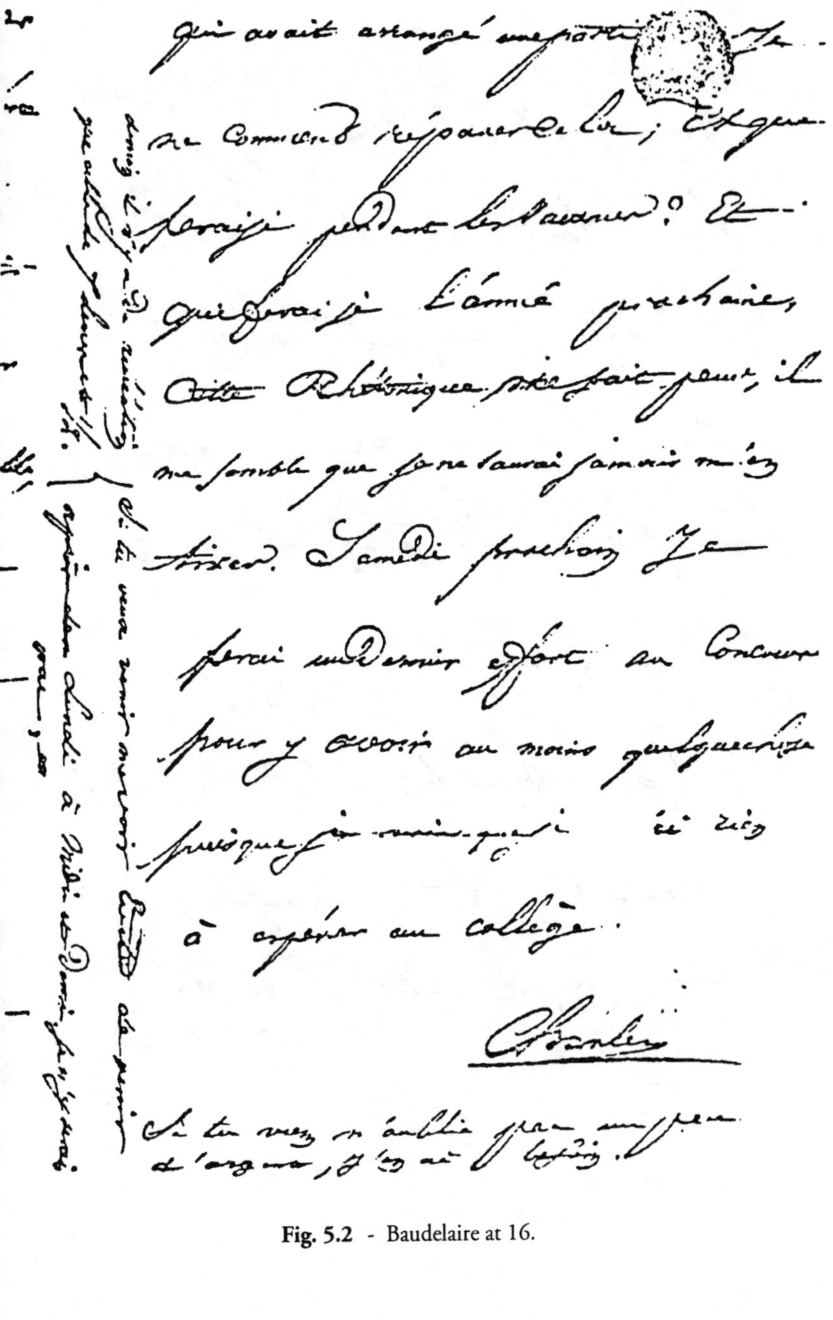

qui avait arrangé une partie [illegible]

ne commence à se passer de lui ; et que

ferai-je pendant les vacances ? Et

que ferai-je l'année prochaine,

cette Rhétorique me fait peur, il

me semble que je ne saurai jamais m'en

tirer. Samedi prochain je

ferai un dernier effort au Concours

pour y avoir au moins quelque chose

puisque je n'ai guère ici rien

à espérer au collège.

Charles

Si tu veux m'oublier pour un peu

de l'argent, j'en ai besoin.

Fig. 5.2 - Baudelaire at 16.

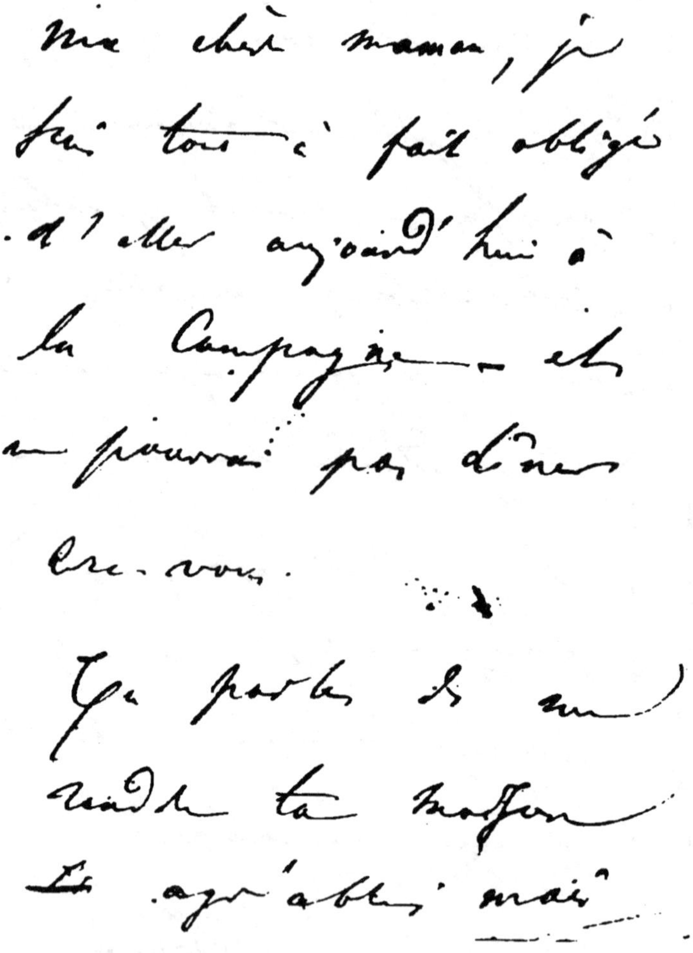

Ma chère maman, je
suis tout à fait obligé
d'aller aujourd'hui à
la Campagne et
ne pourrai pas dîner
chez vous.

Ta parole de ne
rendre ta maison
~~En~~ agréable mais

Fig. 5.3 - Baudelaire at 20.

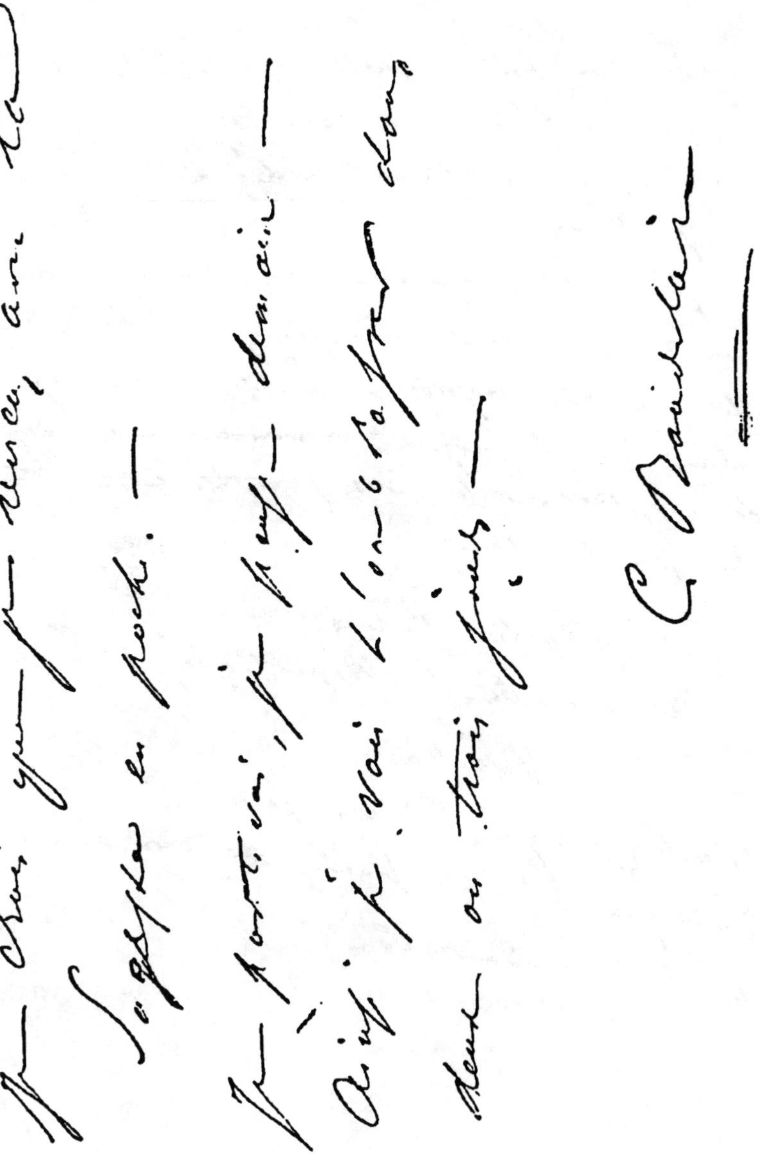

Fig. 5.4 - Baudelaire at 21.

à un homme pressé de travail et
d'occupation comme vous, — Dans
ce cas là, j'attendrai indéfiniment au
café restaurant du coin de la rue de Bourgogne
ayez l'obligeance de me répondre un
mot — votre adresse, vos heures, —
le plus vite possible. La bonté qui règne
dans tous les esprits ~~demande entre~~ appelle
les opérations les plus promptes entre tous
les gens de cœur.

Charles Baudelaire.
avenue de la République 118.
Neuilly

Veuillez agréer ici toujours les témoignages les plus sincères de mon dévouement
et de mon admiration

* **Fig. 5.5** - Baudelaire at 27.

pour moi vis-à-vis de
Mr Ancelle. Je souffre
beaucoup de l'idée de
rencontrer ton Mari; il
faudrait donc que tu
daignasses me marquer
une heure où je ne le
rencontrerai pas chez toi.
Cette visite est indispensable
d'autant plus qu'il se
peut même que je
parte avant vous.

Charles.

Fig. 5.6 - Baudelaire's writing.

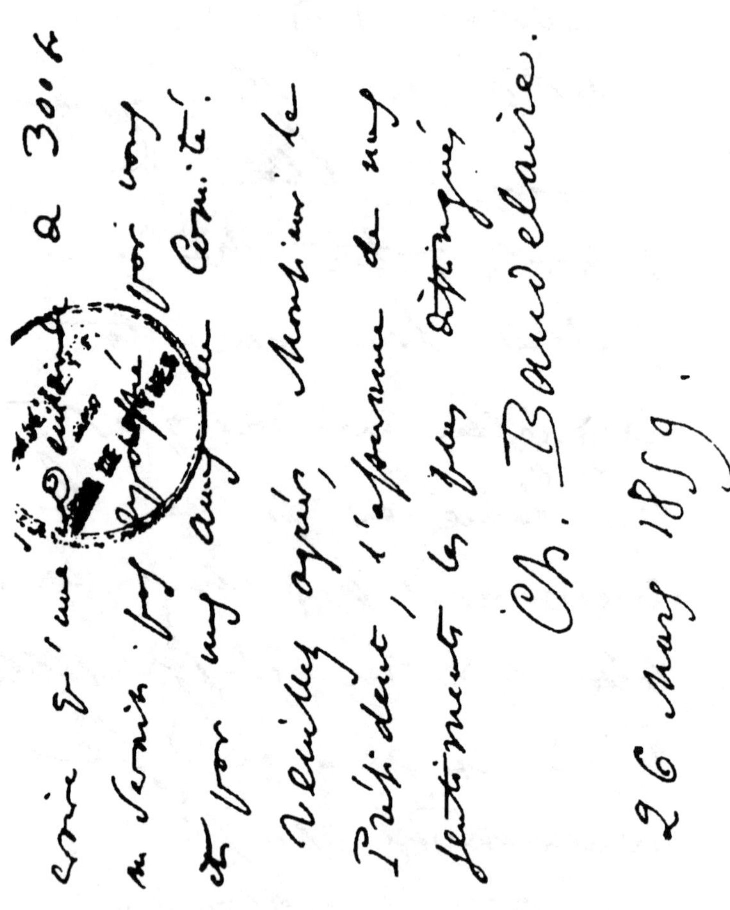

Veuillez agréer, Monsieur le Président, l'expression de mes sentiments les plus distingués.
Ch. Baudelaire.
26 Mars 1859.

Fig. 5.7 - Baudelaire at 38.

— Voilà tout pour aujourd'hui.
Il faudra évidemment que je
retourne à Honfleur à la fin de
ce mois pour retrouver tous mes
manuscrits; mais jamais je ne
changerai de lieu sans vous
avertir.

C. B.

* **Fig. 5.8** - Baudelaire at 39.

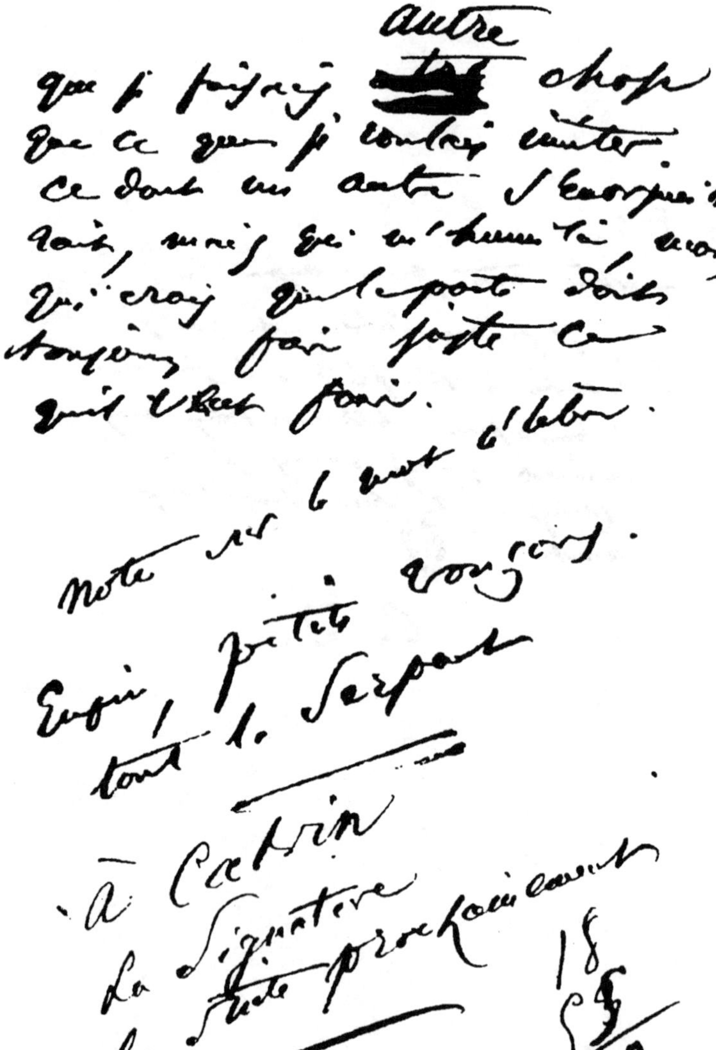

Fig. 5.9 - Baudelaire's personal notes.

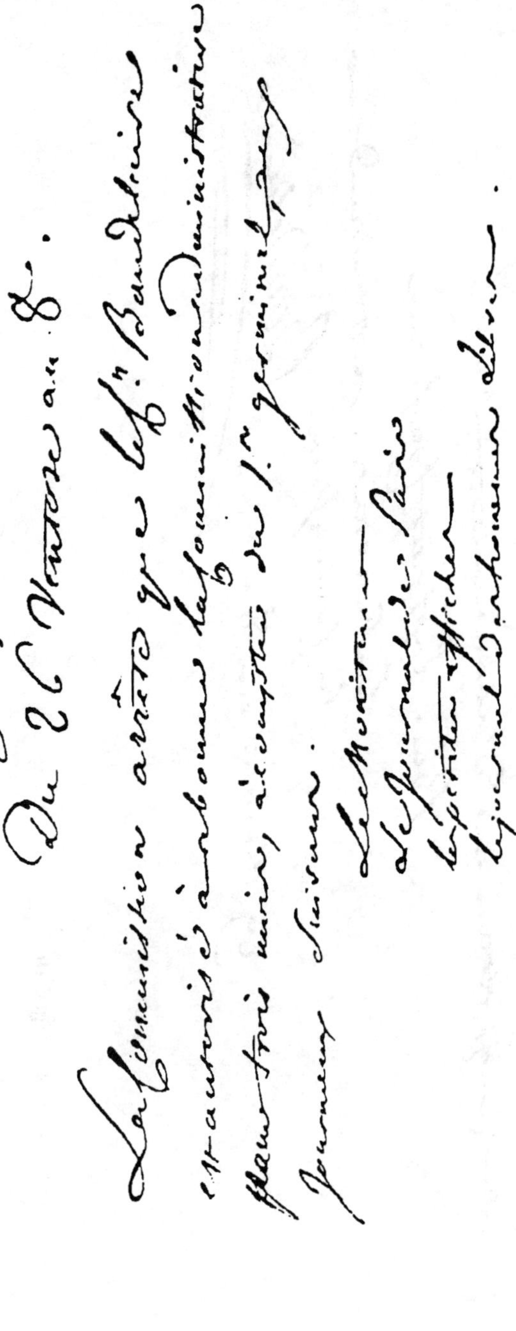

* **Fig. 5.10** - Handwriting of Joseph-François Baudelaire, the poet's father, at 40.
(Sample continued overleaf)

Il lui sera remboursé par le trésorier du Sénat
[illegible] francs d'abonnement.

Pour Extrait Conforme
Le Secrétaire particulier de
la Commission

29 ventôse an 8.

Baudelaire

Continuation of * **Fig. 5.10**

* **Fig. 5.11** - Handwriting of Caroline Dufays, Baudelaire's mother, at 63.

* **Fig. 5.12** - Handwriting of Caroline Dufays at 73 : beginning and end of a letter.

Jacques Aupick-Baudart, Capitaine
adjudant Major au 46ème Régiment de
l'organisation de 1814. a l'honneur d'exposer
à votre Excellence que rentré dans ses
foyers depuis les derniers jours de Juin
expiré, il desirerait que ses services
pussent être agréables au Roi: Il
prend en conséquence l'humble confiance
de vous supplier, Monseigneur, de les
offrir en son nom à Sa Majesté. Il
ose lui Jurer que parmi ses sujets les
plus Dévoués aucun ne lui sera plus
fidèle, aucun ne tiendra plus à
honneur de vivre et mourir pour Elle.

De votre Excellence

Monseigneur

Le très humble et très
Obéissant serviteur

J. Aupick-Baudart

* **Fig. 5.13** - Handwriting of Jacques Aupick, future father-in-law of Baudelaire, at 26.

* **Fig. 5.14** - Jacques Aupick at 45.

* **Fig. 5.15** - Jacques Aupick at 59.

6

Etienne (Stéphane) MALLARMÉ (1842 - 1898)

"Donner un sens plus pur aux mots de la tribu".[1]
(Mallarmé, *Le Tombeau d'Edgar Poe*)

Stéphane Mallarmé was a professor of English, firstly in different French towns, then from 1873 to 1892 in Paris. He lived for art and literature. After several decades of Romantic poetry and in a scientific materialist world, he endeavoured to work out a more refined and complex form of expressing the secrets of the heart. He used symbols, the sound of words and even their form upon the printed page. He did not produce a great quantity of work, and his learned art, its careful and often obscure expression are only accessible to cultured readers. Nevertheless, Mallarmé greatly influenced literary circles, whose younger members at the end of the nineteenth century looked upon him as a master. In France he is considered to be the leader of the Symbolist movement. Paul Claudel and Paul Valéry were his disciples.

(1) Endow with a sense more pure the words of the tribe.

A very great number of studies, both literary and psychological, have been devoted to Mallarmé. Among the latter sort one must mention the second part of *L'Aliénation poétique. Rimbaud-Mallarmé-Proust* by Dr. Jean Fretet (Janin, Paris, 1946) and the *Introduction à la psychanalyse de Mallarmé* by Charles Mauron (La Baconnière, Neuchâtel, 1950). It is to be hoped that a Jungian study will shed new light on the poet's work, in particular *Igitur, Un coup de dés jamais n'abolira le hasard* and the poet's intention of producing a "Great Work".

*

There was an evolution in Mallarmé's handwriting. One can almost use a diagram in comparing the hand of the decade of 1860 (fig. 6.1) when the young poet, newly married, had bouts of melancholic depression, to that of his full maturity (figs. 6.6 to 6.10), with the period of his thirties (fig. 6.2) forming a transition. Moreover the writing in his rough work naturally[(2)] differs from that of his fair copies (figures 6.1, 6.4).

So rich a writing should be examined in depth over every period. Here we will simply analyse the writing of the mature years, adding brief remarks concerning its relationship with the other documents.

The writing has : *a high level of organisation*, with *combined letters*; *harmonious* and with a *high Formlevel* (originality, rhythm, but little warmth);

very homogeneous.

---

(2) Mallarmé was struck by this difference and he saw in it a difficulty for the graphologist's work. Here is his reply to a questionnaire published in the *Revue Encyclopédique* of February 12, 1898 (p.100): "Yes, I think handwriting is meaningful. As in physical movement and facial expression, you convey a sure message. All the same, the professional or amateur writer makes a fair copy or sees it first of all in the mirror of his mind and then transcribes it into a lapidary form. So the immediate effect of his emotions is not seen in his manuscript: but one can form an overall judgement upon his character".

Tension III (concentration, precision, restraint) with some IVb strokes (some tensing and congestion).

Form carried along by *movement* to which it is slightly predominant. The *rhythm* of movement is lively and discreet, with (a) large, soaring strokes springing from a regular middle zone and (b) by a "secondary width" (Saudek) contrasting with nearly squeezed letters : in other words, rhythmic alteration in width and inhibitions both vertically and horizontally, a few disturbances (tensing and congestion). Intense and varied rhythm in creating the form. Pronounced rhythm in the spatial layout.

JAMINIAN DEFINITION

The handwriting is *distinguished, high, vertical, stylised, semi-rounded; aerated, orderly*;

continuity very *uneven* (varying from *juxtaposition* to *over-connectedness*), the same with speed (*constraint* and *slackening*; finals are *soaring centripetally* or *restrained*), and the height varies within words and outside them (*superelevations*);

nuancée in the slight irregularity of width (*narrowing*, but with "secondary width"; *squeezed* at the line-endings), of form, line direction and slant, of pressure (consistent with some ink-filled letters and deviated pressure).

Free gestures : accents are precise and somewhat high; *t*-bars irregular in every respect;

accents and *t*-bars sometimes joined to the following letter and sometimes combined ("head-to-foot" connections)[(3)].

The *signature* is very like the text, somewhat poised and constrained, with narrow superelevations and soaring, centripetal finals; graceful, soaring paraph.

The youthful writing (fig. 6.1) is graceful (*simple, clear*), *sober* and *contained*, slowed up by *inhibitions*, notably by *juxtapositions* with frequent white spaces between letters, creating "holes" inside words.

---

(3) See Note 5.

In the poet's thirties (fig. 6.2), movement is more connected, with the appearance of numerous *combinations* (which often make *head-to-foot linking*) and a tendency to Saudek's *secondary width*; there is a greater difference in height between the exterior letters and the middle zone (*prolonged up and down*), with several soaring strokes, especially in the finals; the forms are *stylised*, with some rounded strokes that one could certainly call "affected".

The writing in figures 6.4 and 6.7 is *neat, limpid* and *elegant*. That of the rough work in fig. 6.10 is *combined* and *tormented.*

This definition is indicative at first sight of superiority (distinguished hand, high Formlevel) of intelligence (aerated, stylised, combined, semi-rounded writing) and of sensitivity (uneven and nuancée).

Aesthetic stylisation (forms that are elegant, sober (except for some capitals, with sharpness and clarity) is well to the fore and controls nearly all the graphic characteristics. The high[(4)], elegant and neat writing, the typical gesture of the soaring finals and the head to foot connections[(5)] speak of an exacting idealism. The love of beauty is a true passion for the writer and is supreme over other tendencies and desires. We have here a strongly intellectualised beauty (aerated, simplified writing with a predominance of form over movement) that has not

---

(4) i.e. letters higher than their width, considerable difference in height between the outside zones and the middle zone. (Not to be confused with superelevation, which is sometimes present).

(5) Notice, for example, in figure 6.8, *P*age, inspira*t*ion, *A*nge, conduisen*t* *m*es and in fig. 6.9 *ill*u*s*tra*t*ions, Apr*ès*, ve*rs*, *Prose*, *An*thologie, po*ëtes*. According to Madame Cerbelaud-Salagnac, this is the sign of religious idealism (to be understood in the widest sense; Mallarmé professed the religion of the Beautiful, but he was not an orthodox believer). References : "Ecriture gothique et calligraphie moderne: liaison de tête en pied et liaison de pied en tête". *Journées graphologiques internationales,* Societé de graphologie, Paris, 1959, pp.32-36 and "Le mode de liaison", *La Graphologie* no.152, pp.28-33, 1978.

however become insubstantial (well-nourished, semi-rounded strokes). Its refined expression (distinguished, neat hand) is evidently more self-conscious (slight constraint, care, initial reinforcements) than spontaneous. We are therefore confronted with the work of a skilful artist.

I have written elsewhere about the odd history of the sign of soaring finals[(6)]. It was discovered by Monsignor Barbier de Montault and was interpreted as a sign of religious feeling by Adrien Varinard to the readers of *La Graphologie* in 1881[(7)]. The following year, following objections, Varinard was less specific and spoke of the sign of a lifting up towards the ideal[(8)]. In his "Graphologie en sept leçons" (*La Graphologie*, Paris, 1884), the same Varinard mentions the sign in question twice, attributing to it the meaning of spirituality, of inborn religiosity if the final upstroke rises vertically or slightly turned to the left, or of susceptibility if it is stiff and with an abrupt ending[(9)]. From the turn of the century the notion has been taken on board by French graphologists. Crépieux-Jamin cites it in *L'Ecriture et le Caractère*[(10)], Madame R. de Salberg in her *Manuel de graphologie usuelle*[(11)], Solange Pellat in *L'Education aidée par la graphologie*[(12)], and J. de Casteljau in *Principes de graphologie rationnelle*[(13)].

This sign was spread abroad with the publication of a Russian translation of Varinard's book in 1889, with a German translation of *l'Ecriture et le*

---

(6) Article in *La Graphologie* quoted at the end of the bibliography of this chapter.

(7) Adrien Varinard, "Portrait de l'abbé Nicole d'Elie, prédicateur italien", *La Graphologie* of Oct. 1 1881 (vol. 11, no. 19) pp.129-132.

(8) *La Graphologie* of January 1, 1882 (vol.,12, no. 1) pp.6-7. Commander Daudel objected that many pious people did not have this sign and suggested it should be interpreted as overexcitement.

(9) *Op. cit.* pp.25 and 76.

(10) Second ed., Alcan, Paris, 1889, p.132 : "Strong religious mysticism, love of the marvellous". Fourth ed., Alcan, Paris, 1896, p.116 : "Mysticism, love of the marvellous, imagination, vision of reality more beautiful that it is in fact, lyricism".

(11) (1901) p.231 of 25th thousand, Hachette, Paris; "aspirations towards the idea".

(12) Hachette, Paris, 1906, pp.147, 175, 177-178. "lyrical feelings","strong lyric or religious aspirations".

(13) Daragon, Paris, 1913, pp.263 - 264: classically, mysticism (if over-excitement, a false vision; if mind narrow, devotion narrow; also artistic and literary idealists; it is the sign of religion in the meaning of a higher altruistic devotion to duty.

Caractère in 1902, and finally by Baroness Ungern-Sternberg, who mentioned it in the *Graphologische Monatshefte* when reviewing the book by Solange Pellat[(14)].

Now, several decades later Klages came across the sign in question. He baptised it *religiöse Kurve* and published his "discovery" in 1927[(15)], basing his interpretation on the theory of expression and the symbolism of space, giving several illustrations and pointing out its greater frequency in the Romantic period than nowadays. Some years later, opposite examples were published by Asmussen[(16)] and above all by Dr. Kloos, who put forward[(17)] several detailed observations about proud, querulous and completely irreligious sociopaths whose writing showed the sign. Klages replied[(18)] by accusing his contradictor of not knowing the foundations of the theory of expression, which always leads to double interpretations. So the sign of stretching towards a high goal indicates here the desire for self-perfection or simply to impose oneself. Klages claimed that if he had only mentioned the positive aspect of the "religiöse Kurve" in his article of 1927, it was because he presumed his readers were cultivated enough to be able to see for themselves the other side of the medal (!)...

It is worth noting that neither Klages nor his two opponents ever mention Barbier de Montault, Varinard, Crépieux-Jamin, Madame de Salberg, Solange Pellat, Baroness Ungern-Sternberg or Casteljau[(19)].

---

(14) P.37 of "Die Graphologie im Dienste der Pädagogik", vol.10, pp.33-40: religious enthusiasm or lyrical exuberance.

(15) Ludwig Klages, "Die religiöse Kurve in der Handschrift", *Zeitschrift für Menschenkunde*, vol. 2, no.5, pp.1-8, 1927.

(16) Arnold Asmussen, "Die religiöse Kurve in der Handschrift eines Raubmörders", Zentralblatt für Graphologie, vol.4, no.3, pp.173-176, 1933.

(17) Medizinalrat Dr. med. and phil. G. Kloos. "Über die sogenannte "religiöse Kurve" (Klages). Kritischer Beitrag zur Ausdruckspsychologie der Handschrift", *Zentralblatt für gesamte Neurologie und Psychiatrie*, vol.162, pp.716-727, 1938.

(18) Ludwig Klages, "Über die sogennante "religiöse Kurve". Nochmals ein kritischer Beitrag", *Zentralblatt für gesamte Neurologie und Psychiatrie*, vol.163, pp.574-582, 1938; a reply by Dr. Kloos in the following pages (583-584) "Stellungnahme zum vorstehenden Aufsatz von L. Klages".

(19) This is not unusual in the course of graphological development. A sign is discovered, published, discussed, clarified, then... it is forgotten. Later, it is discovered again and discussed again. Re-reading former authors, one is reminded of a saying of Saint-Simon "Our children will think they are imaginative when they are only remembering".

Twenty years after Klages, the sign in question was again commented on, this time by the Italian M. Marchesan[20]. He interpreted it as a sign of a fixed idea (*fissazione*) of morbid mental confusion and he considered it important to note the degree of verticality of the direction and its length. He did not claim to be the first to interpret the sign, but he wrote, "Graphology[21] has not properly explained the sign of the fixed idea".

Intelligence is to the fore, supported by great culture (simplified, semi-rounded, limpid hand), refined (nuancée) and original (personal forms and combinations). It is theoretical, more turned to ideas than facts (orderly, vertical, narrow writing) and very personal (some combinations almost illegible). By its structured layout[22] and its forms, which are rhythmic, varied and combined, Mallarmé's writing is a typical example of an intellect capable of generalisation.

Sensitivity is rich and polymorphous (small irregularities in many categories). It is refined (nuancée) and usually is expressed unostentatiously (simple, rather sober and often regular writing), although there is some desire to attract attention (superelevations, centripetal curves). Sensitivity and sensuality (congestion) are even repressed (slight irregularities in width and slant). There is shyness (narrowings) and a sharp susceptibility (superelevatons, verticality and inhibitions). A very deep sensitivity is hidden in its social expression behind a mask of studied serenity (elegant, careful, orderly writing in the fair copies), which give the superficial impression that Mallarmé was unemotional.

His probity is beyond all praise (clear, rectilinear, neat and homogeneous writing with the signature similar to the text). Goodness is present (simple, connected, semi-rounded hand), although not expansive (narrowings : personal character). There

(20) Marco Marchesan, *Dalla grafologia alla grafopsicologia*, La Prora, Milan, 1947, 290p : pp.141-142.

(21) In opposition to the "new" method invented by M. Marchesan : *la grafopsicologia* (which will become *la psicologia della scritura*).

(22) Mallarmé realised the importance of typographical layout. *Un coup de dés* ... is famous and has inspired many a commentary.

is also tactfulness (the writing is nuancée, neat and with a crowding at line-endings); reserve is stronger than warmth and there is much altruism (inhibited, vertical, centripetal, sometimes poised, narrowing writing). Mallarmé has an independent mind.

The full flowering of emotion is not complete. The result is a lack of ease approaching anxiety (verticality and centripetally soaring strokes suggest "receding" writing), and there is a danger of a weakening in aesthetic creation, the richest region of the personality.

*

Chart 6.1 shows the result of the GRAPHOMETRIC study of the letter whose start and finish is shown in figure 6.6.

The analysis of the *stroke* (histogram I) shows a very great differentiation of the sensorial perceptions (variable 1) and great permeability to the environment (strokes with blurred and sometimes porous edges : variable 3). The energetic tension is strong, with a certain lack of elasticity in the rhythm of relaxation (tight and slack: opposition of +3 to -3 in variable 2). Correlatively, there are signs of wear : a drop in the tone and a call upon "nerves" (opposition of +2 to -2 and 4), small signs of forcing and irritation (5).

Thought (II) is precise, capable of simplification (variable 6), and synthetic (15). The intellectual attitude is stretched and introverted (variable charge 7 from +2 to +1). Adaptability is intermittent (bimodality 8 and 9), purely formal, (the figure 28 in +2 of the variable 9 comes from the secondary width of Saudek). But, generally, thought is realistic enough.

The setting up of the histogram of the *Ego* III is difficult. One can only state firmly that there is considerable idealistic ambition (variables 11 and 12), difficulty in harmonising contradictory tendencies (12), and finally an attempt at self-discipline which brings on high emotive tension (14).

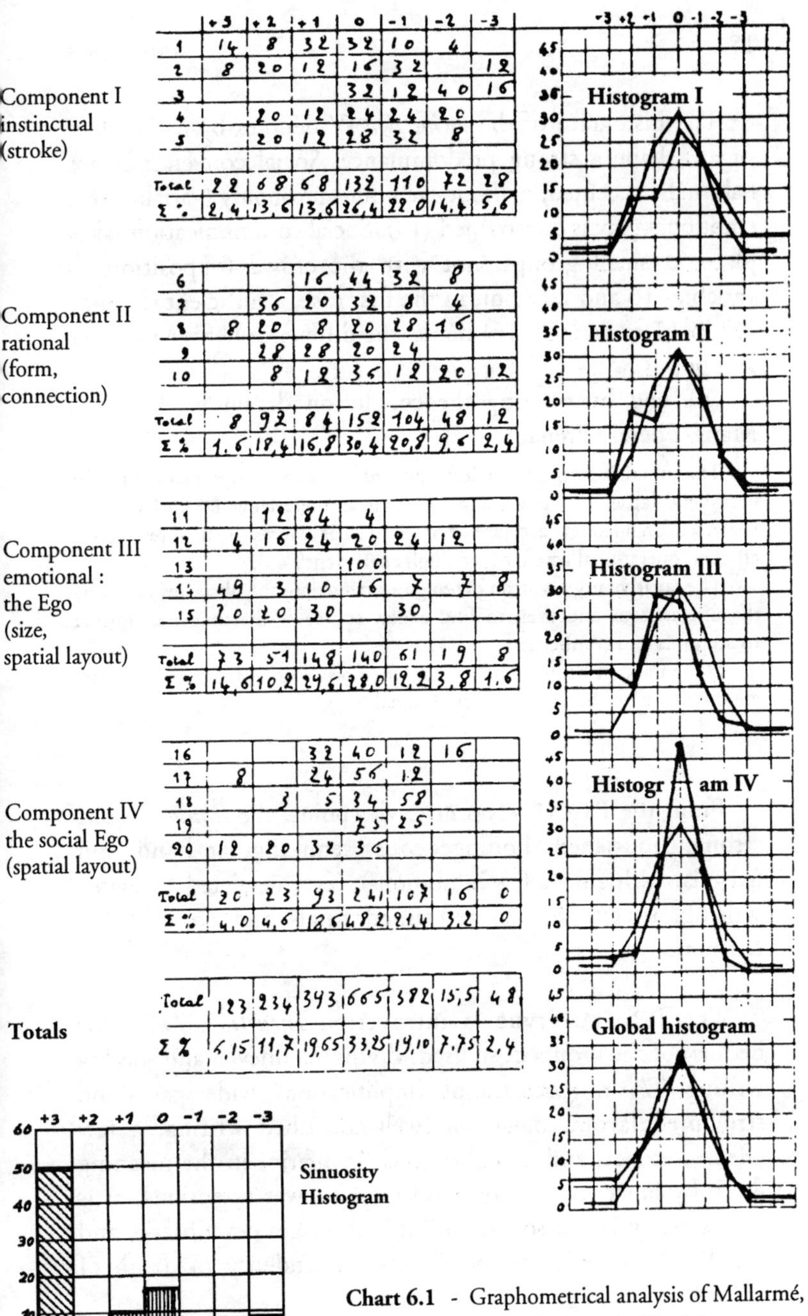

Component I instinctual (stroke)

	+3	+2	+1	0	-1	-2	-3
1	14	8	32	32	10	4	
2	8	20	12	16	32		12
3				32	12	40	16
4		20	12	24	24	20	
5		20	12	28	32	8	
Total	22	68	68	132	110	72	28
Σ %	2,4	13,6	13,6	26,4	22,0	14,4	5,6

Component II rational (form, connection)

	+3	+2	+1	0	-1	-2	-3
6			16	44	32	8	
7		36	20	32	8	4	
8	8	20	8	20	28	16	
9		28	28	20	24		
10		8	12	36	12	20	12
Total	8	92	84	152	104	48	12
Σ %	1.6	18,4	16,8	30,4	20,8	9,6	2,4

Component III emotional : the Ego (size, spatial layout)

	+3	+2	+1	0	-1	-2	-3
11		12	84	4			
12	4	16	24	20	24	12	
13				100			
14	49	3	10	16	7	7	8
15	20	20	30		30		
Total	73	51	148	140	61	19	8
Σ %	14,6	10,2	24,6	28,0	12,2	3,8	1,6

Component IV the social Ego (spatial layout)

	+3	+2	+1	0	-1	-2	-3
16			32	40	12	16	
17	8		24	56	12		
18		3	5	34	58		
19				75	25		
20	12	20	32	36			
Total	20	23	93	241	107	16	0
Σ %	4,0	4,6	12,6	48,2	21,4	3,2	0

Totals

	+3	+2	+1	0	-1	-2	-3
Total	123	234	343	665	382	15,5	48
Σ %	6,15	11,7	19,65	33,25	19,10	7,75	2,4

Chart 6.1 - Graphometrical analysis of Mallarmé, using the letter in Fig. 6.6.

The histogram of the *social Ego* IV denotes by its "barley-sugar" shape a strong predominance. Social conventions are habitually accepted, without excluding autonomy (variable 18); emotional play is constrained (19). Social communication takes place in small groups, not with the crowd (opposition of variables 16 and 20); but, in the first case, a sufficient distance (32 in +1 to variable 16) marks the difference between master and pupils.

We end by quoting the conclusion drawn by Madame Marie-Thérèse Prénat :

> The superior range of intellect, the tension of the energy making up for occasional lapses of vigour, and in so far as the feeling for difference is respected, an adequate acceptance of social rules assures the maintenance of efficient operational activity (very high coefficient : 49).
>
> The creative urge is strong enough to overcome the obstacles raised by the unconscious and even to find a new source of dynamism in former frustrations and conflicts.
>
> He can accept being alone, but never to play second fiddle, even if that entails giving up the security of traditional ways.

*

From the PSYCHOANALYTIC viewpoint, the *libido* is quite strong (nourished, homogeneous, semi-angular hand, but irregular with quite a few inhibitions), very "regulated " (aerated writing, precise forms, restrained finals and considerable tension).

The JUNGIAN type is introverted *Intuition Thinking;* because of the grouped, stylised, rhythmic, uneven and soaring writing, *Thinking* because of simplifications, wide spaces and structured layout. *Sensation* (well-nourished writing, a few affected strokes and complications) is inferior in the meaning given by Janet (congestion and tensed lower extensions) as is *Sentiment* (vertical, sober, "linear", as Klages describes it, and "cold"). From this can be deduced a tendency to depth of thought, a perpetual "quest" for an interior goal, a love of correspondences (introverted Intuition)and strong intellectuality (love of theorising). Sensation is introverted: good sensoriality, attention being paid to the internal resonance of impressions. The inferior *Sentiment* corresponds to a difficulty in warm affective contact (tendency to narrow letters, but with Saudek's "secondary width").

Introversion is strong, to the point of suggesting a tendency to *obsession* : vertical, simplified hand, restrained or centripetal finals, small garlands and arcs; in some documents the writing is small and spaced-out, and elsewhere piled-up on the right. This suggests a strongly *schizoid*[(23)] constitution, for the writing has nearly all its signs (predominance of form, strong tension, original shapes, rather narrow letters, high upper extensions, short or centripetal finals, spacing between words) : a turning-in upon self, a search for an unreal and absolute ideal.

The principal complexes are one of *inferiority* (superelevations, narrowings, tension) and strong *narcissism* (exaggerated, superelevated and ornate capitals, regressive curves). The *Anima* is powerful (rounded movements in the soaring strokes and the capitals, aerated and nuancée hand), but it is not expressed in breadth (vertical, semi-angular, held back, rather constrained, narrow with secondary width), from which may be deduced a moderate development of the life of the affections[(24)]. Notice the unevenness in the lower extensions and the occasional weakness of pressure (congestions, blurred

---

(23) Cf. the study by Dr. Fretet, pp.69-95, mentioned at the start of this chapter.

(24) It is important to mention here the penetrating study in which Mauron shows how deeply Stéphane Mallarmé was affected by the death of his mother when he was five and of his youngest sister ten years later (book mentioned at the start of the chapter, pp.9-44). He points out the link between pictures (so frequent with Mallarmé) of ice, glass and blank paper and the image of the tomb.

stroke edges). This perhaps points to an imperfectly integrated sexuality. One may also infer a fear of confronting life[(25)] and an anxious turning-in on himself (narcissism, inferiority complex). The *Persona*, considerable enough (initial reinforcements, neatness), brings a measure of security, but is also a limitation.

From the SZONDIAN viewpoint, the writing is typically *epileptoid* (*e*+): well-nourished stroke with moderately blurred edges, rhythm constructed, regular and personal, strict layout.

The profile of the *Paroxyslmal* vector is *e+ hy+/-*; this last reaction can be seen in the signs of *hy-* (writing held back and somewhat constrained, simple closed forms and margins often rigid) and of *hy+* variability, exaggerations, ornaments.

The profile *e+ hy+/-* is frequent with poets, the exhibitionist tendency (*hy*+) - making oneself heard, asserting oneself by polarising attention - finding satisfaction in ways admissable to personal ethics (*e*+) and the morality of the group.

The *Ego* is strongly narcissistic: k+ (predominance of form over movement, centripetal tendency of free gestures) with, varying with the documents, *p-* elements (high narrow letters), or *p*+ (large, spread-out, rhythmic movements), whence an *autistic Ego* A_2 *(Sch = k+p- :* life in an unreal constructed world into which the poet projects his aspirations), sometimes tending to an *Ego in peril D (Sch = k+p+* : thirst for the absolute).

The reactions of the *Sexual* vector are very probably *h-* (tense, semi-angular, vertical, with simplified shapes) and s- (Venus component: homogeneous, stylised, semi-rounded hand) showing a certain weakness (inhibitions), still without deficiency and with a successful sublimation (rhythmic writing with a high Formlevel).

---

(25) Mallarmé's first nervous depressions appeared respectively when he decided to get married (spring 1862) and at the birth of his first daughter (November 1864).

The profile of the *Contact* vector contains a reaction *d-* (orderly, constrained, vertical hand with considerable tension, a dark, ink-filled stroke and precise punctuation) and probably a reaction *m+* (nourished, semi-rounded stroke with a strong middle zone): a lasting attachment to the object acting as a mother substitute, jealously idealistic fidelity.

*

The study of temperament and the mythological types is particularly instructive.

The TEMPERAMENTAL dominant is *Nervous-Lymphatic* : Mallarmé is a "Nervous cerebral type" as Dr. Carton says (simplified, connected hand with some irregularity; narrowness, verticality): there is a lively sensitivity behind a cold exterior; an inquisitive, knowledgeable and intelligent mind; vulnerability and a tendency to depression - with a strong, moist Lymphatic component (general regularity, clarity, easiness of certain connections and soaring strokes): refined sensitivity, ability to be kind and even affectionate.

Ranking second, a warm *Bilious* element can be seen in the superelevations and the precise firmness : appetite for reaching outward, idealism, aloofness. There is quasi deficiency in the *Sanguine* element (initial reinforcements), because of the sober movement (simple, contained writing), which is also inhibited (narrow and vertical), and because of the almost below average vitality of the graphic context : lack of expansiveness, of warmth and wide contact.

The general picture is that of a sensitive, dreaming intellectual, receptive rather than active (Nervous -Lymphatic), to whom a Bilious element brings a certain gentle continuity, but who is less than warmly outgoing because of a weak Sanguine element.

From the MYTHOLOGICAL viewpoint, Mallarmé's handwriting evolved remarkably from his youth toward Sun and Saturn.

The manuscripts of 1864 are strongly *Moon* because of the numerous blank spaces and a certain imprecision of forms. There is some measure of *Venus* (moderate rhythm, small garlands), *Mercury* (small writing), not lacking in *Saturn* (sobriety, verticality, interruptions) and *Sun* (distinction).

In his maturity, the dominance of Venus and Moon is replaced by the alliance Sun-Saturn : *Sun*, because of the shapes which are stylised, simplified, distinguished, aesthetic and vertical (aristocratic aestheticism) and because of the super-elevations, tasteful word beginnings and the soaring movements (ambition to reach beyond one's limits, sublimation); *Saturn*, because of the sober vertical hand (typical speculative intellect with a background of moralism), the narrowness and restrained finals (reserve in making relationships), and the rather connected writing (constant activity, reason, fidelity).

Venusian rhythm and Lunar imagination are present, but only in the background, with some elements of *Jupiter* of questionable taste (conventionally elaborate strokes in exaggerated capitals) : desire to be an intellectual leader. There is no deficiency in Mercury (skilful linking) or in *Earth*: precise, regular writing (exactness, a concern for correctness of detail); simple forms (sincerity); head-to-foot connections admirably express the bond between Sun and Earth (incarnation of the ideal). *Mars* alone is deficient (writing that is of a below normal vitality, poised, nuancée and with irregular t-bars: a vulnerable man, not ruled by instinct, and not a fighter).

In the manuscript of *Le Livre* (fig. 6.10) *Saturn* is dominant, because of the black stroke and the tormented progress of the writing (twists, narrowings, backward strokes): solitary reflections and anguished self-questioning.

*

From the viewpoint of the PSYCHOBIOLOGICAL TEMPERAMENTS of Léone Bourdel the writing is *Harmonic* to an exceptionally high degree. This is by reason of the lively, sensitive, spontaneously expressive movement of the rhythm, the simplification, the instinctive aesthetic sense that both the layout on the page and the stylised forms display, the restrained finals and size, the idiosyncratic strokes that diminish legibility and frequently cover several zones (e.g. head-to-foot connections).

Especially with advancing age, the handwriting is *Harmonic-Rhythmic* and *anti-Melodic* because of the semi-angularity, the monomorphism (systematisation), the verticality, the restrained finals and lastly the interruptions in the stroke (at age twenty) and by the high and somewhat narrow letters (from the age of thirty).

It is superfluous to go into the question of how traits of character make up a deeply Harmonic personality centred round a ruling passion: the quest for the Absolute.

*

BIBLIOGRAPHY

Don Felix de SALAMANCA (Lord J. H. INGRAM), *The Philosophy of Handwriting,* Chatto and Windus, London, 1879 : see p.88.
– High quality, beautiful, elegant writing, fluent and graceful. Clarity, perfect attention to detail. Signs of imagination.

Marius DECRESPE, *Manuel de graphologie appliquée*, Guyot, Paris, (1895), vol.I : see pp.125-126.
– The artistic *S*.

R. de SALBERG (Angèle de MONTIGNY), *Manuel de graphologie usuelle enseignée par l'exemple en six leçons et par six cent quarante-neuf types d'écritures (*1901), 46th thousand, Hachette, Paris, 1931 : see pp.213-214.
– Margins to right and to the left (poetic mind), upright hand (inspiration from the head and not the heart), upturned finals (aspiration

towards the ideal). Narrow *M* (shyness) and coiled (literary coterie), the digit 1 written as *l* (intentional oddness).

R. de SALBERG (Angèle de MONTIGNY) "Considérations générales sur la graphologie", *La Graphologie*, vol.33, no.1, pp.152-159, 1903 : see pp.155.
– "Let us look at the surprises that the study of a script can give us. Have you ever wondered how Mallarmé set about writing - this king of impenetrable poets? Don't look for muddled, tangled writing. Mallarmé's hand was that of a typical accountant. This teacher of English was methodical, neat, excessively tidy and his correct vertical writing denotes the Master who has known for a long time how to dazzle the public. They say he used to prepare his evening conversations."

In the next number (vol. 33, no.2) see p.73, there is : "My observations on the poet Mallarmé caused a favourable reply from Mr. Gabriel Favre : I want to make it clear that I have in no way broached the subject of the famous poet's moral qualities or his intellectual standing. All I wanted to do was to point to the contrast between his clear, sober handwriting and the intentional obscurity of his work".

ENIGMA , *Les Secrets de l'écriture,* Société parisienne d'édition, 1929, pp.88-89.
– Blurred, upright paraph : discouragement, mental tiredness.

Suzanne LEMIÈRE, "A propos d'une exposition", *La Graphologie scientifique,* no.86, see p.46, 1936.

"Mallarmé's hand, with its straight, fine, slender handwriting, made up of careful strokes together with long, vertical upper extensions gives an impression of intelligent and harmonious discipline, but suddenly a letter of unexpected shape supplies the proof of great originality".

Edmond JALOUX, *Souvenirs sur Henri de Régnier,* Rouge et Cie., Lausanne, 1941 : see p.19.
– "It was the time (end of the 19th century) when writers indulged in magnificent calligraphy. That of José-Marie de Hérédia was elegant and had majestic capitals. Mallarmé's was fine, supple, straightening up the last letter in each word, like an attentive finger; [...]".

M. D. (Maurice DELAMAIN), "Nos autographes. Stéphane Mallarmé", *La Graphologie,* no.29, see p.31 and IV, 1948.
– Harmonious writing, rather scholarly or calligraphic (notably the signature). Great (morbid) reverence for the page, black and white as in a pattern. Intense and troubled sensuality (muddy [26]and ink-filled,

(26) An odd opinion of the script studied, apparently the only one of Mallarmé's known to Delamain.

although still neat). Graceful curves. Distant from practical life (prolonged writing). "It is difficult to see how such careful, limpid handwriting can belong to the most incomprehensible of our poets. It must be that the literary obscurity is intentional and artificial, having no depth or mental confusion. It has been gradually discovered that most of Mallarmé's enigmas can be explained in a rather matter-of-fact way as being contrived, artificial and pedantic subtleties. Graphology fully supports this view".[27]

G. E. MAGNAT and M. D. (Maurice DELAMAIN), "Sur l'écriture de Mallarmé", *La Graphologie,* no.30, 1948 : see p.20.
– G.E. Magnat took up the defence of Mallarmé, who had little imagination, but who wrote one of the most beautiful lines in French poetry ("Tel qu'en lui-même enfin l'éternité le change"). "Poetry is not made with ideas, but with words", he wrote. Now there are more things in words than we imagine. - M. Delamain acknowledged "the impression of crystalline transparency and sonority, of carving on marble" that the handwriting gives, "the extraordinary elegance of the *l* of the signature (dragonflies!)", and finally, "a monkish clarity and slowness that proclaims the saint of poetry". He does not deny that Mallarmé was a very intelligent man and a great poet. M. Delamain explained that he wanted to point out the contrast between Mallarmé's clear handwriting and the artificial obscurity of his poems... and that he does not particularly like his handwriting.

G. E. MAGNAT, "L'écriture du poète", *La Graphologie,* no.46, p.21, 2nd quarter 1952 and no.47, pp.5-13, 3rd quarter 1952 : see pp.10-11.
– "These four lines illustrate exactly what Pascal meant by the definition "natural". The slow writing, the stroke that is gentle, tender and firm, where the ink looks transformed into a most precious paste which has the power to cause the least bit of paper it has honoured with its presence to look like parchment. Artifice, perhaps rather than art, has been advanced in so far that the least stroke is the unique expression of a unique man, Mallarmé. Sentiment is not expressed in a romantic way, but it seems to manifest its presence in the elegant modesty of the writing line and the stroke. How different from the writing of Victor Hugo! One is tempted to say that Mallarmé is the prince of poetry."

---

(27) Perhaps the unjust inexactitude of this judgement made by an intelligent, cultivated man is caused by a lack of understanding joined to a typological opposition. (Delamain was a strong "extraverted Sensation type".)

La Graphologie, no.39, 3rd quarter 1955 : see p.III.
– (M. DELAMAIN) believes the document from which our fig. 6.9 is taken to be more reliable than the script analysed in no.29.

Jacques SCHERER, *Le "Livre" de Mallarmé. Premières recherches sur des documents inédits*, Gallimard, Paris, 5th ed., 1957, see pp.144, 147-148.
– "He obviously took the first sheet of paper available. But once he had chosen it, he would fill it with the elegant layout that is characteristic of all his manuscripts [...] Mallarmé's writing is often so continuous that it is impossible to decide whether an indecipherable piece corresponds to one word or to several [...] I am not always sure that I have read the text exactly. Mallarmé's writing takes on a very different appearance in different sheets and registers the changing moods of a highly sensitive being. One page is extremely joined-up and the words are no more separate from each other than the letters of a single word. Another page has such chopped-up writing that the letters are like a row of parallel sticks, and are obviously very difficult to interpret. What worries or anxieties sometimes destroy this handwriting that is usually harmonious and supremely elegant?"

Dr. Jean RIVÈRE, *Le Monde de l'écriture*, Gonon, Neuilly sur Seine, 1958, 295p : see p.105.
– Writing prolonged both upwards and downwards. This is rare with artists who usually limit their upper and lower extensions (imitation of printing or a witness to their limited contact with the outside world).

M.(Madame Madeleine) TAVERNIER, "Dispositions et ordonnance des masses écrites dans la page à partir d'une étude sur Stéphane Mallarmé", *La Graphologie,* no.112, 1968 : see pp.20-35.
– Mallarmé's varied gifts: conversationalist, lawyer, journalist, controversialist, lover of language and art. His project for a great work (the *Livre)* which would have expressed the unknowable, the correlation of poetry with the universe, was objective, impersonal and timeless. The importance of white space with Mallarmé: questioning of mystery and the unknown.

His three handwritings (a) the neat, connected, positive and harmonious hand of his correspondence (spontaneous remarks, transcriptions); b) a smaller hand, spread-out with deviated pressure, probably official writing; (c) the more excitable hand, less neat and irregular in continuity of his personal notes, with disturbances in the spatial rhythm, a singular layout and invading white spaces (mystical state: an endeavour to reveal a reality that he has not created).

By contrast, the invasive writings of his contemporaries express a fear of the irrational and the unknowable, and a refuge in day-to-day activities.

R. P. SEILER, "A propos de l'étude de Madame Tavernier de l'ordonnance des masses dans la page", *La Graphologie,* no.114, 1969 : see pp.36-39.
– Analysis and criticism of the preceding article: confirmation of its leading ideas; details and questions about Mallarmé (his intentional lack of clarity, his ability as a talker, the changes in his writing); white spaces interpreted not only as the outside world or the subconscious, but also as rationality; a proposed judgement of the black and white relationship (notably the opposition between Mallarmé's writing and invasive writings) in connection with Pophalian tension.

J.-Ch. GILLE-MAISANI, "Détails d'histoire de la graphologie à propos de l'écriture de Mallarmé," *La Graphologie,* no.157, 1980 : see pp.66-69.
– The head-to-foot connection, discovered by Madame Cerbelaud-Salagnac (1959). The rising final upstrokes discovered by Monsignor Barbier de Montault, discussed in 1881-1882, classic in French graphology, then .... rediscovered by Klages in 1927; such happenings are not rare in the history of graphology.

Encor ! que sans répit les tristes cheminées
Fument, et que de suie une errante prison
Éteigne dans l'horreur de ses noires traînées
Le soleil se mourant, jaunâtre, à l'horizon !

— Le Ciel est mort — Vers toi j'accours ! donne, ô Matière,
L'oubli de l'Idéal cruel et du Péché
À ce martyre qui vient partager la litière
Où le bétail heureux des hommes est couché ;

* **Fig. 6.1** - Handwriting of Stéphane Mallarmé at 22 (fragment of the manuscript of *L'Azur*).

Vendredi 19 Mai 1876
87 rue de Rome

Cher Monsieur,

Je suis confus de votre remerciement, dont je n'accepte que le serrement de mains; car tout ce que j'ai pu faire à l'Athenæum est moins que rien, jugez-en par cette note de deux ou trois lignes placée dans le numéro de la dite encyclopédie, qui accompagne ma lettre. Mais après avoir

* **Fig. 6.2a** - Mallarmé at 34. (Start of a letter).

coupé toute phrase incidente
ici élagué toute épithète, on
a encore l'amabilité de
laisser plus de mes notes
survivre à cette abominable
opération qu'il n'en reste de
toutes celles qui ont trait aux
écrivains anglais les plus
notoires, ainsi que vous
pouvez le voir. J'ai honte
de la sécheresse qu'on impose
à mes télégrammes; or il
paraît que je suis toutefois
favorisé, comme étranger.

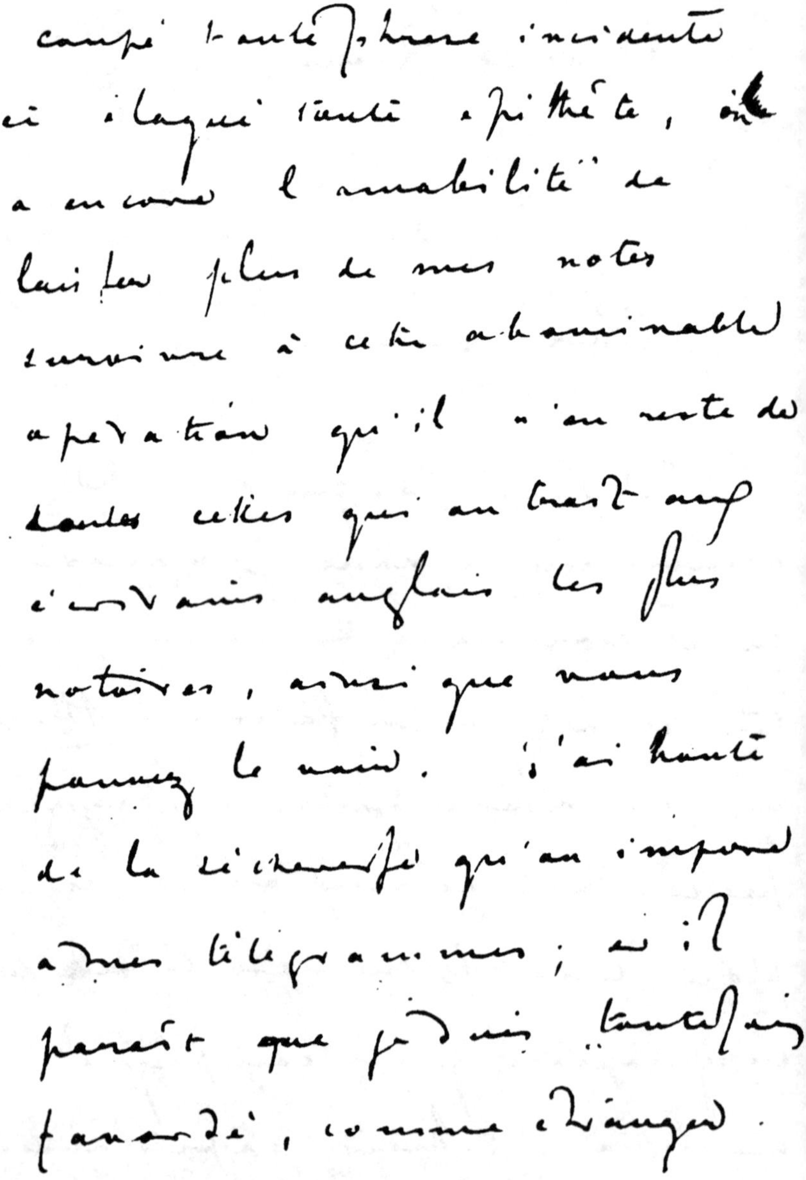

* **Fig. 6.2b** - Mallarmé at 34. (Continuation).

Certainement, j'espère avoir
le plaisir de vous rencontrer
un de ces Jeudis, chez Zola;
en portant à ce Maître un
petit opuscule de critique que
je publie en ce moment; et
dont un exemplaire vous
sera réservé.

Croyez-moi
votre bien dévoué
Stéphane Mallarmé.

* **Fig. 6.2c** - Mallarmé at 34. (End of the letter).

Fig. 6.3 - Mallarmé at 43. (Pencilled letter to Verlaine).

Le Pitre Châtié

Sonnet

Yeux, lacs avec ma simple ivresse de renaître
Autre que l'histrion qui du geste évoquais
Comme plume la suie ignoble des quinquets,
J'ai troué dans le mur de toile une fenêtre.

De ma jambe et des bras limpide nageur traître,
À bonds multipliés, reniant le mauvais
Hamlet ! c'est comme si dans l'onde j'innovais
Mille sépulcres pour y vierge disparaître.

Hilare or de cymbale à des poings irrité,
Tout à coup le soleil frappe la nudité
Qui pure s'exhala de ma fraîcheur de nacre :

Rance nuit de la peau quand sur moi vous passiez,
Ne sachant pas, ingrat ! que c'était tout mon sacre,
Ce fard noyé dans l'eau perfide des glaciers.

Stéphane Mallarmé

Fig. 6.4 - Manuscript of *Le Pitre châtié*.

Fig. 6.5 - One of the famous envelopes that Mallarmé used to send with the address in verse and which, it is said, always arrived safely. (43 years).

(D) Valvins, par Avon (Seine et Marne)
Dimanche 22 Août 1886

Mon cher Monsieur d'Orfer,

Je trouve votre lettre au retour
d'une petite absence que j'ai faite
de la campagne même. Quel
dommage que M. Raynaud
votre ami qui, en effet, a,
m'a-t-on dit, publié l'ensemble
des vers d'Hérodiade dans

* **Fig. 6.6** - Start of a letter sent by Mallarmé at 44.
(Sample continued overleaf).

Agréez mes amitiés et
présentez à Monsieur Raymond
avec mes regrets de ne pas
faire mieux, les vœux
qu'il y a lieu de faire pour
le succès de sa publication.

Stéphane Mallarmé

Vous m'enverrez, n'est-ce pas,
des épreuves, pour changer un mot ou d

Continuation of * **Fig. 6.6** - End of a letter sent by Mallarmé at 44.

Paris 89 rue de Rome

Monsieur

Votre oeuvre amicale
en faveur de Villiers de l'Isle-Adam
reste anonyme, rien, chiffres,
indications, vous le comprenez,
qui l'ait portée à la connaissance:
aussi le grand remerciement
qu'il y a lieu de vous faire,

* **Fig. 6.7** - Start of a letter sent by Mallarmé at 47.
(Sample continued overleaf).

de souvenir.

Je suis votre

reconnaissant et dévoué

Stéphane Mallarmé

Mardi 19 Mars 1889

Continuation of * **Fig. 6.7** - End of a letter sent by Mallarmé at 47.

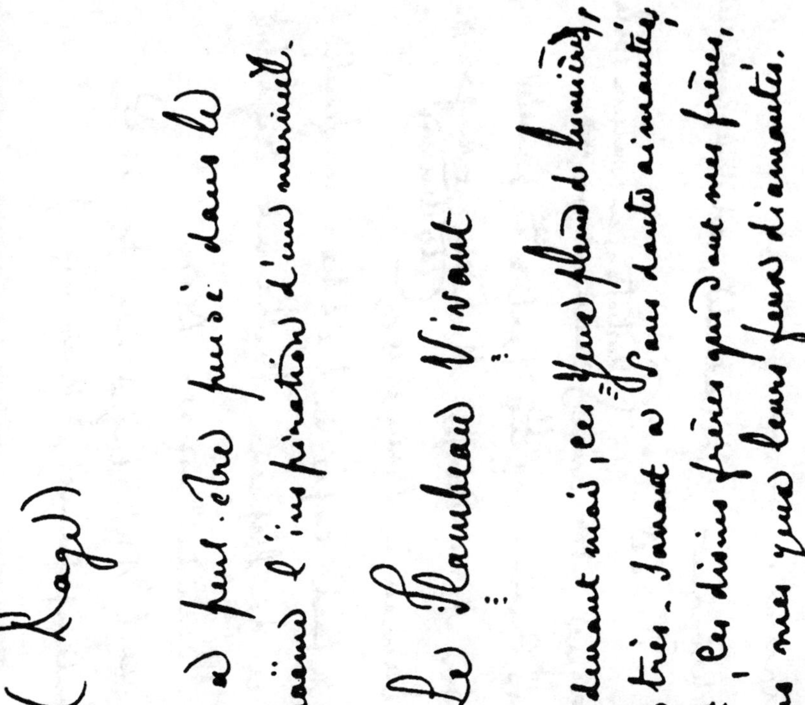

Fig. 6.8 - Mallarmé after his fiftieth year.

définitive, à la librairie [illegible] ,

— Prochainement : Hérodiade, édition complète

Prose

Le Tiroir de Laque, avec [illustrations en couleur sur la] commentaire,

Aquarelles de John Lewis Brown ; eaux-fortes [à la] pointe

sèche de Mme Berthe Morisot et Degas : [, de Renoir]

10 cahiers, chez Deman, à Bruxelles.

Le Vathek de Beckford, copie de l'édition originelle

de 1787, avec Préface de Stéphane Mallarmé, chez Labitte.

Album de Vers et de Prose

(fascicule 10e de l'Anthologie des poètes et

prosateurs Contemporains, Bruxelles.)

Fig. 6.9 - Mallarmé at 55.

Fig. 6.10 - Rough notes made by Mallarmé of the plan for *Le Livre* (reduced by about 30%). (Sample continued overleaf).

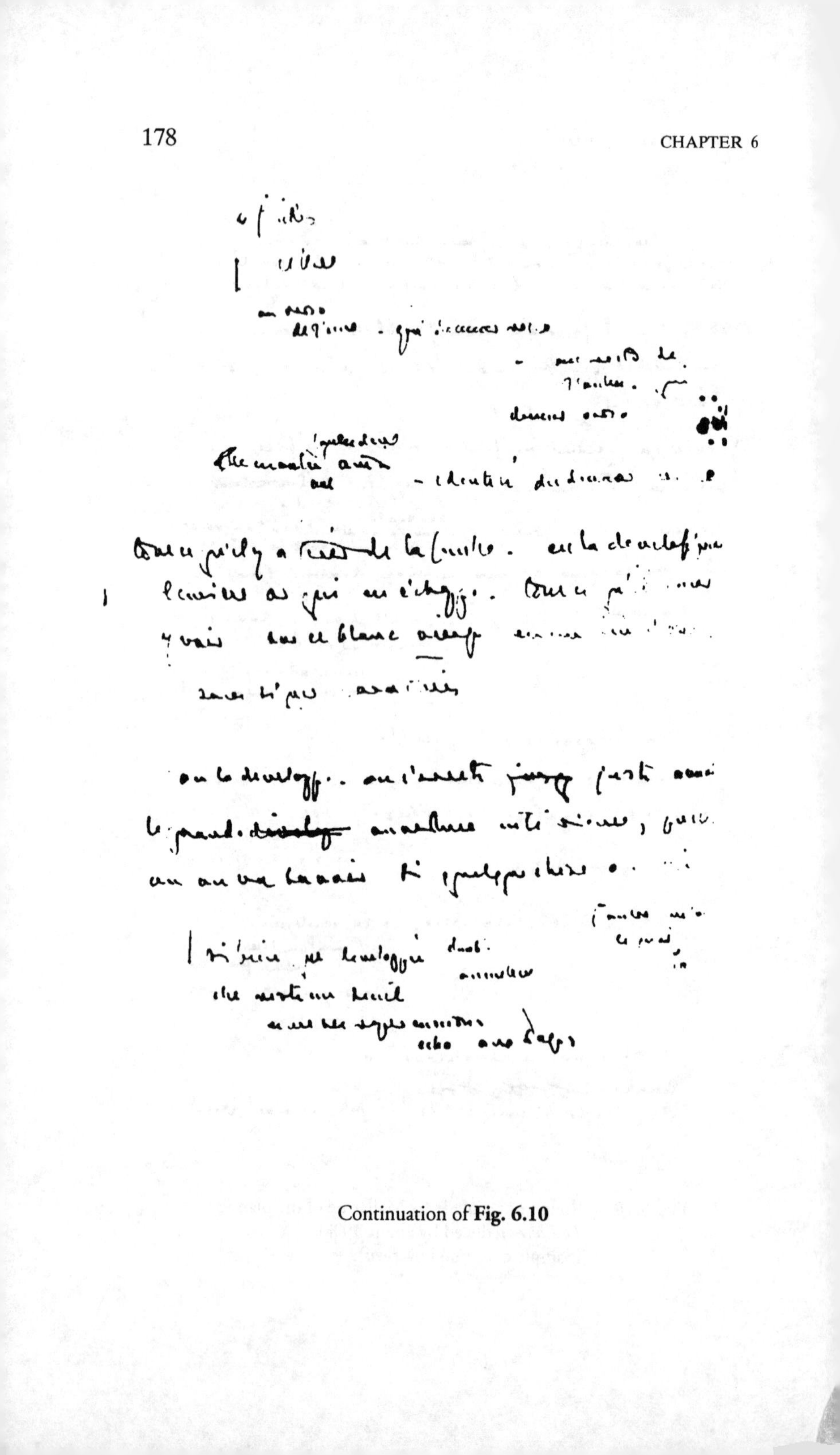

Continuation of **Fig. 6.10**

7

Paul Marie VERLAINE (1844 - 1896)

A low grade Paris clerk, Paul Verlaine early published some graceful verses (*Fêtes galantes*). His home life (1870) was destroyed by his relationship with the young poet, Arthur Rimbaud, with whom he lived in Belgium and England. Imprisoned for two years (1873 - 1875) for having fired at his friend, Verlaine came to himself, was converted (*Romances sans paroles, Sagesse*) and led an ordered life. But after the death of his mother (1886) he fell back permanently into drinking and debauchery.

If the man was pitiable, the poet was great by the sincerity of his emotional impulse, his regrets and the incomparable music of his verses. Verlaine, elected "prince of poets" in 1894, is today not only famous, but popular.

We will study the writing of the young Verlaine (figs. 7.1 to 7.3). Then we will compare the writing after his conversion (figs. 7.4 to 7.6) and finally that of his last years.

Examples 7.1 and 7.2, taken as typical of the young poet's writing, come from the manuscript of *Fêtes galantes* (1869). Figure 7.3 (partly enlarged in 7.9) is a dedication written by Paul to his fiancée in 1870.

As ORIENTATING SYNTHESES and in the foreground of the JAMINIAN definition for figure 7.1, we put forward :

Organised writing with idiosyncratic letters (*d, g, q, s*).

Harmony lessened by the poor quality of the stroke and the somewhat exaggerated flying strokes.

Formlevel quite high.

Irregular, easy, rhythmic movement with precise, though not well structured forms; only disturbed at stroke level.

Pophalian tension III, with disturbed strokes IVb.

Spontaneous, accelerated, semi-rounded, right-slanting writing; *animated, irregular* in all categories; very *connected, compact.*

Initial emphasis; *enlarging* with *soaring* and often *centripetal finals*; "lyrical *d*".

Pastose stroke, *amendments, spasms, congestion.*

Irregular left-hand margin.

Closed ovals, but sometimes open to the left with a small loop.

T-bars done from right to left, long, flying, horizontal or rising; accents regular.

The lines of poetry (fig. 7.2 and 7.3) are written more *carefully*, with a better formed and more *angular* middle zone, but the *t*-bars are *irregular*, and the stroke is *thick, congested* and almost *muddy.*

The signature (fig 7.3 and 7.9) is *inhibited* and quite *reduced.* Its direction, generally *upward*, has many *hesitations* (step-like). The *ensiform* (sword-shaped)[(1)] paraph is *light.* In the initials, P.V., there is the same opposition between the general *ascending* direction and *inhibitions* (narrow letters, regressive paraph).

*

(1) i.e. made by a straight stroke going down and to the left. (The term was used by l'abbé Michon, but not often since.)

Verlaine's handwriting is of the sort that justifies the opinion of the German graphologist, Heinrich Pfanne, that the stroke should be considered as an aspect of writing of the same order as the three aspects of Gross which Heiss adopted: movement, form and spatial layout.

The *stroke* in this writing (cf. the enlargements in fig. 7.9) is indeed rich in meaning, with the extra interest that it is very different from the writing line, that is the other aspects of the writing, constituting a counter-dominant in Saudek's meaning.

The average pressure on the pen is not very strong, the stroke in fig. 7.1 being very light. In fig. 7.2 the downstrokes are certainly thicker, but that is because the pen nib is rather wide[(2)] which congests many letters : therefore "Breitfeder-wechselzug", according to the happy expression of Müller-Enskat, and not heavy pressure. Moreover, numerous congestions appear irregularly, generally as a sign of spindle-shaped strokes and exceptionally of writing punctuated by dots. (fig. 7.1 : *32*; 7.2 : *E*t ce vicomte; 7.3 : *p*etit, *p*lein, es*p*oir) or of clubbed writing (fig. 7.1 : final upstroke of Pantomim*e*)[(3)].

The edges of the strokes are unclear (Crépieux-Jamin's blurred stroke and Hegar's pastose.) Under the magnifying glass (fig 7.9) they seem made on blotting paper and in some places the stroke is broken (e.g. in the paraph). The flow of ink gives the impression of the messiness that characterises the porous or granulated stroke of Brotz and Pophal.

---

(2) This is apparent from the fact that the stroke also becomes wider when ascending, whence a widening in the north-eastern side of the loops of the letters *l*, *b*, etc. (see fig. 7.1 : Pantomim*e*, *h*erbe; fig. 7.2 : *b*riquet, *b*as, *l*a, cl*é*; fig. 7.9 : Mat*hild*e Maut*é*, Ver*l*aine). On this subject the reader is referred to General H. Menjaud, "Détermination de la pression de l'écriture", *La Graphologie,* no.23 : pp.13-17, July 1946 and to W. Müller and A. Enskat, *Graphologische Diagnostik. Ihre Grundlagen, Möglichkeiten und Grenzen*, Huber, Bern, 1961, pp. 31-32.

(3) Document 7.2 may have been written under the influence of alcohol.

The stroke is generally curved, but sometimes straight. It is quite rapid. In a word it is close to Hegar's types XIV and X.

This light, blurred, curved stroke shows to what extent the intense sensuous impressions stimulate the imagination. The presence of delicately soaring upstrokes in writing with such a wide nib inclines one to suspect the existence of a delicate aesthetic feeling directed by the brain and not only by instinct. On the other hand, strong pastosity (blurred edges, congestions) bears witness to a considerable sensuality, which is demanding and not always refined and which permeates the personality and risks unbalancing it (porous stroke) more especially because the senses are capable of initiating activity in an impulsive manner (light, rapid and sometimes straight strokes).

The *movement* of the writing is rich by reason of its elastic, easy, unfettered rhythm (overconnections). Right-slanting, rather rapid and soaring, it speaks of a mind both lively and capable of initiative and looks very spontaneous, the enlarging and centrifugal finals suggesting impulsiveness.

Analysis reveals more complexity. The movement has tension enough (Leitbild III - though this tension falls here and there to II: note the middle zone of fig. 7.1) and takes on forms that are undifferentiated, but precise (even in the enlarged finals) and quite varied. This proves that the writer's activity is directed towards a clearly perceived goal that conforms to his deep tendencies (harmony between movement and form). The first impression of open spontaneity is modified, however, by the ovals closed or open to the left with the occasional loop, irregular speed, regressive strokes, a generally decreasing left-hand margin, the sword-shaped paraph, and the full stop after the signature. The writer is very self-centred and capable of considerable dissimulation, which is linked to his lack of self-confidence (reduced, hesitant and step-like signature).

Spatial layout is intensely rhythmic : the individualism is original - but it is not aerated (compact writing with overconnections between the words and some tangling between the lines) : a demanding need for contact.

Intelligence is of high quality (rapid, connected hand) with the ability both to assimilate and to create (semi-rounded writing with some individualistic shapes) and with a good psychological sense (nuancée). On the down-side, judgement is sometimes hasty (size and speed too irregular, with both initial and final emphasis). Will-power is capable of initiative (rapid, semi-angular, thrown writing with long t-bars) and of the following-up of ideas (connected hand), but it lacks resistance (light, curved strokes, an uneven writing trail).

To sum up, graphology broadly confirms the picture of Paul Verlaine preserved by posterity. An intelligent and sensitive man, inclined to act on impulse, having much sensuality and an overriding need of contact and warmth. It does not confirm the hackneyed idea of the careless Bohemian, because it reveals his anxiety, his propensity to hide his feelings[(4)] and most important, beyond his impulsiveness, a clear and even obstinate following-up of ideas.

*

Typological study confirms and perfects this description.

From the viewpoint of the TEMPERAMENTS, Verlaine's writing reveals a moist lymphatic (or Lymphatic-Sanguine), with a dry component (Nervous -Bilious).

The *Lymphatic-Sanguine* element is revealed by the connected, irregular, easy and graceful hand with its initial emphasis : fanciful, dreamy, sensitivity, need for tenderness and approval, i.e. communication. The *Nervous* component appears in the speed and the unevenness (a sharp mind and a feeling for the nuance), the *Bilious* component in the strong but unstable *t*-bars

(4) According to biographers, more than one of Verlaine's "impulsive" actions had really been carefully and secretly prepared.

(will-power and consistency in the stream of ideas are present, but do not rule the personality).

The poet appears clearly behind this temperamental mixture : the Lymphatic element corresponds to the part of him that is instinctive and immaturely sensory; the Sanguine element to the need to communicate by exteriorising; the Nervous-Bilious to the process of conscious intellectual structuring.

From the MYTHOLOGICAL angle, we have prominently *Moon* (curves, slender upstrokes), *Jupiter* (capitals, exaggerated finals), *Mercury* (accelerated, easy, light, irregular in direction), and *Saturn* (dark strokes, a certain stiffness in figure 7.3), but the other types are not altogether lacking : *Mars* (cruciform *t*-bars), *Sun* (tall letters), *Earth* (forms very unvarying, thickening stroke) and *Venus* (curves).

The resultants are easily established. For example : a nature that is Bohemian (Moon and Mercury), hungry for warm contact (Jupiter and Venus), anxious and pessimistic (Saturn) and disconcerting in behaviour (the association Moon-Mercury-Saturn, Martian impulsiveness).

The JUNGIAN Type is hard to determine. Madame Ania Teillard, to whom I submitted this writing, diagnosed an introverted *Intuitive* type (light, uneven, rhythmic hand) with a good balance between *Sentiment* (wide, semi-rounded writing) and *Thinking* (accelerated hand with individualistic forms), the inferior *Sensation* being strong and perturbing (poor quality of stroke, spasms).

From the SZONDIAN viewpoint, the general appearance is hysteriod *hy*+ (rapid, "flowing" movement, whimsical irregularity, inflated exaggerations, Sanguine and Nervous temperamental components): a vibrant, excitable nature desiring to "make a splash" (a seeking-after an audience to shock, astonish or amuse), parading its selfishness. This reaction *hy+* is associated, in the paroxysmal vector profile, with reaction *e*0 (a weak "oozing" stroke lacking internal density, irregular left-hand margin) : impulsiveness, lack of resistance to the instinct for pleasure, fits of anger. The *Ego* is probably *ideal-seeking* B_2D (*Sch* = *k+/-p+* : *k+/-* because of an irregular middle zone and the occasional idiosyncratic forms, which, however, are generally undifferentiated; *p+* because of the animated, rhythmic hand and the large movement in the upper zone). The man is an anxious worker who knows what he is seeking.

The profile of the *Sexual* vector is *h+s+* : *h+* because of the stroke which is pastose, warm, semi-rounded, and usually gentle and because of the Lymphatic-Sanguine temperament (sensuousness, a feeling for kindness, a need to be trusting, to be understood and to reach satisfaction). The profile is *s+* by reason of the semi-angularity, the frequently strong *t*-bars, the connected lower extensions, the vertical pressure, the spasms - spindles and clubs - and the needle-points (fighting spirit, lively and violent reactions).

The profile of the *Contact* vector is *d*0 *m+*, because of the thoroughgoing oral character (warm, comfortable strokes, garlands, easy, concave and high finals, ovals, sometimes open to the left). A considerable sociability that is brotherly and devoid of aggressiveness, but fickle and with a Bohemian disregard for rules. This profile often means an addiction to alcohol and an immature parental fixation.

Lastly, from the point of view of the PSYCHOBIOLOGICAL TEMPERAMENTS, Verlaine's writing is typically *Harmonic*. When I showed the script to Jacques Genevay without revealing the name of the writer, he exclaimed straightaway "A rough Harmonic type!" The hand is indeed lively, sensitive and "vibrant", uneven in all categories, spontaneous and with very little *Melodic* adaptation and *Ryhthmic* regularity. But this

Harmonic temperament is somehow badly displayed, existing at a visceral level (overconnections, exaggeratedly thrown and a poor quality stroke).

*

In 1880 - 1881, after the drama of the years 1871 - 1875 (life with Rimbaud, broken home life and imprisonment in Mons) , Verlaine was converted. Figures 7.4 to 7.6 are from *Sagesse.*

The higher quality of the stroke (fewer spasms, absence of signs of aggression) bear witness to a real change. But there is still the initial emphasis and the flying *d* and finals : excitement, rather disquieting for the stability of his overall balance.

From the SZONDIAN viewpoint, *p+* is now stronger than *hy+* at first sight. The partial reaction *k-* (banal forms: adaptation), is strong in the Ego *k+/-p+*. The profile of the paroxysmal vector has become *e+hy+/-* (*e+* because of the firmer stroke, the rhythm of the more stable movement, the more orderly margins, and the signature underlined more strongly; *hy-* because of the restrained rhythmic movement and the simplicity of the forms). This profile is frequent with poets. It shows (*hy+*)[5] in fact an excessively affective life (*e+hy+*) in a manner admitted by both conscience (*e+*) and the social group (*hy-*). We have pacification, but not sublimation.

As for the psychobiological temperament, there is a considerable Melodic element which can be seen in the horizontal flow, in the lessened tension and in the better extraversion. It goes with an act of adaptation and implies rather a fading-away than an expansion.

*

(5) After his conversion, Verlaine was ostentatious about his religious convictions.

Figures 7.7 and the rest come from the LAST PERIOD of the life of Verlaine, leader of the "Décadents", and then Prince of poets. Figure 7.7 dates from the darkest moral time (Verlaine lost his wife in 1886. Sick and poor, he took to drinking again and then to debauchery. He even thought of suicide). Figures 7.8 and 7.10 are from the time when, by dint of working, he managed to pick himself up.

These examples show considerable differences. In the correspondence the harmony and the simplicity of the forms are striking. But vitality is missing, as can be seen in the imprecise movements and the shakiness of 1888 and the smallness and the cramped strokes of 1892. The Melodic element is gone (except for the emphasising of some capitals in 7.8).

Figure 7.11 was done six months before the poet died at the age of fifty-two years. It shows signs of disorganisation (lack of co-ordination, breaks, letters unfinished, aborted strokes: cf. the lower part of figure 7.12).

*

Figure 7.8 [(6)] has been examined GRAPHOMETRICALLY (cf. chart 4.1).

The striking anomaly in the histogram of the stroke (I) bears witness to the physical and nervous breakdown. The sign both of a deeper wear and tear, especially visible in the poor quality of the stroke (variable 4 with high co-ordinates -2 and -3), and of extreme impressionability, with attacks of overpowering anxiety (variable 3 with very high ordinates -2 and -3). Sensory perception (variable) remains rich and varied.

---

(6) It has not been possible to do a graphometrical study of handwriting from either the youthful or the *Sagesse* periods, because the documents obtained are facsimilies and the only exception (fig. 7.3) is not suitable for such an examination, since it consists of octosyllabic lines and the original manuscript was on poor quality paper.

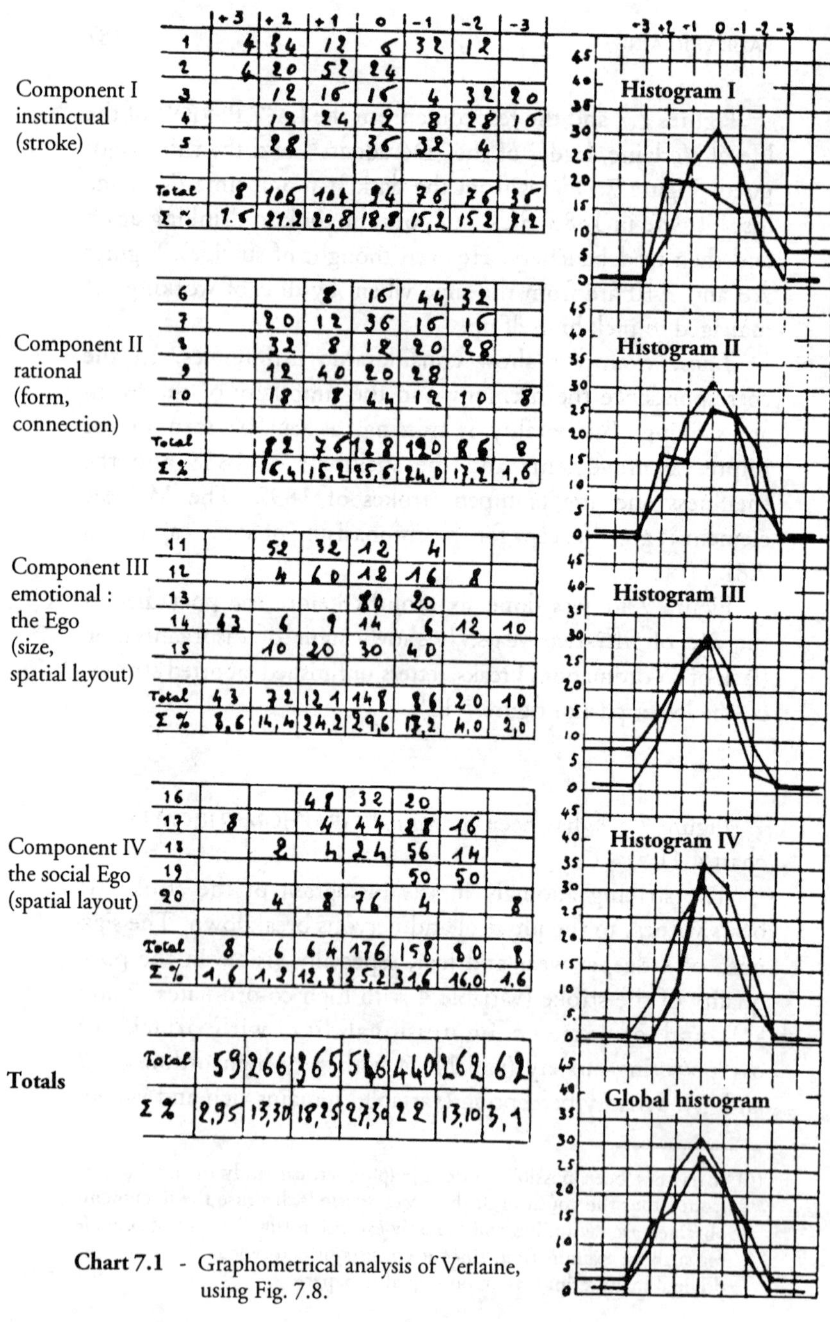

Component I
instinctual
(stroke)

	+3	+2	+1	0	-1	-2	-3
1	4	34	12	6	32	12	
2	4	20	52	24			
3		12	16	16	4	32	20
4		12	24	12	8	28	16
5		28		36	32	4	
Total	8	106	104	94	76	76	36
Σ %	1.6	21.2	20,8	18,8	15,2	15,2	7,2

Component II
rational
(form,
connection)

	+3	+2	+1	0	-1	-2	-3
6			8	16	44	32	
7		20	12	36	16	16	
8		32	8	12	20	28	
9		12	40	20	28		
10		18	8	44	12	10	8
Total		82	76	128	120	86	8
Σ %		16,4	15,2	25,6	24,0	17,2	1,6

Component III
emotional :
the Ego
(size,
spatial layout)

	+3	+2	+1	0	-1	-2	-3
11		52	32	12	4		
12		4	60	12	16	8	
13				80	20		
14	43	6	9	14	6	12	10
15		10	20	30	40		
Total	43	72	121	148	86	20	10
Σ %	8,6	14,4	24,2	29,6	17,2	4,0	2,0

Component IV
the social Ego
(spatial layout)

	+3	+2	+1	0	-1	-2	-3
16			48	32	20		
17	8		4	44	28	16	
18		2	4	24	56	14	
19					50	50	
20		4	8	76	4		8
Total	8	6	64	176	158	80	8
Σ %	1,6	1,2	12,8	25,2	31,6	16,0	1,6

Totals

	+3	+2	+1	0	-1	-2	-3
Total	59	266	365	516	440	262	62
Σ %	2,95	13,30	18,25	27,30	22	13,10	3,1

Chart 7.1 - Graphometrical analysis of Verlaine, using Fig. 7.8.

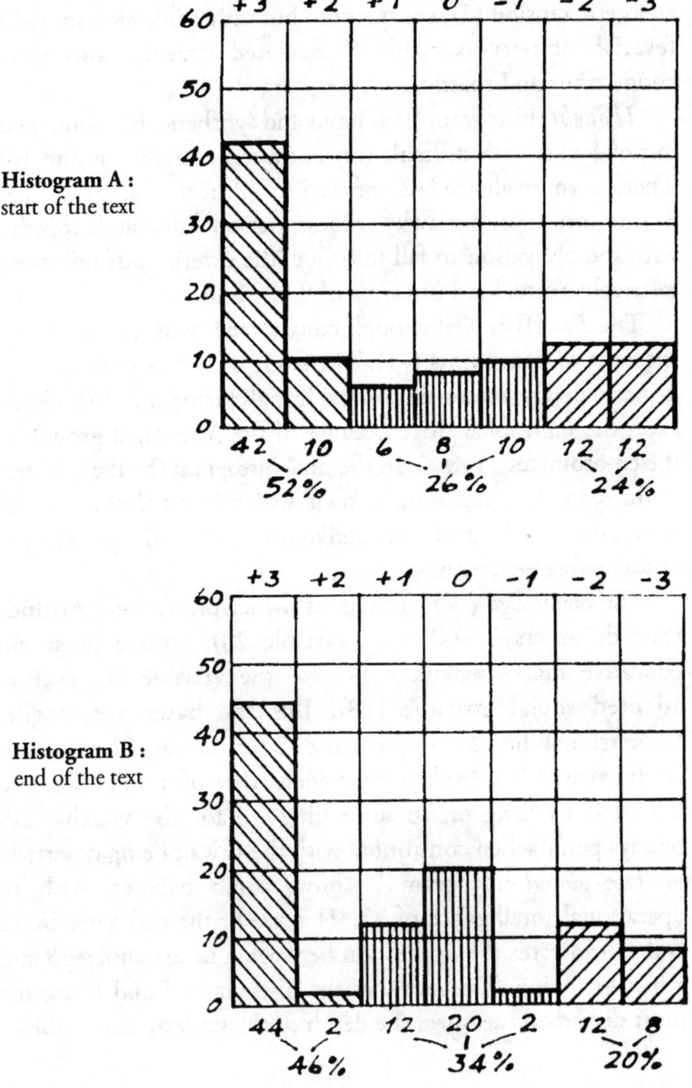

Chart 7.2 - Graphometrical analysis of Verlaine : sinuosity histograms

The writer tries to compensate for his loss of vitality by an energetic tension (2), contraction, but only achieves a sporadic, feverish activity (variable 5: deviated pressure and many congestions and spasms).

Thought (histogram II) is rapid and synthetic, but sometimes out of focus, with difficult concentration (variables 6 and 10). There is ambivalence (+2 opposed to -2) in the variables 7 and 8: exteriorisation but awkwardness, personal demands together with the obligation to fall into line, the exterior attitude being relatively normalised (maxima of 9 in +1 and -1).

The *Ego* III is well enough constructed, with the accent on the zone of constraints (+1). The study of sinuosity (chart 4.2) is particularly interesting. The initial histogram (A) clearly expresses emotional drive because of the continued growth of the co-ordinates +1 to -3. In the final histogram (B) the "cluster" in the reasoning zone is on its own, with a false balance between repression (+3) and impulsiveness (-2, -3), generating unforseeable behaviour.

The *social Ego* (IV) sustains its owner pretty well. Attitude towards others is still easy (variable 20), with a persistent educative mark (maximum +1 for the variable 16) and an adapted social attitude (18). But the bases are fragile. Impressionability is strong (-1 and -2 for the variable 19), self-confidence (17) is broken by sudden crises of doubt (+3), and the need to hang on to something (-3 for the variable 20) betrays panic when confronted with the risk of being deserted.

The *global* histogram V shows a fair balance, with an operational intelligence of 37. The rise of the ordinates in +2 and -2 indicates the opposition between a severe superego and a lust for living. The fact that the histograms I and II are the most disturbed measures the depth of the underlying troubles.

*

BIBLIOGRAPHY

J. CRÉPIEUX-JAMIN, *La Graphologie en exemples*, Larousse, Paris, 1899 : see pp.102-104. [On the manuscript of the verse "Dans ce hall trois fois circulaire" (1893) with signature.]

– "What is chiefly striking about the handwriting of Paul Verlaine, especially when several specimens are examined, is its variability. Irregularities in every category reveal the neuropath and show a nervous system too easily influenced, a morbid susceptibility, and, in a word, a certain lack of equilibrium. But intelligence is active and subtle. Perhaps his ideas, like his writing, lack clarity, but this disorder can be put down to the abundance of his impressions. This must be the cause of his hesitant hand, the difficulty in selection from several conflicting solutions.

"All the extremely varied features of his scripts which do not always seem to be executed by the same person, betray his poor health, his sensitiveness and his painful yet delicate inspiration. Living in straitened circumstances, vanity alone could give him heart. He was ambitious but had no practical sense.

"We have no grounds to speak ill of his character. He was not interested in money (rightward-turning and generally quite large writing), and his selfishness was limited to questions of fame (very high capitals, rising writing, rarely small but often light) for which he was avid.

"He was neither prudent nor circumspect, seeing very clearly what was to be done and giving advice to others about it, but never being able to accomplish things himself because he was so neglectful. (neglected punctuation, unbarred *t*). His energy was weak and ill-directed and that confirms the salient points of his nature:plenty of ideas and pictures, little concentration, nerves in a poor state and a certain break-up of the character".

Magdalene THUMM-KINTZEL, *Der psychologische und pathologische Wert der Handschrift*, Paul List, Leipzig, 1904, 208pp.

– Double curve (*L* see p.56, *m* p.63, *e* p.64) : aesthetic sense. Triple curve (*E* see p.64). Distinctive shape of the aesthetic curve pointing to a poetic gift (*L* see p.72). Right-turning connection (*sang* see p.85): wit. Non-ascending lower extensions (*gl* see p.136) : apathy.

Magdalene KINTZEL-THUMM, *Psychology and Pathology of Handwriting*, Fowler and Welles, New York 1905.

– Characteristic curve of the artistic talent in *n, e,* and *E* (see pp.40, 48, 49) and of poetic talent specifically in *D* (see p.57).

Ernest DELAHAYE, preface to the facsimile edition of *Sagesse* in the collection "Les manuscripts des maîtres", Messein, Paris, 1913 : see pp.26-28.

– Verlaine's handwriting might mislead a graphologist because of the schoolboy way he held his pen and formed his letters, (especially the capitals and the childlike *d*). "A man of thirty five with the mind of a teenager, one would say on seeing his writing". Capitals always start at the top: idealism; *e* never ink-filled: sensitiveness; rounded hand: enjoyment more important than duty or necessity; upward tendency: instinctive optimism; connected writing: "quick judgement, ready and easily-flowing speech"; letters fully formed: modesty; separate initials: "reflections first, then a very ready verbal expression of the idea". The *t*-bars are varying and light: gentleness. When they go down : stubbornness. Sudden heavy pressure : poor health.

Ernest DELAHAYE, preface to the facsimile edition of *Fêtes galantes* in the collection "Les manuscripts des maîtres", Messein, Paris, 1920 : see pp.I-II.

– The same general writing characteristics as in the manuscripts of *Sagesse* especially in the capitals. But in *Fêtes galantes* the writing is more "hasty, emotive, irregular, independent, with now and then, abrupt nervous jerks". The writing in *Sagesse* flowed more calmly and had a copy-book look, with childlike capitals. "The writer is twelve years older but he has become young again: We see the "irrepressible childhood" of which he speaks in *Amour,* and the "new Christian" who has regained his purity by becoming a small boy".

ENIGMA, *Les Secrets de l'écriture,* new edition, Société parisienne d'édition, 1929 : see pp.95-96.

– (Concerning the signature) Sword-like paraph[7], obliquely leftwards.

Suzanne LEMIÈRE, "A propos d'une exposition", *La Graphologie scientifique* no.86, see p.46, July-Aug 1936.

– Verlaine's very open, gentle and plaintive handwriting".

H. de BOUILLANE de LACOSTE and Edouard de ROUGEMONT, "Verlaine éditeur de Rimbaud", *Mercure de France* of June 15, 1937 (no.936, 48th year, vol. 276), see pp.477-502.

– This article deals with the changes, in reference to the 1871 manuscripts that Verlaine's faulty memory made to the poems of Rimbaud that he published. The only graphological observation (see p.496) concerns the alteration in Verlaine's writing between 1871 and 1886 in respect of a copy of *Premières Communions* : "The handwriting is certainly that of Verlaine, but how woefully it has changed since the time when he carefully copied Rimbaud's poems into an exercise-book!

(7) See note at the start of the chapter.

Deadened, shapeless, it bears witness to years of suffering and poverty, and its very look is chilling".

G.E. MAGNAT, "L'écriture de poète", a lecture given in Paris on April 23, 1952, *La Graphologie* no.46, see p.21, 2nd quarter 1952 and no.47, see pp.5-13, 3rd quarter 1952, see p.10.
– [Concerning four lines from *Bateau Ivre* (22nd verse), that the speaker believed were in Rimbaud's hand when they were really executed by Verlaine, as had been ascertained long before by R. Bonnet and M. Chalvet, and later confirmed by E. de Rougemont, H. de Bouillane de Lacoste and P. Izambard: cf. the article written by the last three in the Mercure de France of November 1, 1936 (quoted in the bibliography of chapter 8), see pp.459-461.]

"*Rimbaud* [...] The text that appeared on the screen was that of the end of *Bateau Ivre*, and was extraordinarily lively, pitching and rolling, the very image of a "drunken" boat. The secret of Rimbaud's *enlightened* art is the way he goes along and identifies with the words that he writes especially when they concern the elements of fire, earth air and water. So terribly is the poet at one with things, his pen[(8)] seems to follow the changing shapes, leaning now rightwards, now leftwards, going up or down in a rhythm that is not that of calligraphy, but of the world he is conjuring up. This ability to be at one with a stone, a bird, the wind or a flower must have at length become unbearable. He must have felt identified with things. No wonder that at the age of nineteen he totally abandoned[(9)] a life so divine by its omnipresence that it had become, for the man he was, *Une Saison en enfer.*"

Klara G. ROMAN, *Handwriting. A key to Personality,* Routledge and Kegan Paul, London, 1954 : see p.370.
– (Concerning eight lines with signature. Relationship between text and signature). Signature smaller than text: under-estimation of self. This humility can be artificial (desire to appear modest) or neurotic (self-devaluation, generally corroborated by other signs, notably, in English, by small pronoun *I*).

Matilde RAS, Lo *que sabemos de grafopatología (estudio de los escritos patológicos),* Gregorio del Toro, Madrid, 1968 : see pp.100, 103.
– Figures and sketches by Verlaine, presented (without comment) as a typically unbalanced personality.

---

(8) Typical example of the way suggestion can lead astray intuition, even that of a great graphologist. Magnat thought he was looking at Rimbaud's handwriting.

(9) Pure speculation (caused by the same suggestion): actually, Verlaine never gave up literature, but earned his living through writing, was named "the Prince of poets", and wrote verses until his death in 1896.

Silvia RAS, *Grafotécnica. Grafologia interpretativa*, Paraninfo, Madrid, 1973, 153p : see pp.78-79.
– A Nervous character (emotive, non-active, primary).

Myriam MENNESSON, *La Graphologie en 10 leçons*, Hachette, 1975, 254p : see p.150.
– "Writing which is irregular, unstable, jerky, thrown and narrow". A Nervous character (emotive, non-active, primary).

Nicole BOILLE, "Le geste créatif" in Anne-Marie BOETTI and Nicole BOILLE, *Romances sans paroles, Variations calligraphiques*, Edizioni Carte segrete, Rome, 1983, pp.15-45 : see p.17.
– The comments are reproduced (scaled down by 15%) in figure 7.13.

Luc UYTTENHOVE, *Dictionnaire de Graphologie*, Garancière, 1985, 319p : see p.150
– Small sober writing, with calligraphic tendencies.

Marie BERNARD, *Sexual Deviations as seen in Handwriting*, Whitston, New York, 1990, 408p : see pp.210-213.
– (Youthful handwriting). Passive, right-slanting : weakness, a need for support. Leftward turning lower extensions : mother fixation. Weakness in the letter *J* : lack of resistance. Simplified, pure shapes: poetry, idealism. Writing of the last years: pastose, congested, wavering t-bars, amended strokes.

Christian GOTH, *Écrivans. Écritures. Manuel de graphologie appliqué à l'écriture des gens de lettres,* Bordas, 1990, 256p : see pp.246-247.
– "The pen claws the paper just as misfortune has clawed his life. The man is wounded, the victim of great interior suffering, but possessing a fantastic creative power which urges him to understand his state. The need for affection is strong but despairing".

Table

1	Clair de lune	12.
2	Pantomime	12.
3	Sur l'herbe	12.
4	L'allée	14.
5	A la promenade	20.
6	Dans la grotte	12.
7	Les ingénus	12
8	Cortège	20.
9	Les coquillages	13.
10	En patinant	64.
11	Fantoches	12.
12	Cythère	12.
13	en bateau	15 / 8
14	Le faune	16
15	Mandoline	20
16	à Clymène	32
17	Lettre	18.
18	Les indolents	36
	Colombine	16.
19	. . . . .	
20	L'amour par terre	20
21	en sourdine	16
22	Colloque sentimental	
		412

Fig. 7.1 - Handwriting of Paul Verlaine aged about 25.
(Manuscript of *Les Fêtes Galantes*). (Reduced 15%).

13

En bateau

L'étoile du berger tremblote.
Sous l'eau plus noire et le pilote
Cherche un briquet dans sa culotte

C'est l'instant, messieurs, ou jamais
D'être audacieux et je mets
Mes deux mains partout, désormais.

Le chevalier Atys qui gratte
Sa guitare, à Chloris, l'ingrate
Lance une œillade scélérate.

L'abbé confesse bas Eglé
Et ce vicomte déréglé
Des champs donne à son cœur la clé.

Cependant la lune se lève
Et l'esquif en sa course brève
File gaîment sur l'eau qui rêve.

Fig. 7.2 - Verlaine at about 25. (Manuscript of *Les Fêtes Galantes*).

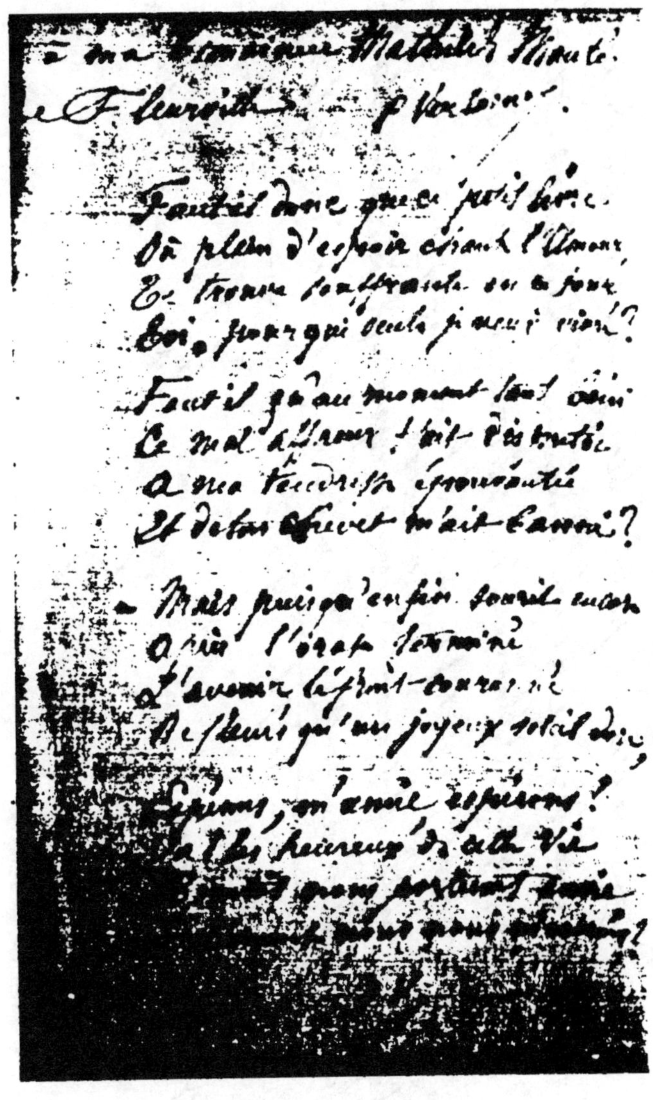
À ma [illegible] Mathilde Mauté
de Fleurville — P Verlaine.

Faut-il donc que ce petit livre
Où plein d'espoir chante l'Amour,
Te trouve souffrante en ce jour,
Toi, pour qui seule je veux vivre?

Faut-il qu'au moment tant [illegible]
Ce mal [illegible] [illegible]
À ma tendresse [illegible]
Et de ton chevet m'ait banni?

Mais puisqu'enfin sourit encor
[illegible] l'orage terminé
L'avenir [illegible] couronné
De [illegible] qu'un joyeux soleil dore,

Espérons, ma [illegible] espérons!
[illegible] heureux de cette vie
[illegible]
[illegible]

* **Fig. 7.3** - Verlaine at 26. (Addressed to his fiancée).

Fig. 7.4 - Verlaine, aged 36.

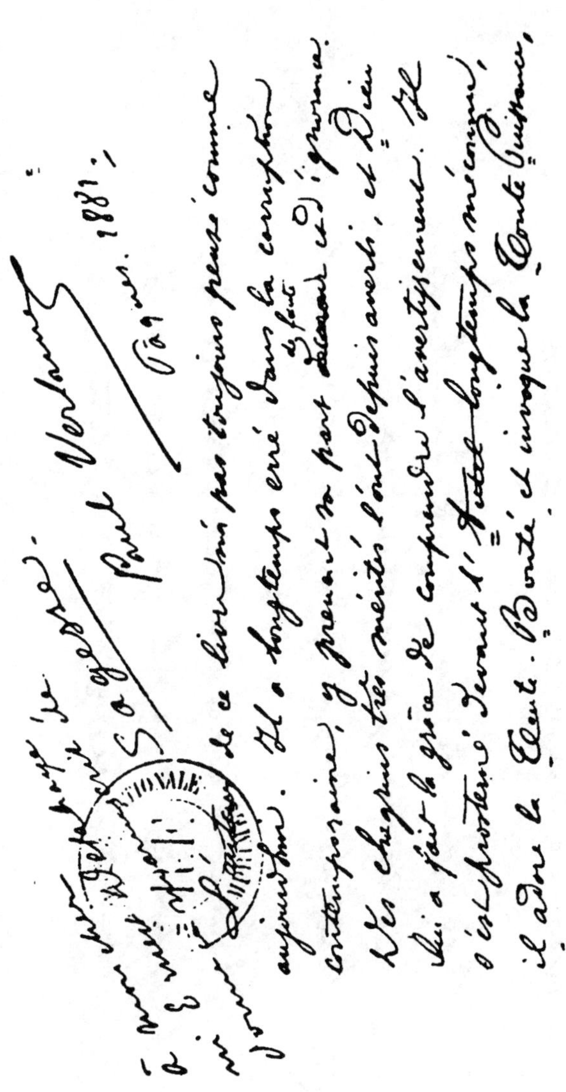

Fig. 7.5a - Verlaine at 37.

Hélas, ce noir abîme de mon crime,
Dieu de terreur et Dieu de sainteté,

Vous, Dieu de paix, de joie et de bonheur,
Toutes mes peurs, toutes mes ignorances,
Vous, Dieu de paix, de joie et de bonheur,

Vous connaissez tout cela, tout cela,
Et que je suis plus pauvre que personne,
Vous connaissez tout cela, tout cela,

Mais ce que j'ai, mon Dieu, je vous le donne.

Fig. 7.5b - Verlaine at 37 : end of the manuscript of *O mon Dieu, vous m'avez blessé d'amour.*

Le ciel est, par dessus le toît,
Si bleu, si calme!
Un arbre, par dessus le toît,
Berce sa palme.

La cloche, dans le ciel qu'on voit
Doucement tinte.
Un oiseau sur l'arbre qu'on voit
Chante sa plainte.

Mon Dieu, mon Dieu, la vie est là
Simple et tranquille.
Cette paisible rumeur là
Vient de la ville.

— Qu'as tu fait, ô toi que voilà
Pleurant sans cesse,
Dis, qu'as-tu fait, toi que voilà,
De ta jeunesse?

Fig. 7.6 - Written by Verlaine.

Paris le 13 Juin 88.

(D) Mon cher d'Orfer,

J'ai été terriblement occupé tous ces jours-ci, terriblement souffrant aussi bien que forcé d'être dehors.

Je serai demain ~~jeudi~~ vers 10 heures [illegible] chez moi. Si donc vous pourrez recopier Mr Aubin [illegible] et envoyez-moi.

Votre dévoué

P. V.

* **Fig.** 7.7 - Verlaine at 44.

Vendredi 12 février. [1892]

* **Fig. 7.8** - Verlaine at nearly 48.

Monsieur,

Il me revient seulement à présent, que le manuscrit dont vous parlaient deux de mes lettres aurait été l'objet de tels délictueux tripotages, et qu'une lettre (est elle de vous?) ~~aurait~~ m'aurait été interceptée par un logeur aidé d'une fille, — une lettre venue de Londres.

Je me fais fort de r'avoir le manuscrit si vous voulez bien m'écrire un mot qui rassurât ma délicatesse et me mît à même de témoigner de mon mécontentement à l'endroit de ces gens et de leurs procédés à votre et à mon égard, comme à celui de la Justice.

Agréez, Monsieur, l'expression de ma vraie gratitude — et de mon impatience à être éclairé par vous sur des agissements dont j'ignorais à l'Hôpital Broussais

P. Verlaine

15 (et non plus 18) Quinze, rue Descartes.

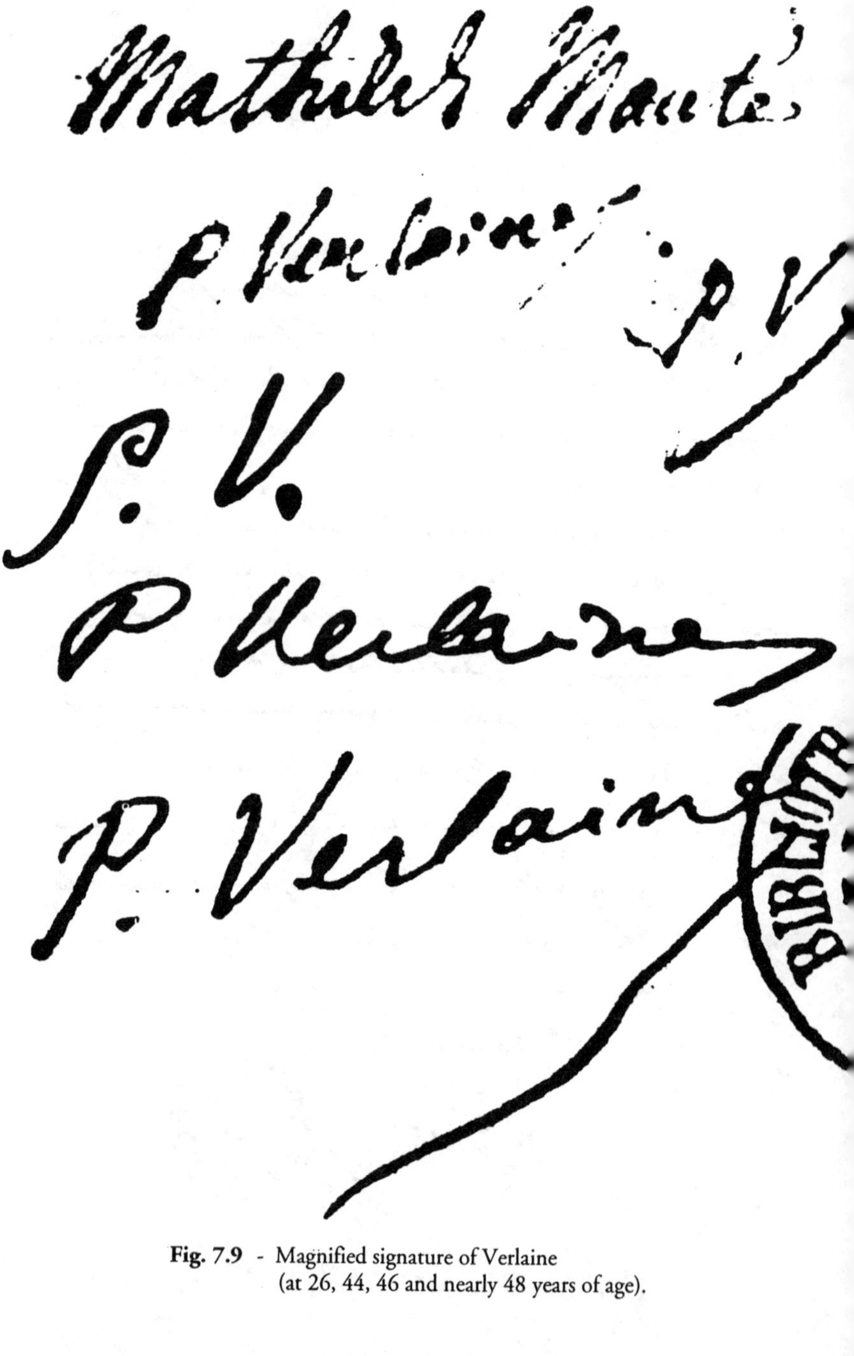

Fig. 7.9 - Magnified signature of Verlaine
(at 26, 44, 46 and nearly 48 years of age).

Pièce XX de Parallèlement

Limbes.

I

Explication

« Je vous dis que ce n'est pas ce
que l'on pensa. »
(P. V.)

Le bonheur de saigner sur le cœur d'un ami,
Le besoin de pleurer bien longtemps sur son sein,
Le désir de parler à lui, bas à demi,
Le rêve de rester ensemble sans dessein!

Le malheur d'avoir tant de belles ennemies,
La satiété d'être une machine obscène,
L'horreur des cris impurs de toutes ces lamies,
Le cauchemar d'une incessante mise en scène!

Mourir pour sa patrie ou pour son Dieu gaîment
Ou pour l'autre, en ses bras, et baisant chastement
La main qui ne trahit, la bouche qui ne ment!

Vivre loin des devoirs et des saintes tourmentes
Pour les seins clairs et pour les yeux luis-

* **Fig. 7.10** - Verlaine at 48.

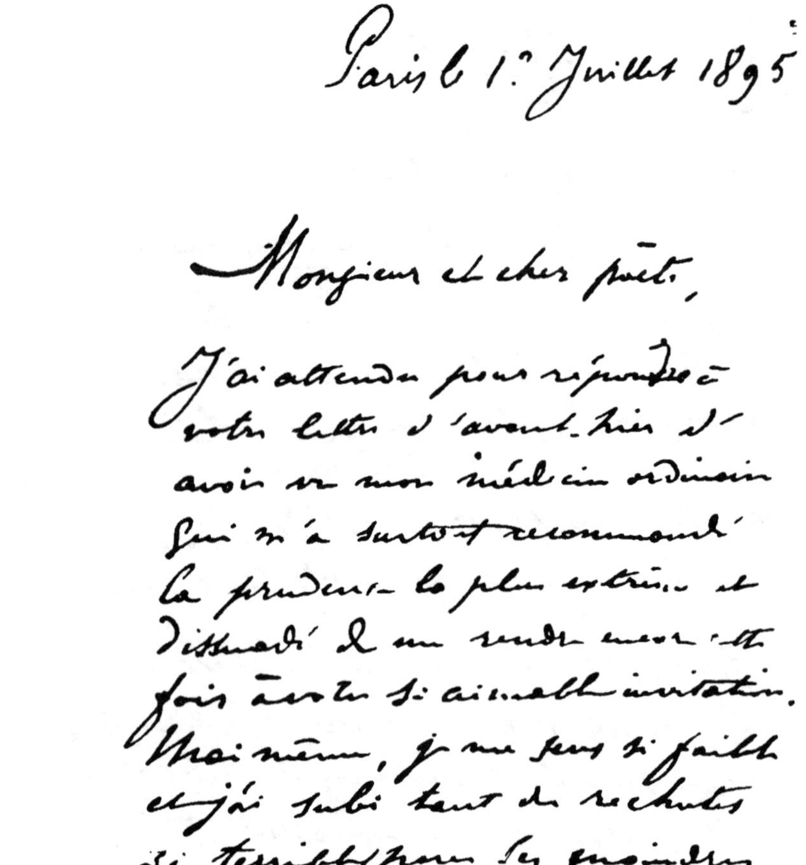

Paris le 1er Juillet 1895

Monsieur et cher poète,

J'ai attendu pour répondre à votre lettre d'avant-hier d'avoir vu mon médecin ordinaire qui m'a surtout recommandé la prudence la plus extrême et dissuadé de me rendre encore cette fois à votre si aimable invitation. Moi-même, je me sens si faible et j'ai subi tant de rechutes si terribles pour les moindres imprudences qu'à mon grand regret, croyez-le bien, je partage ses craintes.

Excusez donc mon absence la semaine prochaine et croyez à tous mes plus vifs regrets réitérés de ne pas pouvoir vraiment sortir si prématurément

* **Fig. 7.11** - Verlaine at 51.

Fig. 7.12 - Breakdown in Verlaine's handwriting.

La douceur puérile dans l'écriture de Verlaine, se situe en empreinte douçâtre et laconique, dans la langueur des enroulements régressifs, en quête maternelle, dans la courbure de liaison, lorsqu'elle chemine, morose

ou

s'étire en finale, ardente de désirs "de ce qui ne l'exile pas".

Puérils les grossissements de pluriel impulsif!

Mais la volonté combattive par instants devient angles durcis, barres de T lançées, cinglantes, ou crochets centripètes de possessivité rageuse, ressacs de l'impatience.

Et l'arcade surélevée des lettres initiales, sans même savoir qu'elle

protège l'intimité orgueilleuse, secrète, se plante en ample majuscule hiératique, "Dans" l'emphase recommencement.

Fragile, poreux, spasmodique, saturnien, le *"trait"* substance psychophysique de la mort dans l'âme, de l'appel sensuel, trivial, le "trait" des "Refusés" se met à "nu",

et dans le frais oubli, puéril, obscène, tombe la feuille de vigne.

Au delà du rythme de rêve, toujours vibre la tension graphique, sourde anxiété pour une vision lucide, malgré l'insatiable oralité première, où se complait avec ses âmes soeurs, ô jeunes filles pardonnées,

Paul Marie Verlaine

Fig. 7.13 - Commentary on Verlaine's handwriting, written by Madame Nicole Boille (reduced in size in order to fit the page).

8

Jean-Nicholas-Arthur RIMBAUD (1854 - 1892)

Rimbaud occupies a unique place in the history of French literature, shooting across it like a meteor. This brilliant poet, who at the age of fifteen opened up fresh paths for French poetry, gave up writing at the age of nineteen in order to travel the world and devote himself to commerce.

He is one of the most interesting poets of our time; witness the enormous number of books about him. Firstly, he is the precursor of Surrealist poetry. But non-literary motives come into play as well, creating a regular "Rimbaud myth" (1). Many anarchistic rebels see themselves in the adolescent who rejected the authority of his family, insulted Christ in filthy terms and joined the revolutionary movement in the Paris Commune. Existentialists claim kinship with him. Young drug users look upon him as their forerunner. There are those who emphasise

(1) It is surely disquieting that present day society should take so great an interest in a being who was so mentally and morally debased.

the metaphysical, satanic side of the revolt led by a young man desirous of "changing life itself"; others believe they can see in him traces of spirituality and try to prove that he could have been a mystic if only things had turned out differently. Some turn to the poet's experiments in "second sight" and look for deep, hidden meaning in his every utterance. Yet others insist however that Rimbaud had a taste for practical jokes. Finally, one may ask how much of the interest in Rimbaud is motivated by his dissolute relationship with Verlaine.

From the psychological point of view, which concerns us here, Rimbaud is a very typical and rich "case". This perverted sociopath is the prototype of the *disharmonic* person, in the meaning of classic French psychiatry. This high level of imbalance derives from the family background (unstable father and maternal uncles), from a life riddled with passing infatuations and sudden breakaways[(2)], and from the contrast between the lack of general acceptance and his exceptional gifts. Rimbaud is constitutionally the prototype of the *paranoiac* by reason of his unbounded pride, his faulty judgement, his scorn for others, his non-conformity, his spirit of revolt, his solitude, his endless dissatisfaction and his fitful delving into

---

(2) The list of occupations that Rimbaud took up and the "professions" he tried is quite frightening. After giving up literature, he taught French in England, was a tutor in Stuttgart, tramped about Italy, became an interpreter in Genoa, volunteered for the Carlist army and obtained a teaching post in Maisons-Alfort. He developed a craze for music in Charleville, then joined the Dutch army, deserted in Java, became a coast sailor in the North Seas and a street-hawker in Vienna, from which city he was expelled by the police. He then became an interpreter in a circus in Hamburg and Scandinavia. In Charleville he studied Arabic, locking himself in a cupboard for hours on end. He went to Cyprus, where he became a foreman. His wanderings took him to Palestine and the shores of the Red Sea, before he at last settled in Abyssinia.

Seen in this light, it would appear that Rimbaud's abandoning literature, about which so much has been written, was similar to the giving up of his numerous passing crazes.

books. His lonely lack of toleration or of any affection towards others, and many features of his poetry betray signs of a *schizoid* personality. From the psychoanalytical point of view, Rimbaud's entire personality is saturated with *anality*. As a teenager he wrote "Shit to God" on the benches at Charleville, was constantly foul-mouthed and composed obscene verses. Later in his greedy business years he had a special belt made so that he could sleep with his gold; with anality went sadism, paranoia and an absence of any heterosexual feeling(3).

*

Scripts by Rimbaud dating from his adolescence till his last days have been conserved. They strikingly reflect the evolution of his life.

Figures 8.1 to 8.3 were written by the brilliant schoolboy whose Latin and French verses had already been published and who was aiming at literary glory. Figure 8.6 comes from the famous "letter of the seer" in which the sixteen and a half year old Rimbaud wrote his profession of literary faith, the charter of a whole school of modern poetry. Figure 8.7 was done a year later, after the poet had become initiated into debauchery and drug-taking in Paris. Figure 8.8 is from the manuscript of *Les Illuminations*, his last literary work.

(After a seven year leap, figures 8.12 to 8.18 show the writing of Rimbaud the businessman).

In the young Arthur's handwriting at the start of the great period of the poetic inspiration of his sixteenth year (figs. 8.1

---

(3) To the objection that Rimbaud spent some time in Aden with an Abyssinian woman, here is the way he rejected her (in order to set about a commercial expedition) : "I have done with this woman altogether. I shall give her some money so that she can take the boat from Rasali to Obock, where she can go where she pleases. I have had enough of this pantomime. I should not have been so foolish as to fetch her from Choa and I certainly won't take her back there".

and 8.2) there is no harmony between form and movement, the latter being still schoolboyish, with a lot of impromptu, complicated embellishments. Moreover this movement has sudden bursts of speed and size which break the overall regularity and upset the rhythm. The resultant tangling disturbs the spatial layout.

In the foreground of the JAMINAN definition we have :

Lively, wide and exaggerated writing;

discordant in pressure (*spasms*), in speed (*wild soaring strokes)*, in height (*superelevations*), in form (sometimes schoolboyish, sometimes *complicated, ornate* or *vulgar*);

connected to grouped convex with *descending steps; tangled.*

Free gestures : t-bars flying and proteiform; proteiform accents, generally rather emphasised and irregular in size; precise, emphatic *punctuation.*

Signature *superelevated, complicated, ornate, thrown, jerky;* paraph with *complicated* and *strong lassos.*

Such handwriting is very "graphogenic", i.e. "speaking aloud" to the graphologist. The latter will immediately notice intense, exalted vitality (lively, thrown writing), but disturbed (exaggeration, irregular pressure and speed, excessive variability in some forms), a noisy desire to attract attention (capitals that are inflated, ornate, superelevated, centripetal strokes) and lack of clarity (tangled lines). We have the complete picture of the young Rimbaud possessed of a boundless imagination (wide, lively writing; notice the variety of flying strokes in the *d, t* and final *n*), by strong sensoriality [writing enriched (Klages), slightly pastose] and by a troublesome sensuality (numerous spasms and some twists). Self-assured, egotistical and vain (wide writing, capitals superelevated, inflated and spirally ornate, leftward strokes), he has no objective view of himself (connected writing, schoolboy forms, compact and tangled layout).

The reader of a literary turn of mind will here see the graphic portrait of an exceptional surge of inspiration which overturns and engages all the strength of the writer. A doctor would see an obvious disorder with at least potential irregularities in the sexual domain (spasm, irregularities in several categories - signs of sexual disorder, as André Lecerf has shown - a few twists and congestions). A moralist, disturbed by the violence and abundance of the gifts displayed, but uncertain of their orientation (varying direction of thrown finals, discordances and vulgarity), will be reminded of the comment of the headmaster of the college at Charleville where Rimbaud was a pupil : "Nothing commonplace will come out of this mind. He will be either the spirit of evil or of good".

*

A TYPOLOGICAL study refines these results.

The *Temperament* is warm *Sanguine*, with a *Nervous* component.

"Warm Sanguine" (i.e. Sanguine tending towards Bilious), visible in the strokes that are exaggerated, lively, inflated, wide and high, corresponds to a nature that is emotive and impetuous, authoritarian and subjective, eager to play an important role. The Nervous component is the "sensitive Nervous" described by Dr. Carton : writing that is thrown, carried-away and spasmodic; the component goes with considerable greed and a potentially great instability; joined to the Sanguine dominant it means a strong over-enthusiastic imagination and reinforces the subjectivity.

The fixing of the JUNGIAN type is rather difficult. Probably a *Sensation* type because of the banal forms, the rhythmic stability of the middle zone and the pastose stroke. There is an auxiliary *Sentiment* function (width, slant, "pathos") and some *Thinking* (fairly rapid writing, some original forms).

From the SZONDIAN viewpoint, we are evidently dealing with an "Ego in peril" (*Sch* = *k*+*p*+) wanting "to be all and to have all" (prominent and well-formed middle zone; enlarged and widened capitals; individualistic forms; Sanguine-Bilious temperament). The profile of the *Paroxysmal* vector is *P* = *e*+*hy*+: *e*+ because of the strong stroke, the fairly stable rhythm of the middle zone, the sustained slant, the plunging finals, the underlined signature and the Bilious component in the temperament; *hy*+ because of the dominance of movement over form, the flying strokes, exaggerations, inflations and ornaments, and the Sanguine component in the temperament. This means an emotional surge ("a storm of movement" in the area of affectivity) : desire is intense and spills out onto social behaviour.

Less prominent is the reaction *hy*- (because of the persistent schoolboy forms), signalling a certain conformity. In fact the youthful Arthur had to obey his mother at home and was a well-behaved pupil at college. He wanted to be a socially acceptable celebrity as a Parnassian poet.

The profile of the *Sexual* vector is *S* = *h*+*s*+/- : *h*+ because of the well-nourished, slightly pastose writing, the curved finals, the display of Sensation and Sentiment; *s*+/- because the activity (*s*+ : writing that is firm, spasmodic, right-slanting, soaring and above average in vitality, Bilious temperament of the type Mars) is directed towards the imaginative zones (prominence of the exterior zones). This profile, frequent in adolescents corresponds to an intense need for affection (*h*+) and an ambivalent attitude towards the body (*s*+/-), usually a cause of upset and connected to homosexual themes.

In the *Contact* vector *C*, the writing shows the reaction *m*+ (well-nourished stroke, slightly pastose, a strong middle zone with wide ovals, comfortable finals, but regressive strokes : a desire to mix, but difficulty in making contact) and gives a negative or weakly charged reaction *d* (infantilism *d*0 : rejection of any law or reciprocity, coarse modes of expression - Rimbaud's writings and speech were markedly filthy).

From the point of view of MYTHOLOGICAL TYPES, figure 8.1 is ruled by Jupiter and Mars. *Jupiter* brings an enormous social ambition (exaggerated, inflated and ornate capitals), precocious for a fifteen year old boy, and an expressive self-assurance (carefree forms, strokes inflated and over-wide). *Mars* shows an impulsive need for conquest (right-slanting and thrown writing) with violent authority (spasms and super-elevations, sharp points).

Of secondary importance, the trite and sometimes vulgar forms, the stability of the basic rhythm and the compactness correspond to an *Earth* component (sincerity, the almost obsessive importance of his preoccupations, vulgarity); the imprecision of certain forms (the *t*) and the wide, rounded writing correspond to a *Moon* component (inventiveness, aesthetic feeling) - here a kind of "dark moon", morbid rather than angelic, because of the spasms and sharp points that mark the rounded strokes, the downward orientation of the latter and lastly because of the graphic context.

Saturn is not absent (dark strokes, arcades : Rimbaud is really very closed in upon himself). There is little of *Mercury* (accelerated speed, needle points : causticity, close to Mars), but there is a little *Sun* (the superelevations result from the vanity of Jupiter and not from a unifying Sun); lastly, there is a complete *lack of Venus* (writing exaggerated, uncontrolled, spasmodic and with arcades : lack of kindness and tact).

Figure 8.3 shows the end of the manuscript of *À la musique.* The weakness of movement in the last line is striking : pressure less strong, size smaller (complex *E*t with *E*lles a line higher, vienne*nt* with trouve*nt* or parle*nt*) : the finals are less thrown. This last line has a story behind it. Rimbaud had at first written :

Et mes désirs brutaux s'accrochent à leurs lèvres[(4)],

but his master, Izambard, thought the line too crude and had him replace it by the more dignified alexandrine (which is given in all editions of the poem):

---

(4) And my stark desire hangs upon their lips.

Et je sens les baisers qui me viennent aux lèvres[5].

The sudden slackening, in this spot, of the vigour of the writing shows how dull the poet thought the correction was, which he only half-heartedly accepted.

Figure 8.5, produced slightly later, has the same characteristics, with great variety in form : a rich and unbridled imagination.

Figure 8.6 comes from the famous letter in which the sixteen and a half year old Rimbaud mapped his programme : to become a "seer" by the reasoned deranging of the senses, in order to explore the unknown.

> I say that one must be a *seer*, make oneself a *seer* by a long, boundless and reasoned *disordering of all the senses.* Every form of love, of suffering, of madness [...]. Unspeakable torture in which one needs all faith and superhuman strength in which one becomes, above everyone else, the most sick person, the greatest criminal, the most cursed, - and the Supreme knower! - For one has arrived at the *unknown*!

This example differs from the preceding ones because there is less movement and less exaggeration of the large, spread-out movements, by forms that are more personal and less schoolboyish, by the tormented and "frémissant" [quivering] look[6], which is due to irregularity in width and continuity and to numerous little jerky movements. Still present are the discordances (in speed and form) and the aggressive signs (finals, often needle-like, thrown towards the right). Psychologically, one can deduce a break with conventions and a matured *thinking* process.

As to MYTHOLOGICAL TYPES, Jupiter's social avidity has given way to Mercury's analytical mind (dry stroke, small dimension, easy acceleration, irregularity, with small jerks), with a certain amount of *Sun* (high *t*-bars). The relational

---

(5) And I feel the kisses brush my lips

(6) By this term is meant nuancée, animated, slightly jerky and with a "vibrant" stroke.

importance of the other types has hardly changed : Mars is especially to the fore with the needle-like, flying strokes. It is odd that this aggressive solitary who affects to despise others, needs their presence (compact orderliness : need for affection in the "ballooning" shapes).

How Rimbaud set about following his programme is well-known : a life cut off from others, work done at night, drug-induced hallucinations and homosexual debauchery. The result can be seen in figure 8.7. There is hardly any movement. What there is is in isolated patches rather than by ebbing and flowing (Pophal), stiffness; form is now more important. Ink-filled letters, a disturbed stroke (breaks, twists and mistakes) betray the poor physiological state, and the descending lines and the tormented writing indicate depression. As for the mythological types, *Saturn* is stronger than in 1871 (a stiffened, tormented writing : a retreat into self, deepening of thought, pessimism, solitariness). Other types are present, especially Mars-Moon : aggression led on by the imagination.

After the dramatic conclusion of the association with Verlaine and the partial catharsis brought about by the composition of *Une Saison en enfer*, Rimbaud's writing had, in 1874, become that of figure 8.8. which comes from the manuscript of *Les Illuminations*. In this example we see the blossoming of intelligence (simplification, sober individualistic forms) and of feeling (writing irregular in all categories). It represents the summit, graphologically speaking, of the young poet's developing writing.

*

Rimbaud's PSYCHOBIOLOGICAL TEMPERAMENT, so typically *Rhythmic* in accordance with his behaviour (and also in accordance with the spirit behind his poetry), is only progressively evident in the course of the evolution in the youth's handwriting. That is not exceptional in the "HMR

(Complex) period", in which Harmonic, Melodic, Rhythmic and Complex tendencies habitually appear. Sometimes one tendency or another is momentarily to the fore, before the fundamental temperament takes over, in such a way that a Rhythmic subject behaves during his adolescence as a Rhythmic-Complex[(7)] or as a Complex-Rhythmic.

Figure 8.1 is certainly Melodic-Rhythmic : Melodic by its component of Jupiter, by the exuberance of its over-enrichment which is easy and rounded. It is Rhythmic because of the constant stability of movement in the middle zone. This stability appears more clearly in figure 8.3, which is more Rhythmic with its angular arcades. In the drawings done at about the same time (fig. 8.4) the Rhythmic temperament is visible (stereotyped repetition of straight, hatching strokes giving a note of irony), associated with a Complex touch.

In figures 8.6 and 8.7 - Rimbaud has refused to return to college and lives as he pleases - the Rhythmic element (Nervous-Bilious temperament, angular arcades) appears to be dominant. In the first example the Complex touch is still visible (disharmonic rhythm) and the second is anti-Harmonic (hardness, ugly forms) and anti-Melodic (angles, sharp points).

*

"The seer's letter" (fig. 8.6) has been examined GRAPHOMETRICALLY (cf. Chart 8.1).

The histogram of the *instinctual* component I seems[(8)] very "damaged", with a deviation of energetic potential (a hindrance of +2), which cannot be used as a support of self-awareness (falls to +1 and -1) and seems[(8)] to be unfettered in its

---

(7) Remember that Rhythmic-Complex subjects take a particular delight in humbugging the public.

(8) A facsimile was used in the analysis which makes the study of the stroke unsure (particularly the variables 3 and 4) and of size (variable 11).

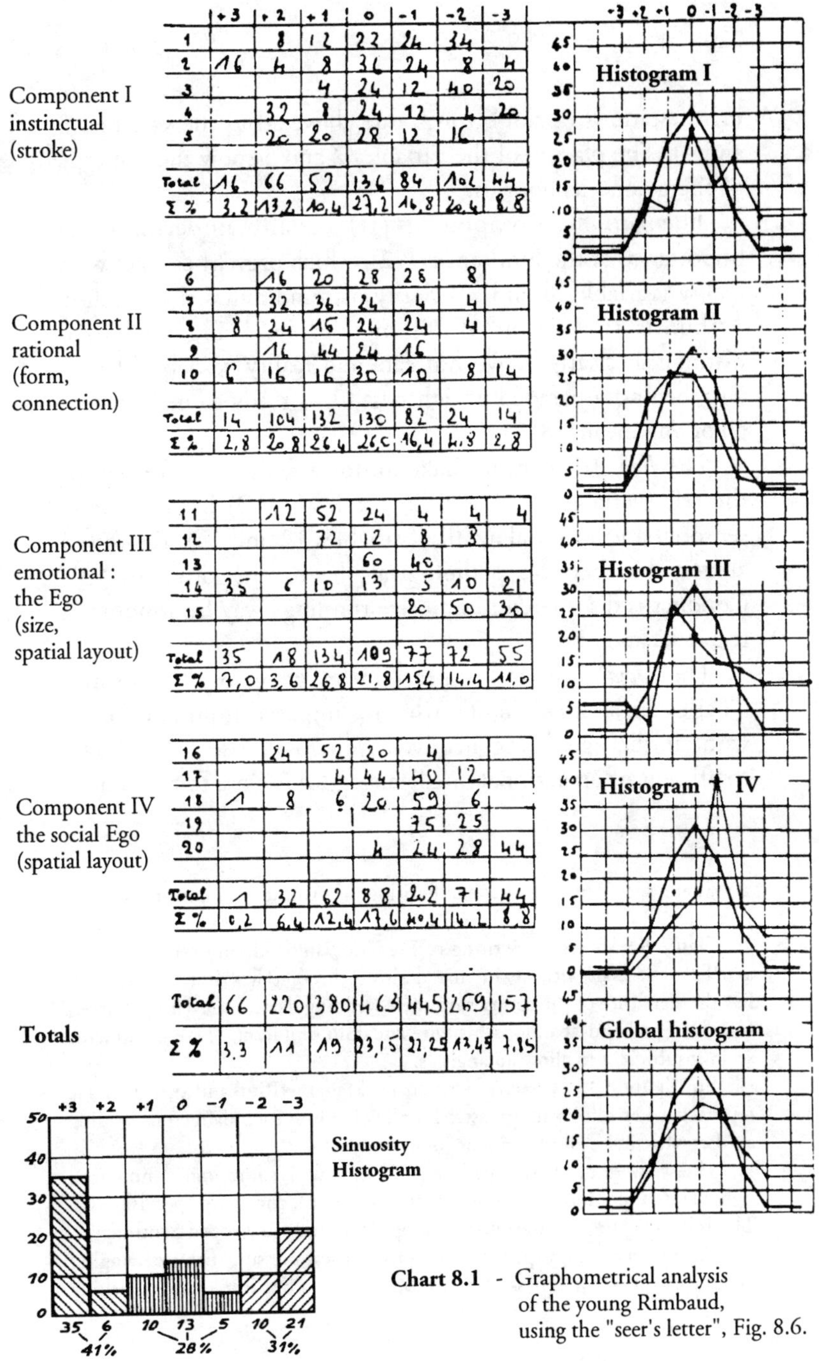

Component I instinctual (stroke)

	+3	+2	+1	0	−1	−2	−3
1		8	12	22	24	34	
2	16	4	8	36	24	8	4
3			4	24	12	40	20
4		32	8	24	12	4	20
5		20	20	28	12	16	
Total	16	66	52	136	84	102	44
Σ %	3,2	13,2	10,4	27,2	16,8	20,4	8,8

Component II rational (form, connection)

	+3	+2	+1	0	−1	−2	−3
6		16	20	28	28	8	
7		32	36	24	4	4	
8	8	24	16	24	24	4	
9		16	44	24	16		
10	6	16	16	30	10	8	14
Total	14	104	132	130	82	24	14
Σ %	2,8	20,8	26,4	26,0	16,4	4,8	2,8

Component III emotional : the Ego (size, spatial layout)

	+3	+2	+1	0	−1	−2	−3
11		12	52	24	4	4	4
12			72	12	8	8	
13				60	40		
14	35	6	10	13	5	10	21
15					20	50	30
Total	35	18	134	109	77	72	55
Σ %	7,0	3,6	26,8	21,8	15,4	14,4	11,0

Component IV the social Ego (spatial layout)

	+3	+2	+1	0	−1	−2	−3
16		24	52	20	4		
17			4	44	40	12	
18	1	8	6	20	59	6	
19					75	25	
20				4	24	28	44
Total	1	32	62	88	202	71	44
Σ %	0,2	6,4	12,4	17,6	40,4	14,2	8,8

Totals

	+3	+2	+1	0	−1	−2	−3
Total	66	220	380	463	445	269	157
Σ %	3,3	11	19	23,15	22,25	13,45	7,85

Chart 8.1 - Graphometrical analysis of the young Rimbaud, using the "seer's letter", Fig. 8.6.

manifestations (a climb to -3, due above all to the variables 3 and 4). The placing of the variables 2 and 5 show the dispersal of energy and its poor use.

The *rational* component (II) equally underlines the importance of the hindrances (+2), which prevent contact with reality (variables 6 and 7), clarity of mind and a moral sense. Arthur is the victim of his own game, being unable to distinguish clearly between dream and reality (variables 10, 6) and, behind a paraded uprightness (9) is ready to make use of all or any means (8).

The *Ego* (III) tries to make up for a fluctuating feeling for the self (variable 11 descending as low as -3) by an intense sensorial and material avidity (variables 12 and 14). Repressed anxiety has become pathological (histogram raised to +3). Conduct is disordered : impulsive running away from home (a rise in -2 and -3).

The *social Ego* (IV) appears in an obligatory conformity ("barley sugar stick" in -1), which is imposed from day to day without the ego being involved (fall to 0, rise to -3). The coefficient of operational intelligence (30) is close to morbidity.

*

Some specimens of the handwriting of Arthur's parents have been preserved.

Figure 8.9 shows the writing of Frédéric Rimbaud, an ex-army officer, a self-taught man with an intense desire to become a writer. Figure 8.10 has the signature of the spouses on their wedding day ...... seven years later, Captain Rimbaud abandons his wife and four children. These documents seem insufficient to allow an analysis.

But figure 8.11 is a letter written by Madame Rimbaud in which she reproaches her son's schoolmaster for allowing him such dangerous reading as "Les Misérables" by V. Hugot (*sic*).

The writing, of an average level, is simple with some angles (honesty), right-slanted (conformity), in relief (authoritarian), and sharp (peevishness). The Jungian type is Sensation-Thinking, with underdeveloped Sentiment.

The temperament is primarily Bilious (vertical pressure, firmness, angles) : courage and an awareness of her responsibilities, but intolerance (slashing strokes) and fixed ideas (angles). Then there is as much evidence of the cold, Nervous type (strong pressure, developed lower extensions : practical, serious intelligence) and the Sanguine type (wide, right slant : importance of social values).

Earth comes first of the mythological types (simplicity, diving lower extensions). Then, noticeably, and in equal proportions Mars (relief with sudden stops and heavy vertical strokes, right slant), Moon and Jupiter (arabesques in *d*), Sun (height) and Saturn (dark writing, juxtaposed). Whence we conclude a hard-working, serious character who does not toy with principles and beliefs. She has a high sense of responsibility evidenced by trenchant reactions, and circumstances sometimes oblige her to act with masculine severity.

It is not surprising to learn that this worthy, but short-sighted woman should by her sternness crush the personality of her eldest son and drive the younger to revolt.

*

The series of letters from 8.12 to 8.18 tells the story of Rimbaud's life in Abyssinia.

Figure 8.12 (1881) was written during an illness. Rimbaud was low in spirits, and suspicious of everybody. A year later (fig. 8.13) he has recovered his energy, is eager to make discoveries and to write works for the Geographical Society. The writing in 8.14 dates from the feverish period when Rimbaud hoped to make a fortune selling weapons of war. After the disastrous end of the expedition, in which he lost half his capital, Rimbaud rested for a time in Egypt (fig. 8.15), then came back in resignation to Harar (fig. 8.16), where he led a hard, active life (fig. 8.17). In 1891 he developed cancer of the lower end of the femur. Figure 8.18 is an extract from the painful diary of his journey from Harar to the coast of Somalia. He was repatriated and died in France at the end of the year.

There is a striking contrast between the writing in 1882 (fig. 8.13) and the examples from 1870.

The former differs from the latter particularly (a) by the

more developed forms (though the difference is still slight), (b) by the disappearance of the exaggerations in the capitals, in the *d* and in the signature, the now moderate difference in height between the middle and outer zones (upper and lower extensions are both shorter), and lastly (c) by the ease of connected to over-connected writing. Nevertheless, the reader will notice that the graphic description of figure 8.1 still applies, in spite of these alterations.

Thus, (a) intelligence has matured, (b) imagination is at play in a more realistic area and is less concerned with attracting attention, (c) activity is more methodical. But Rimbaud remains Rimbaud. Thrown finals are exaggerated and proteiform, now attacking the right-hand margin (aggression) and now regressive and crossing preceding letters (as if the writer sought self-destruction). This is indicative of an impulsiveness that is all the more dangerous because the writing is right-slanted, often getting larger and tangled (absence of lucidity)[9].

The writing is now typically Rhythmic-Melodic. See especially examples 8.13 and 8.17, regularly right-slanted, connected, resolute and quite angular (Rhythmic), with some spread-out capitals and finals (Melodic). There are forms and layout which are anti-Harmonic. The drawings in the African period (figs. 8.19 and 8.20) confirm the Rhythmic dominance by their structure (rectilinear stroke, repetition) and by the precision of their execution without any affective sign. The ostrich in the second drawing is Rhythmic, anti-Harmonic and anti-Melodic.

From the psychoanalytical viewpoint, the main change is the presence in the foreground of *anality* (the stroke is smeary, congested and with aggressive, flying strokes, angles and narrowings). Rimbaud lives only for money, sleeps with his gold and sees himself surrounded by fools and knaves.

---

(9) Tangled lines are the classic sign of an intense appetite for contact. Is this indicative of the desire experienced by this solitary poet?

This regression is evidence of several SZONDIAN vectors. In the Ego vector the reaction p- comes first (compact, thrown writing with narrow exterior letters) : accusatory projection. In the *Paroxysmal* vector the reaction of the epileptoid factor has become *e+/-* (unsustained stroke, with spasmodic stiffening, conjuring up the picture of rocky ground or the light of a stormy day), or even *e-* (strong signs of revolt : angles, receding, thrown, needle points, compactness). In the *Contact* vector there is the reaction *d-* (compact, tense, often angular writing, heavy stroke with congestion). To sum up, Rimbaud is looking for rescue by clutching anxiously at *material possessions* (*d-*) which fill up the void left by his former ideals and ambition (*e+, hy+, p+*).

The sequence of examples shows the ups and downs of Rimbaud's career in business. The writing in 1886 (fig. 8.14) is full of imprudent enthusiasm (easy, over-connected writing, thrown, growing larger and rising at the end). The writing in 1887 and 1888 (figs. 8.15 and 8.16) reveals a downward trend (the writing is reduced, more sober and rounded, and with inhibitions. At about this time Rimbaud noticed that his hair had gone grey). In 1890 (fig. 8.17), the writing is more animated and similar to that of 1882 (fig. 8.13), but with some noticeable differences : the reared, receding strokes are rarer (less destructive rage), there is no tangling in the compact layout (normal social contacts), and the somewhat lifeless stroke reveals general exhaustion.

To sum up, the evolution in the years 1882-1890 is a kind of repetition of that between 1870 and 1872. There is an initial enthusiasm (fig.s 8.1 to 8.3, 8.13), then disorder (figs. 8.6, 8.14) and finally bitterness and loss of vitality (figs. 8.7, 8.15 to 8.17). Madame E. Koechlin (H. Saint-Morand) to whom I submitted this connection between the evolution of the poet and the businessman confirmed it in the following terms :

> It is obvious that the initial grouping of the temperaments has varied but little, except in the way they combine. The warm Sanguine type is

aroused when everything looks rosy and he acts confidently, sustained by the imaginative Moon. He then falls back into the vulnerable, reasoning Nervous state (Saturn). - Basically Rimbaud is a Mars-Jupiter man of action as well as an imaginative Moon type. He is sustained by the vanity of the emotive and enterprising Sanguine, but will have no more balance at the end of his life than at the beginning.

The curve of this evolution, repeated twice, is certainly a result of Rimbaud's temperament. Compare the manner in which, in *Le Bateau ivre*, a great inflation is followed by a lower extension which ends in a desire for annihilation. Nearly all commentators have read in this poem the foretelling(10) of the author's fate : his literary ambition that he himself renounced, and the distant journeys from which he would return to die in his motherland.

To come back to our examples, notice, in the same order of ideas, the persistent *convexity* in the direction of the lines(11). This age-old sign of excitement followed by depression is a summary of all that has been said. If the reader objects that the future cannot be read in handwriting, let him consider the words of Heraclitus : "Man's character is his future". It is useful to re-read the passage(12) written on this topic over a hundred years ago by the founder of our science of graphology :

There is a fate which is the logical consequence of causes that we create freely. *We are ourselves the unwitting makers of our future. We construct it like a workman builds a house or a savage sets up his hut. It is our own work*, and

---

(10) "Poetic work does not always reflect the life of the poet, but sometimes it prefigures and heralds it", said Charles Baudouin (*Psychanalyse du symbole religieux*, Fayard, Paris, 1957, p.62 and *Jean Racine ou l'enfant du désert*, Plon, Paris, 1963, p.54). Analogously, the prospective value of the initial dreams of an analysis are well known.

(11) I have noticed this in nearly one hundred scripts.

(12) J.-H. Michon, "De la fatalité rendue par les écritures. Le Prince Impérial", *La Graphologie* of August 15, 1876, vol.8 (16) : 121-126 (see pp.124 and 126). (The italics are mine). It is not fair, without following the reasoning, to liken the Abbé Michon to a common fortune teller claiming to read the future in the direction of lines of handwriting.

we alone are responsible for the happiness or the misfortune which embraces us, as a result of the moral causes we have piled up. [....] It is not surprising that when graphology says that *descending handwriting is the sign of discomfort, of a false situation into which one obstinately puts oneself, in spite of the certainty of disaster*, it is predicting this disaster, not as a fortune teller does, but by following the logical path which discloses *the mental state of the writers who refuse to follow a calm, normal life* in which no danger need be run, and one only has to behave as a normal person.. [...] That is why I uttered an involuntary cry, on seeing for the first time the signature of the Prince Imperial in his early manhood. It was descending.

*

The result of the GRAPHOMETRICAL analysis of figure 8.17 is given in Chart 8.2.

The *instinctual* component I shows (sudden peak to 0) the conscious reception of sensations and impressions which are no longer lived at their instinctive level (blocking +2, lapse of the means of adapting +1 and -2). The cleanness of the stroke (variable 3) means a strong barrier to sensitiveness; its conduct (5) shows a high probability of consciously lived sadism. The quality of the stroke betrays a great temperamental tiredness.

The *rational* component II is characterised by a fall in adaptability to daily life (-1), therefore a running away (ordinates rising to -2 and -3), with a lively caustic (variable 6) intelligence, but animated and very irregular in its activity (7 and 10) with a non-existent ethic.

In the *Ego* III component, the refusal of affection (+3, due to the variable 14) gives an appearance of stability (variable 13), but the break (fall to -1 and the hollow of the histogram to +2) produces a painful isolation ("plane of anxiety" from 0 to -1). The ego does not rule desire, but takes arms against proud rigidity and an abandonment to the appetites (note the layout of the variable 12).

The histogram IV (*social Ego*) underlines the poverty of actual contact (a rise to +2, -1), and the desire to run away (a peak to +2) : gloomy pride (variable 17), lack of affection (19) and absence of any moral control (18 and 20).

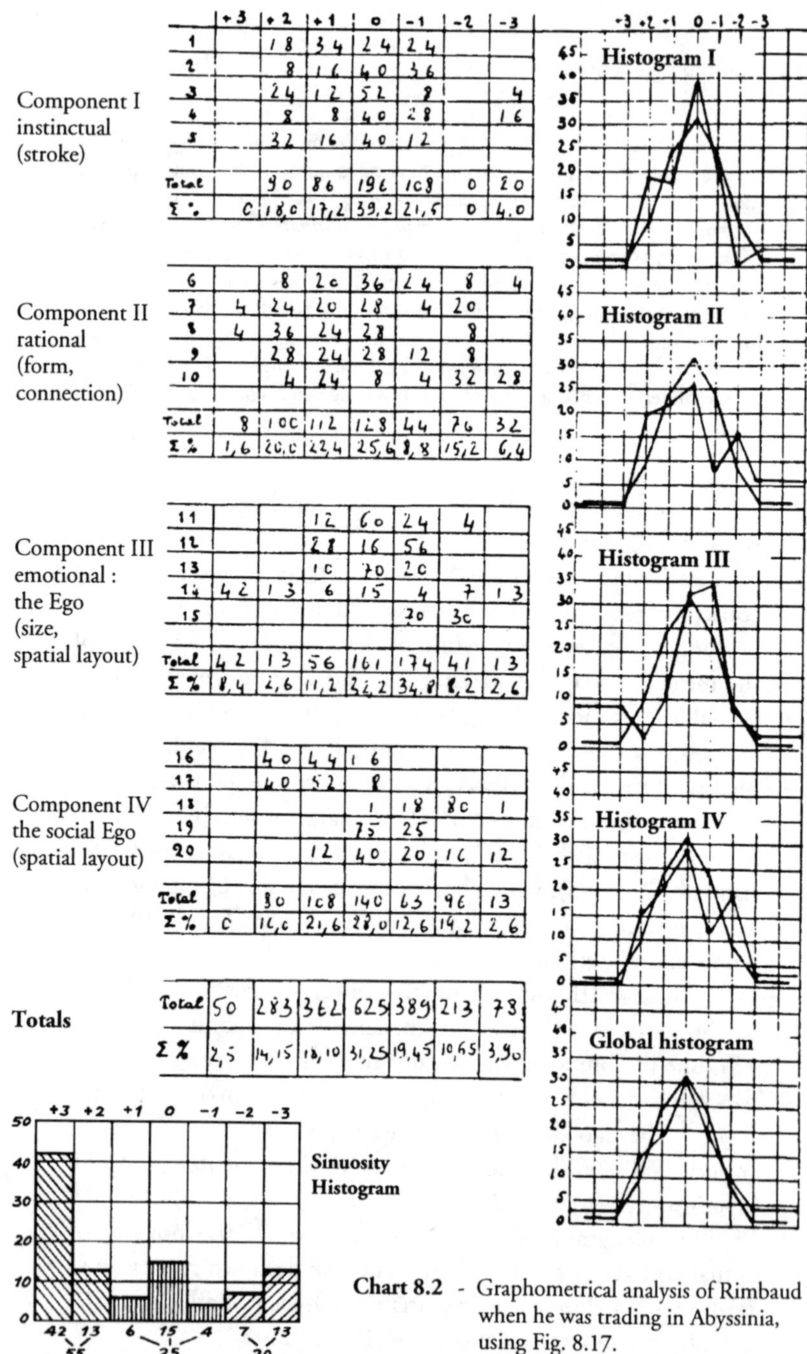

Component I instinctual (stroke)	+3	+2	+1	0	-1	-2	-3
1		18	34	24	24		
2		8	16	40	36		
3		24	12	52	8		4
4		8	8	40	28		16
5		32	16	40	12		
Total		90	86	196	108	0	20
Σ %	0	18,0	17,2	39,2	21,6	0	4,0

Component II rational (form, connection)	+3	+2	+1	0	-1	-2	-3
6		8	20	36	24	8	4
7	4	24	20	28	4	20	
8	4	36	24	28		8	
9		28	24	28	12	8	
10		4	24	8	4	32	28
Total	8	100	112	128	44	76	32
Σ %	1,6	20,0	22,4	25,6	8,8	15,2	6,4

Component III emotional : the Ego (size, spatial layout)	+3	+2	+1	0	-1	-2	-3
11			12	60	24	4	
12			28	16	56		
13			10	70	20		
14	42	13	6	15	4	7	13
15					70	30	
Total	42	13	56	161	174	41	13
Σ %	8,4	2,6	11,2	32,2	34,8	8,2	2,6

Component IV the social Ego (spatial layout)	+3	+2	+1	0	-1	-2	-3
16		40	44	16			
17		40	52	8			
18				1	18	80	1
19				75	25		
20			12	40	20	16	12
Total		80	108	140	63	96	13
Σ %	0	16,0	21,6	28,0	12,6	14,2	2,6

Totals	+3	+2	+1	0	-1	-2	-3
Total	50	283	362	625	389	213	78
Σ %	2,5	14,15	18,10	31,25	19,45	10,65	3,90

Chart 8.2 - Graphometrical analysis of Rimbaud when he was trading in Abyssinia, using Fig. 8.17.

The *global* histogram V gives an appearance of equilibrium, with a high coefficient of operational intelligence (45). But the state of the four components shows upon what fragile and submorbid bases this construction exists.

*

BIBLIOGRAPHY

Édouard de ROUGEMONT, H. de BOUILLANE de LACOSTE, P. IZAMBARD, "L'évolution psychologique d'Arthur Rimbaud d'après son écriture", *Mercure de France*, Nov. 1, 1936 (no.921, 47th year, vol.271) : see pp.458-495.

– The following is a summary of a noteworthy longitudinal study based on the examination of eighty documents.

(1) *Rimbaud the poet* - In 1870 : a rich nature, a powerful and impulsive temperament, a mixture of idealism and sensuality, mulishness (lively writing, discordant in pressure, with arabesques, irregular in size, right-slanting, leftward turning, condensed); unconcernedly selfish (right-slanted, with rounded strokes); meticulousness (careful writing); reserved character. In some scripts : signs of anger (sharp-pointed, flying strokes), of physiological imbalance (twists), of excitement (exclamation marks), and of intellectual evolution (simplifications, grouped letters). In 1871 : better culture (simplifications) and judgement (sober, less compact hand); selfishness and self-satisfaction are still present (regressive strokes, coils : but there are some progressive movements), as are sensuality and lack of civility (vulgar capitals), but there is a more refined sensitiveness (lighter and smaller writing). In 1872 the writing is simpler and more sober : reflectiveness, intellectual growth, influence of Verlaine. In 1873 the writing is discordant in direction, speed and size. There are amendments and some disorganisation in the letters at the time of the break with Verlaine (disorder, alcohol). - To sum up, we have an impetuous temperament, an observant and thoughtful intelligence, imagination and independence, self-centredness, sensuality, and idealism. Later there is culture and an inquisitive mind. "This man is an artist and not an abstract thinker or a scientist".

(2) *Rimbaud the trader* - 1880 : simplified, combined and rounded writing (less selfish and less coarse), sinuous (suppleness), rapid and simplified (active mind, culture), tapering (critical sense), descending, amended, occasional imprecision (tiredness), needless dots, interruptions (circulatory disorders). "He undergoes his lot rather than being in charge of it". 1883 : he ceases to be a rebel (precise, progressive writing), becomes sociable and altruistic; impressionability (irregular writing), a

lessening of resistance (slackening of the stroke) and sensuality. "An honest, worthy man with lofty concerns : a fine character". 1885 : large writing (more vitality) with regressive strokes (concern for acquisitions), progressive, rounded, spontaneous, light (generosity, sensitivity). 1888 : gentler, generous and serene. The spirit of enterprise has lost its fine edge; defensiveness (regressive paraph, centripetal endings).

(3) Conclusion : in 1871 and 1872 Verlaine's influence on Rimbaud was salutary intellectually. In Africa, Rimbaud became kinder.

Henry de BOUILLANE de LACOSTE, *Rimbaud et le problème des Illuminations*, Mercure de France, Paris, 1949, 269p.

– The author of this thesis claims to prove that *Les Illuminations* were composed after *Une Saison en enfer*, contrary to the opinion generally accepted. His main argument consists in showing that the manuscript of *Les Illuminations* was written between the end of 1873 and 1875. This rests on the change in Rimbaud's handwriting. His study is concerned essentially with the shape of the letters culled from 39 scripts from 1870, 21 from 1871, 14 from 1872, 6 from 1873, 4 from 1874 and 6 from 1875. Several graphological remarks are made in passing.

– 1870 : co-existence of a conservative, scholarly discipline that simplifies everything and a tendency to prettify, whence a mixture of ugly and elegant capitals (p.22); extreme changes in the shape of the small letters (intellectual richness, imagination desirous of change), shortening of quotations (order, clarity) (p.25); clubbed paraph sloping upwards (ardour, self-confidence) (p.27); "frightful" signatures ("pride and vanity combined, coarseness, insolence and over-weening mind", lack of a sense of the ridiculous) (p.36); a greater maturity in November than in March and April, the vagaries and fire of youth : "everything speaks of an abundance of energy, but not of balance and reason" (p.42).

– 1871 : a lessening of excitement (p.49); a sudden change in July ("emancipated, liberated writing" : a running away) (p.53).

– 1872 : the writing, like the poetry, reflects the change in life (p.63); some scripts show the effect of alcohol (pp.75-76, Rimbaud's writing becomes like Verlaine's, proof of susceptibility to others (pp.80-82); printed capitals : Rimbaud is becoming more cultured (p.83).

– 1873 : vagaries in the writing with a return to former shapes and the adoption of new ones (creative imagination) (p.91). At the time of the break with Verlaine there are letters written with sincerity (pp.92, 97) and those written under the influence of alcohol (p.99). The writing of the final break confirms the absence of bitterness (p.104). In Roche, there are signs of nervous exhaustion (excitement and asthenia, perhaps intoxication (p.105). After, there is harmony and an easy simplicity (the cure) (p.109).

– 1874-1875 : harmony at the start of the year, then discouragement and finally vigour, albeit without harmony (p.136).

– *Illuminations* : handwriting more evolved than in 1873 : a taste for life and for work (p.162).

M. DELAMAIN, "La graphologie appelée au procès Rimbaud". *La Graphologie*, no.38, pp.18-24, 1950 and no.46, see pp.20-21, 2nd quarter 1952.

– [1950] An account of the thesis of Bouillane de Lacoste. After having surveyed the work in general, Delamain criticises the graphological conclusions, especially the perception of growing harmony, because the size is normalised and forms are simplified. On the contrary, the excessive energy of the first scripts, typical of Le Senne's Nervous character, reveals the creative demon in the young poet. Formlevel is lower in the subsequent evolution, which causes the appearance of trivial feelings and practical concerns, the rightful balance between inspiration and reason occurring in *Les Illuminations*. "Graphology properly so-called, would therefore end in perceiving Rimbaud's "farewell to literature" not as the effect of a Romantic paroxysm, but on the contrary, as the result, perhaps painful, of a critical appreciation of the emptiness or the danger of an effort pushed too far".

– [1952] A script from 1884 confirms the "depoetisation" of the handwriting which has now become elegant in a commercial way.

G.-E. MAGNAT, "L'écriture du poète", *La Graphologie*, no.46, see p.21, 2nd quarter 1952 : see pp.7, 10.

– Analysis of the manuscript of *Le Bateau ivre*. Magnat thought it was in the hand of Rimbaud, although it was a copy written out by Verlaine. For this reason I have given a summary of the analysis at the end of chapter 7, which concerns Verlaine.

Jean-Charles GILLE-MAISANI, *Psychologie de l'écriture. Etudes de graphologie*, Payot, Paris, 1969, 270p : see pp.61-63.

– Designed, exaggerated and spasmodic handwriting of *Soleil et Chair* : imagination, disorder.

André LECERF and Jean-Charles GILLE-MAISANI, "Die sexuellen Regelwidrigkeiten (Anomalien) in der Handschrift", *Graphologisches Spektrum '70*, pp.11-23, 1970 : see pp.18, 20.

– (On the last six lines of *Ma Bohème* with signature). Writing discordant in form, size, direction, speed, pressure : strong probability of sexual anomalies.

Jean-Charles GILLE-MAISANI, *Psychologie de l'écriture. Suite à l'ABC de la graphologie*, 2nd ed., Payot, 1978, 308p. English edition : *The Psychology of Handwriting*, Scriptor Books, London, 1992, 349p :

– Repetition of the commentaries, analysed above, of *Soleil et Chair* (see pp.58/78-79) et de *Ma Bohème* (see pp.71/95).

Michel MORACCHINI, *ABC de graphologie*, Jacques Grancher, 1984, 288p.
– P.199 : Rimbaud, Sensation type.
– P.276 : (letter from 1888, *fig.* 8.16) : "The handwriting of the 'poète maudit' furnishes an example of a completely discordant character : tense, tormented, excited, with marked attraction for the lowest depths, stirred up at once by a disgust for life as by a certain need to overreach himself. Frustrated, violent and conceited, he has none the less been able to run his fantasies into imagery and make a remarkable literary work ... (large writing, discordant in all categories, disordered, carried away, with flying strokes in several directions, animated)".

Marie BERNARD, *Sexual Deviations as Seen in Handwriting*, Whitston, Troy (New York), 1990, 408p : see pp.214-215.
– (Analysis of the last three lines of *Ma Bohème* with signature). Writing done in the ungrateful time of life, but well organised, twisted, *t* left-turning : clinging to the mother. Clubbed lower extensions : the search for an "anchor". Pastose middle zone : need to love; lyrical *d* : poetic sense. Simplified *R* in the signature which is superelevated : pride.

Monique DEGUY, "Centenary of the Death of Arthur Rimbaud", *The Graphologist 10* (2), no.35 : see pp.67-75, 1992.
– At 15-16 years of age : exaggerated capitals, odd elaborations in letters producing a changing general appearance which is, however, consistent (great vitality, awareness of his genius). In about 1870 : discord (strength of ambiguous urges), a contraction in the size of writing (intellectualism), jerkiness and sharpness.

When in Ethiopia, his writing became consistent, sober, connected and semi-angular.

Claude BOURREILLE, "Le graphologue et la psychanalyse", *La Graphologie* no.214, pp.69-77, 1994.
– See pp. 71-77 - Graphological study of the sonnet *Voyelles,* considered from a psychoanalytical point of view : Inner oppositions : introversion-extraversion, feminine-masculine, past-present, personalised and copybook forms. This last example constitutes "a tentative organisation which the Transcendental Force can use".

Arlette LOMBARD, "Concerning the writing of Rimbaud", *La Graphologie* no.215, pp. 59-64, 1994.
– The permanent characteristics of Rimbaud's writing : determined effort, intransigent pride, but becoming banal in Abyssinia".

J.-Ch. GILLE-MAISANI, "Another look at Rimbaud's writing", *La Graphologie* no.217 (in print), 1995.
– Variations of the writing : at the start of the 1870's as well as in the 80's : enthusiasm, then demoralised withdrawal. Connected with the theme of *Bateau ivre* and the nearly-constant convex direction of the lines in the writing.

Je regrette les temps de la grande Cybèle
Qu'on disait parcourir, gigantesquement belle,
Sur un grand char d'airain, les splendides cités;
Son double sein versait dans les immensités
Le pur ruissellement de la vie infinie.
L'Homme suçait, heureux, sa mamelle bénie,
Comme un petit enfant jouant sur ses genoux.
Parce qu'il était fort, l'Homme était chaste et doux.

Misère! Maintenant il dit: Je sais les choses,
Et va, les yeux fermés et les oreilles closes:
Et pourtant, plus de dieux! plus de dieux! l'Homme est Roi,
L'Homme est Dieu! Mais l'Amour, voilà la grande Foi!
Oh! si l'homme puisait encore à ta mamelle,
Grande mère des dieux et des hommes, Cybèle;
S'il n'avait pas laissé l'immortelle Astarté

Fig. 8.1 - Arthur Rimbaud's handwriting at fifteen and a half.

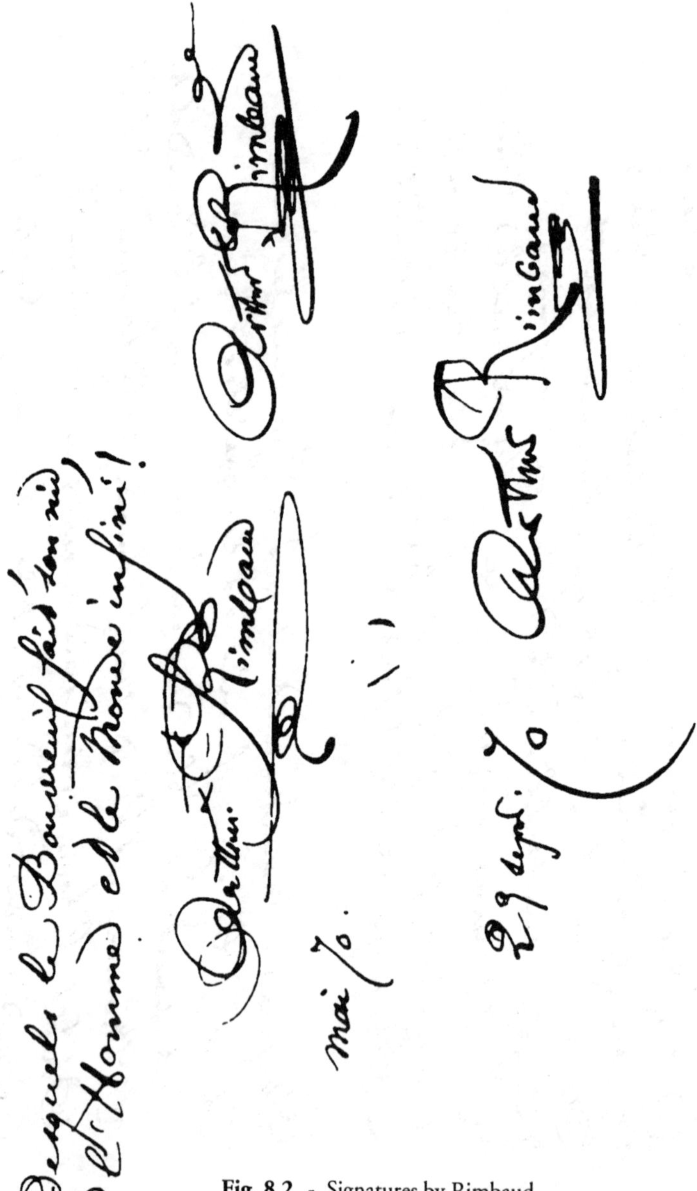

Fig. 8.2 - Signatures by Rimbaud between fifteen and a half and sixteen.

— Moi, je suis, débraillé comme un étudiant,
Sous les marronniers verts les alertes fillettes :
Elles le savent bien ; et tournent en riant,
Vers moi, leurs yeux tout pleins de choses indiscrètes.

Je ne dis pas un mot : je regarde toujours
La chair de leurs cous blancs brodés de mèches folles :
Je suis, sous le corsage et les frêles atours,
Le dos divin après la courbe des épaules ;

J'ai bientôt déniché la bottine, le bas...
— Je reconstruis les corps, brûlé de belles fièvres.
Elles me trouvent drôle et se parlent tout bas...
— Et je sens les baisers qui me viennent aux lèvres...

Arthur Rimbaud

Fig. 8.3 - Rimbaud at fifteen and a half.

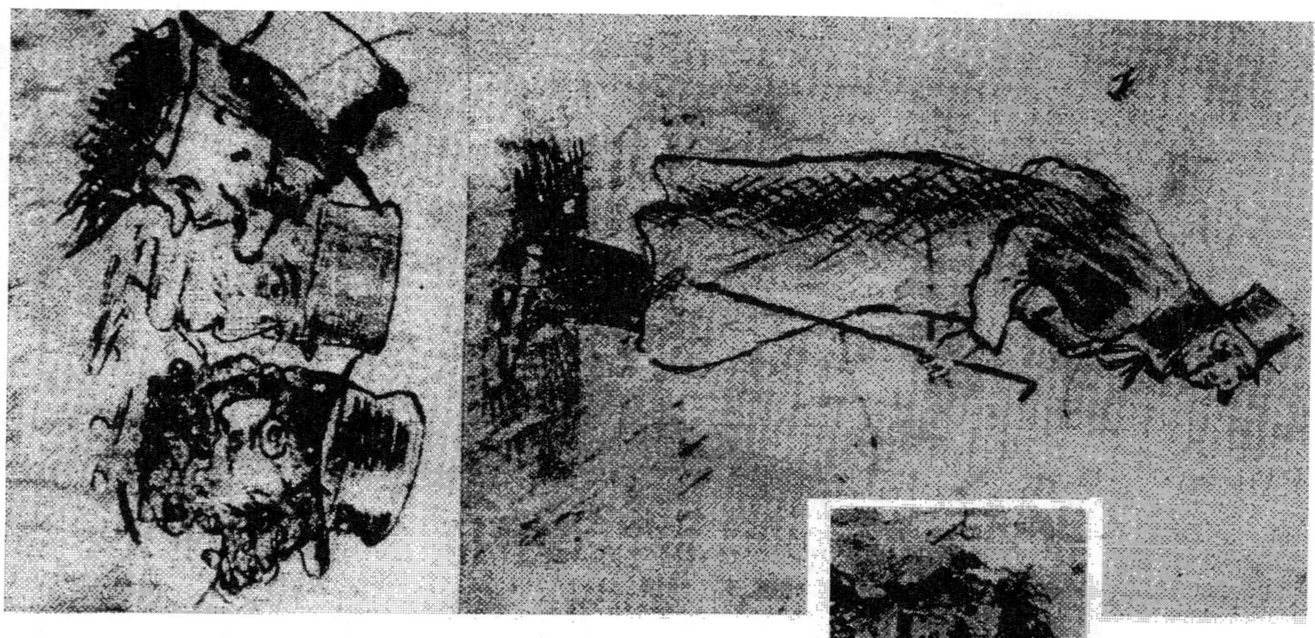

Fig. 8.4 - Drawings by Rimbaud at school.

Ma Bohème (Fantaisie)

Je m'en allais, les poings dans mes poches crevées ;
Mon paletot aussi devenait idéal ;
J'allais sous le ciel, Muse ! et j'étais ton féal ;
Oh ! là là ! que d'amours splendides j'ai rêvées !

Mon unique culotte avait un large trou.
— Petit-Poucet rêveur, j'égrenais dans ma course
Des rimes. Mon auberge était à la Grande-Ourse.
— Mes étoiles au ciel avaient un doux frou-frou

Et je les écoutais, assis au bord des routes,
Ces bons soirs de septembre où je sentais des gouttes
De rosée à mon front, comme un vin de vigueur ;

Où, rimant au milieu des ombres fantastiques,
Comme des lyres, je tirais les élastiques
De mes souliers blessés, un pied ~~tout~~ près de mon cœur !

Arthur Rimbaud

Fig. 8.5 - Rimbaud nearly 16.

l'instar des comprachicos, quoi ! Imaginez un homme s'implantant et se cultivant des verrues sur le visage.

Je dis qu'il faut être *voyant*, se faire *voyant*.

Le Poète se fait *voyant* par un long, immense et raisonné *dérèglement* de *tous les sens*. Toutes les formes d'amour, de souffrance, de folie ; il cherche lui-même, il épuise en lui tous les poisons, pour n'en garder que les quintessences. Ineffable torture où il a besoin de toute la foi, de toute la force surhumaine, où il devient entre tous le grand malade, le grand criminel, le grand maudit, — et le suprême Savant ! — Car il arrive à l'*inconnu* ! Puisqu'il a cultivé son âme, déjà riche, plus qu'aucun ! Il arrive à l'inconnu, et quand, affolé, il finirait par perdre l'intelligence de ses visions, il les a vues ! Qu'il crève dans son bondissement par les choses inouïes et innommables : viendront d'autres horribles travailleurs ; ils commenceront par les horizons où l'autre s'est affaissé !

— La suite à six minutes —

Fig. 8.6 - Rimbaud at nearly sixteen and a half : the so-called "seer's letter".

Bannières de mai

Aux branches claires des tilleuls
Meurt un maladif hallali.
Mais des chansons spirituelles
Voltigent parmi les groseilles.
Que notre sang rie en nos veines,
Voici s'enchevêtrer les vignes.
Le ciel est joli comme un ange
L'azur et l'onde communient.
Je sors. Si un rayon me blesse
Je succomberai sur la mousse.

Qu'on patiente et qu'on s'ennuie
C'est trop simple. Fi de mes peines.
Je veux que l'été dramatique
Me lie à son char de fortune.
Que par toi beaucoup, ô Nature,
– Ah moins seul et moins nul! – je meure.
Au lieu que les Bergers, c'est drôle,
Meurent à peu près par le monde.

Je veux bien que les saisons m'usent.
À toi, Nature, je me rends;
Et ma faim et toute ma soif.
Et, s'il te plaît, nourris, abreuve.
Rien de rien ne m'illusionne.
C'est rire aux parents, qu'au soleil,
Mais moi je ne veux rire à rien;
Et libre soit cette infortune.

Mai 1872

Fig. 8.7 - Rimbaud at seventeen and a half.

Bottom

La réalité étant trop épineuse pour mon grand caractère, — je me trouvai néanmoins chez ma dame, en gros oiseau gris bleu s'essorant vers les moulures du plafond et traînant l'aile dans les ombres de la soirée.

Je fus, au pied du baldaquin supportant les bijoux adorés et ses chefs d'œuvre physiques, un gros ours aux gencives violettes et au poil chenu de chagrin, les yeux aux cristaux et aux argents des consoles.

Tout se fit ombre et aquarium ardent.

Au matin, — aube de juin batailleuse, — je courus aux champs, âne, claironnant et brandissant mon grief, jusqu'à ce que les Sabines de la banlieue vinrent se jeter à mon poitrail.

Fig. 8.8 - Rimbaud at 19.

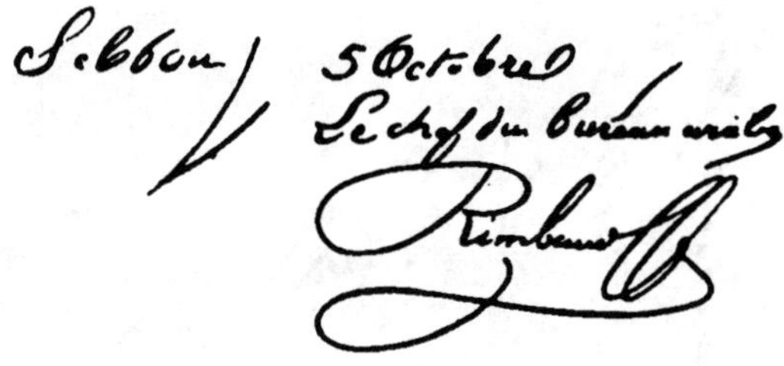

Fig. 8.9 - Handwriting of Arthur Rimbaud's father at about 30.

Fig. 8.10 - Signatures of Arthur Rimbaud's parents (Frédéric Rimbaud and Vitalie Cuif, 38 and 27 respectively) as seen on their marriage certificate.

* **Fig. 8.11** - Handwriting of Madame Rimbaud, the poet's mother, at 44. (Sample continued - see opposite)

Continuation of * **Fig. 8.11**

Harar le 5 aout 1881

Chers amis

Je viens de demander que l'on donne l'ordre à la maison en France de payer entre nos mains en monnaie française, la somme

tour à la côte ou à Aden me referont tout à fait. Et qui diable sait encore sur quelle route nous conduira notre chance ?

Avons

Rimbaud

* **Fig. 8.12** - Rimbaud at 26.

Aden 10 Juillet 1882

(D) Chers amis,

J'ai reçu vos lettres du 14 juin et je vous remercie de vos bons conseils.

J'espère bien aussi voir arriver mon repos avant ma mort. Mais d'ailleurs à présent je suis fort habitué à toute espèce d'ennuis et si je me plains, c'est une espèce de façon de chanter.

Il est probable que je vais repartir dans un mois ou deux au Harrar si ces affaires d'Egypte s'arrangent. Et cette fois j'y ferai un travail sérieux.

* **Fig. 8.13** - Rimbaud at 27 (Sample continued overleaf).

C'est dans la prévision de ce prochain voyage
que je vous prie d'envoyer à sa destination la
lettre ci jointe, dans laquelle je demande une
bonne carte du Harar. Mettez cette lettre sous
enveloppe à l'adresse y indiquée, affranchissez
et joignez un timbre pr la réponse. On vous
dira le prix et vous enverrez le montant
une dizaine de francs en un mandat poste
et sitôt arrivée envoyez moi la carte.
Je ne puis pas m'en passer et personne
ne l'a ici. Je compte donc sur vous.
Nouvelles prochainement
à vous
Rimbaud.

Continuation of * **Fig. 8.13**

Tadjourah 8.3.86

(D) Chers amis

J'attends toujours ledit
Volume, je trouve
que le retard s'accentue.
Je ne pars pas d'ici
d'ailleurs avant mai
Ecrivez moi toujours
à l'adresse ci dessous —
Voici 2 mois sans nouvelles
de vous

Arthur Rimbaud

~~Hôtel Suel~~
Hôtel de l'univers
à Aden

* **Fig. 8.14** - Rimbaud at 31.

compter les recommandations que l'on veut b

me donner pour Zanzibar.

Je laisserai mon argent ici à la banque, et comme il y a à Zanzibar des négociants faisant avec le Crédit L. je toucherai toujou les intérêts.

Si je retire le dépôt à présent, je perdrai les intérêts, et en outre je ne puis plus transporter continuellement cet argent sur mon dos, c'est trop bête, trop fatigant et trop dangereux.

Je te demande donc, comme il ne

et 8 jours pour la réponse.

Envoie-moi cela en une lettre chargée, adressée ainsi

Monsieur Rimbaud

au Consulat de France

Caire

Egypte.

*** Fig. 8.15** - Rimbaud at 32.

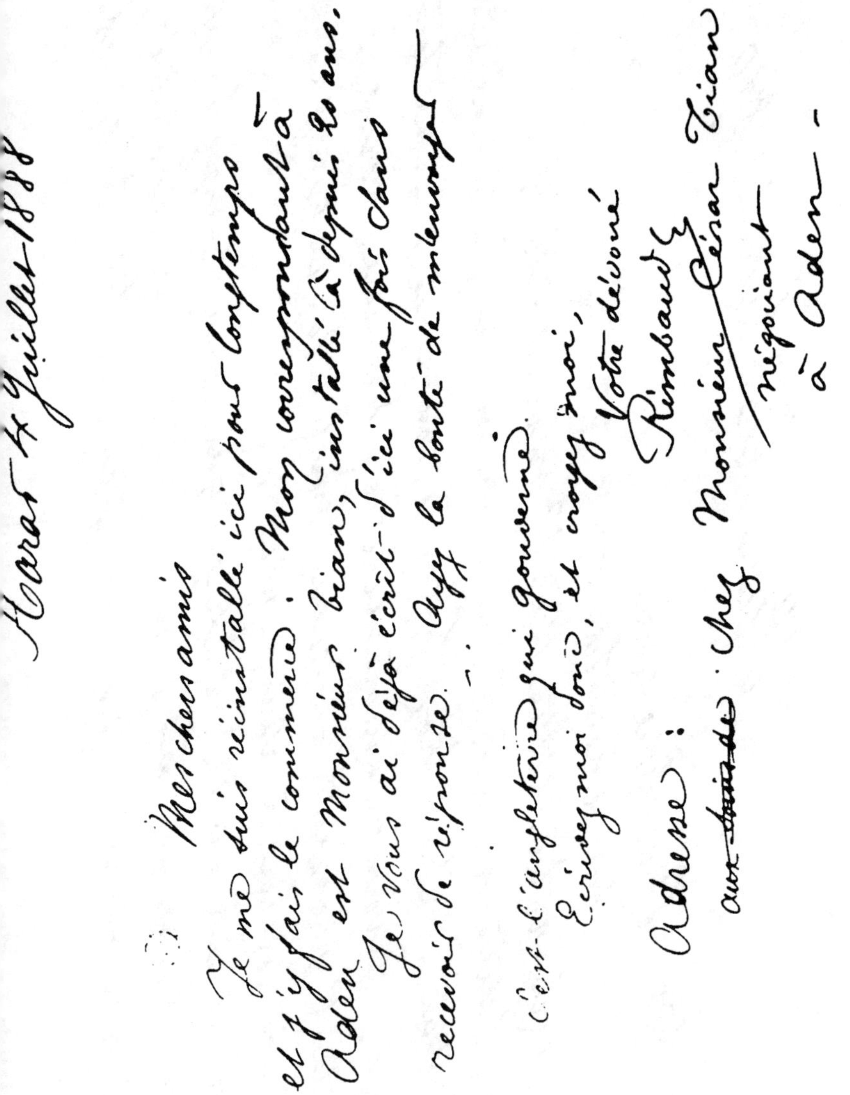

Harar 4 Juillet 1888

Mes chers amis

Je me suis réinstallé ici pour longtemps et j'y fais le commerce. Mon correspondant à Aden est Monsieur Tian, installé à Aden depuis 20 ans. Je vous ai déjà écrit d'ici une fois sans recevoir de réponse. Ayez la bonté de me [illegible]

C'est l'Angleterre qui gouverne. Écrivez-moi donc, et croyez-moi, Votre dévoué Rimbaud

Adresse : aux ~~soins de~~ chez Monsieur César Tian négociant à Aden.

* **Fig. 8.16** - Beginning and end of a letter from Rimbaud at 33.

Harar le 3 janvier 1890

Ma chère mère
Ma chère sœur

J'ai reçu votre lettre du 19 novembre 1889
Vous me dites n'avoir reçu de moi depuis une lettre
Du 18 mai ! C'est trop fort ; je vous écris presque tous
les mois, je vous ai encore écrit en décembre, vous
souhaitant prospérité et santé pour 1890, ce que j'ai
d'ailleurs plaisir à vous répéter.
Quant à vos lettres, je crois bien que
je n'en laisserais pas passer une sans y répondre ;
mais rien ne m'est parvenu, j'en suis très fâché ; et

* **Fig. 8.17** - Rimbaud at 35 (Sample continued, see opposite).

Quant à vos lettres de chaque quinzaine, croyez bien que
je ne les laisserais pas passer une sans y répondre,
mais rien ne m'est parvenu, j'en suis très fâché, et
je vais demander des explications à Aden, où je suis
pourtant étonné que cela se soit égaré.

Bien à vous, Votre fils votre frère.

Rimbaud,
chez Monsieur Tian
Aden (Arabie)
Colonies Anglaises.

Continuation of * **Fig. 8.17**

Les chameaux n'arrivent qu'à 6h1/2

(7)

Lundi 13 — Levés à 5 1/2 arrivés à Dâbo-Kaboba à 9h campé —

Mardi 14 (8)

Mouned Saugri | 1
Abdullahi | 1
Abdullas | 1
Bakker | 1

Levés à 5 1/2. Les porteurs marchent très mal. à 9 1/2 halte à Arrouina. On me jette par terre à l'arrivée. J'impose 4 thalers d'amende.

Levé à 2 heures arrivé à Samado à 5 1/2

72.5 à 5 1/2

319.14

Mercredi 15 (9)

Levé à 6h arrivé à Ensa à 10h relevé à 2 1/2 arrivés à Kombavoren à 6 1/2

Jeudi 16 (10) levé 8 1/2

... Halte à Bouroubassa à 9h. trouvé là 10 ... — levé 2h. Dadap 6 1/4

112 Dabouleh ... 2 ...

Fig. 8.18 - Rimbaud at 36.

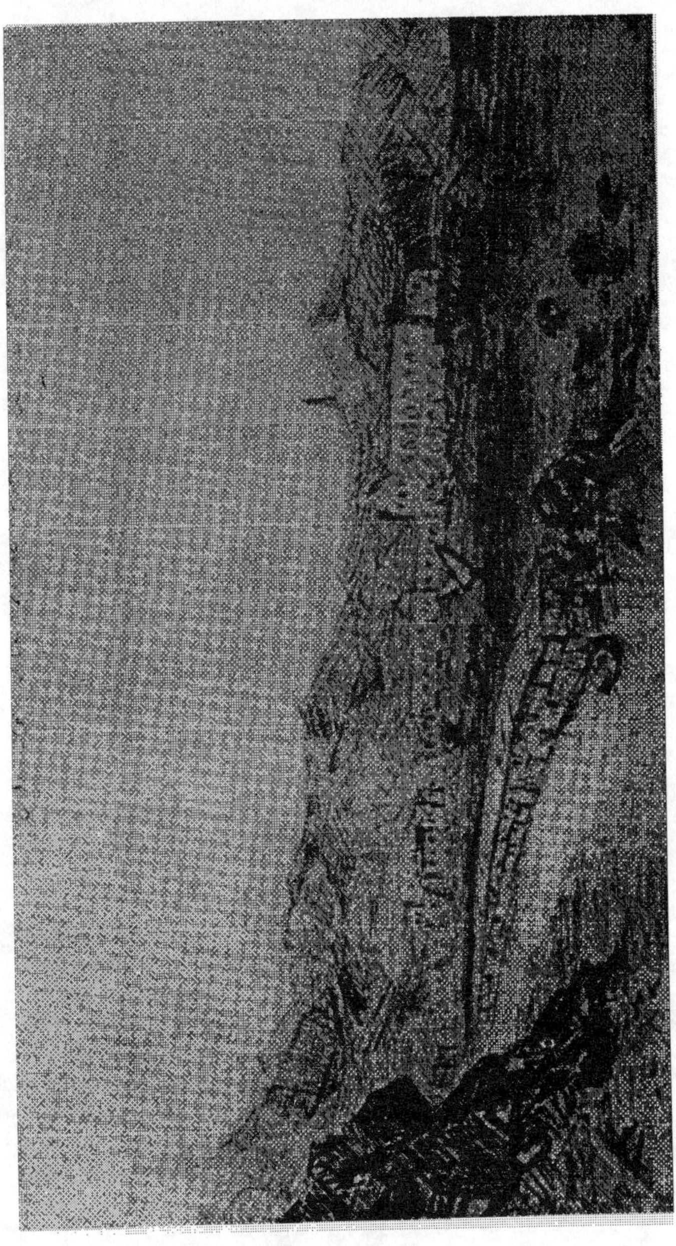

Fig. 8.19 - Drawing by Rimbaud in Aden.

Fig. 8.20 - Drawing by Rimbaud in Africa.

BIBLIOGRAPHICAL REFERENCES

(1) BOOKS DEVOTED to POETS' HANDWRITINGS

Adolf HENZE, *Die Handschrift der deutschen Dichter und Dichterinnen*, Bernhard Schlicke, Leipzig, 1855, 161p.

Edouard de ROUGEMONT, *Commentaires graphologiques sur Charles Baudelaire*, Société de graphologie, Patis, 1923, 65p.

Paul CASPAR, Gertrud von KUEGELGEN, *Dichter in der Handschrift. Graphologische Deutungen zeitgenössischer Dichtwerke*, Sponholtz, Hanover, 1937, 187p.

Hermann GERSTNER, Karl SCHWORM, *Deutsche Dichter unserer Zeit*, Eher, Munich, 1940, 622p.

Léonore de POMBAL, *Poésie et Graphologie. Étude sur le graphisme de poètes portugais modernes et contemporains*, self-published work, Lisbon, 1971, 418p.

J.-Ch. GILLE-MAISANI, *Écritures de poètes de Byron à Baudelaire*, Dervy-Livres, Paris, 1977, 191p.

Jean-Charles GILLE-MAISANI, *Écritures de poètes. Graphologie et poésie. Deuxième série : de Sully-Prudhomme à Valéry*, Dervy-Livres, Paris, 1981, 267p.

Jean-Charles GILLE-MAISANI, *Poésie, Musique et Graphologie. Écritures de poètes et de compositeurs : compléments*, Dervy-Livres, Paris, 1988, 332p.

(2) GENERAL BOOKS on GRAPHOLOGY in ENGLISH

Rosa BAUGHAN, *Character Indicated by Handwriting*, 2nd ed., Upton Gill, London, 1886, 139p; new edition, MacKay, New York, 1920.

Magdalene KINTZEL-THUMM, *Psychology and Pathology of Handwriting*, Fowler and Welles, New York, 1905, 149p.

L.K. GIVEN-WILSON, *The Psychology of the Movements of Handwriting from the works of Crépieux-Jamin*, George Routledge and Sons, London, 1926, 196p.

Robert SAUDEK, *The Psychology of Handwriting*, Allen and Unwin, London, undated [1925], 394p; 2nd edition, 1954, 288p.

Louise RICE, *Character Reading from Handwriting*, Frederick A. Stokes, New York, 1927, 374p.

Robert SAUDEK, *Experiments with Handwriting*, Allen and Unwin, London and Doubleday, Doran, New York, 1928, 394p.

C. Harry BROOKS, *Your Character from Your Handwriting. A guide to the new graphology* [....] *An explanation of the method of Robert Saudek*, Allen and Unwin, London, 1930, 159p.

Gordon W. ALLPORT, Philip E. VERNON, *Studies in Expressive Movement*, Hafner, New York, 1933, 269p; reprinted, 1967.

Nadya OLYANOVA, *Handwriting Tells,* Wilshire Book Co., Hollywood (California), 1936, 371p; re-edited.

Alfred O. MENDEL, *Personality in Handwriting. A Handbook of American Graphology,* Stephen Day Press, New York, 1947; 4th ed., 1971, 375p.

Werner WOLFF, *Diagrams of the Unconscious. Handwriting and Personality Measurement, Experiment and Analysis*, Grune and Stratton, New York, 1948, 423p.

Frank VICTOR [GRUENFELD], *Handwriting, a Personality Projection*, Charles Thomas, Springfield (Illinois), 1952, 149p.

Ulrich SONNEMANN, *Handwriting Analysis as a Psychodiagnostic Tool*, Grune and Stratton, New York, 1953, 276p.

Klara G. ROMAN, *Handwriting. A key to personality*, Routledge and Kegan Paul, London, 1954, 382p; new ed., Noonday Press, New York, 1962.

M.N. BUNKER, *Handwriting Analysis, the art and science of reading character by Grapho Analysis*, Nelson Hall Co., Chicago (Illinois), 1959, 256p; re-edited.

Irene MARCUSE, *The Key to Handwriting Analysis*, 2nd ed., McBride, New York, 1959, 180p.

Nadya OLYANOVA, *The Psychology of Handwriting,* Sterling Publications, New York, 1962, 224p.

Hal FALCON, *How to Analyze Handwriting*, Cornerstone Library, New York, 1964, 160p; re-edited.

Billie PESIN ROSEN, *The Science of Handwriting Analysis. A guide to Character and Personality,* Crown Publishers, New York, 1965, 223p.

Rudolph S. HEARNS, *Handwriting. An Analysis Through Its Symbolism*, Vantage Press, New York, 1966, 171p; 2nd ed., 1973.

Eric SINGER, *A Manual of Graphology*, Duckworth, London, 1969, 245p.

John SILVI, *Handwriting and the Human Mind*, Harlo Press, Detroit (Michigan), *Book I*, 1973, 278p; 2nd ed., 1979; *Book II*, 1978, 270p.

William Leslie FRENCH, *The Psychology of Handwriting*, Putnam, New York, 1922, 226p; new edition with the title *Your Handwriting and What it Means*, Newcastle Publishing Co., Van Nuys (California), 1976.

Karen AMEND, Mary S. RUIZ, *Handwriting Analysis. The Complete Basic Book*, Newcastle Publishing Co., North Hollywood (California), 1980, 196p.

Patricia MARNE, *Graphology*, Hodder and Stoughton, London, 1980, 170p.

Paula SASSI, Eldene WHITING, *Fundamentals of Handwriting Analysis. A beginning Course*, Handwriting Consultants, San Diego (California), 1982, 177p.

Paula SASSI, Eldene WHITING, *Personal Worth. Intermediate Course in Handwriting Analysis*, Handwriting Consultants, San Diego (California), 1983, 198p.

Paula SASSI, Eldene WHITING, *Personality Evaluation. Advanced Course in Handwriting Analysis*, Handwriting Consultants, San Diego (California), 1983, 156p.

Marie BERNARD, *The Art of Graphology*, Whitston Publishing Co., Troy (New York), 1985, 416p.

Margaret GULLAN-WHUR, *The Graphology Workbook*, Aquarian Press, Wellingborough, 1986, 110p.

Betty LINK, *Advanced Graphology*, Personnel Consultants and Publishers, Chicago (Illinois), 1986, 263p.

Renna NEZOS, *Graphology. The Interpretation of Handwriting*, Rider, London, 1986, 315p; 3rd ed., Scriptor Books, London, 1992.

Gabrielle BEAUCHATAUD, *Learn Graphology. A Pratcial Course in 15 Lessons*, (translated from the French), Scriptor Books, London, 1988, 279p.

Patricia MARNE, *The Concise Graphology Notebook. An Introduction to the Basic Principles of Handwriting Analysis*, Foulsham, London, 1988, 128p.

Hubert DESENCLOS, *Understanding Graphology. How to Interpret Handwritings*, Collins, London, 1990, 144p.

Helmut PLOOG, *Basic Graphology*, Professional Association of Certified Graphologists/Psychologists, Munich, 1991, 10 volumes with cassettes.

Jean-Charles GILLE-MAISANI, *The Psychology of Handwriting*, (translated from the French), Scriptor Books, London, 1992, 347p.

Renna NEZOS, *Advanced Graphology. 20 Lectures on selected topics*, Scriptor Books, London, 1993, 388p.

Renna NEZOS, *Judicial Graphology*, Scriptor Books, London, 1994, 176p.

Max PULVER, *The Symbolism of Handwriting*, (translated from the German), Scriptor Books, London, 1994, 364p.

(3) BOOKS and ARTICLES on TYPOLOGIES

Chapters on typologies are found in the books by Marie BERNARD (1985), Renna NEZOS (1986) and G. BEAUCHATAUD (1988).

The following books and articles are especially devoted to that subject.

(a) On Galen's temperaments :

Paul CARTON, *Diagnostic et Conduite des tempéraments : la connaissance synthétique et clinique de l'homme* (1926), 4th ed., Le François, 1972, 194p.

Suzanne DELACHAUX, *Écriture et Psychologie des tempéraments*, Delachaux et Niestlé, Neuchâtel, 1955, 184p.

Augusto VELS, "The four vectors in the Vels method of graphoanalysis", *Graphology*, no.4, pp.17-20, 1988.

(b) On planetary, or mythological types :

H. SAINT-MORAND (Mrs. E. KOECHLIN), *Typologie planétaire : les complémentaires*, 1964, 90p; *L'Écriture et la Typologie planétaire*, 1973, 70p, self-published papers, Paris.

Sylvie BORIE, *Introduction à la typologie planétaire. Entretien avec Mauric Munzinger*, 1973, 45p; *Graphologie. Typologie planétaire : Uranus, Neptune, Pluton*, 1983, 83p, self-published papers, Paris.

Hélène de MAUBLANC, *L'Écriture par la méthode Saint-Morand*, Masson, Paris, 1989, 192p.

Anne-Marie SIMOND, *La Graphologie planétaire. Une typologie de l'écriture et de la personnalité*, Albin Michel, 1990, 349p.

J.-Ch. GILLE-MAISANI, "The Planetary Types in Handwriting", *Graphology*, no.15, pp.4-36 and no.16, pp.3-29, 1991.

(c) On character after Heymans and Le Senne :

Renna NEZOS-IATROU, "Graphology in practice. Part 3 : the characterology of Heymans and Le Senne", *The Graphologist* 2(3), pp.12-14, 1984.

Emile CAILLE, *Characters and Handwriting* (translated from the French), Scriptor Books, London, 1991, 307p.

(d) On Jung's types

Renna NEZOS-IATROU, "Graphology in practice : the classification of C.G. Jung", *The Graphologist* 2(2), pp.7-15, 1984.

Milton MOORE, *Jungian Psychology : Graphological Applications*, self-published paper, Charlottesville (Virginia), 1988, 30p.

Ania TEILLARD, *The Soul and Handwriting. A Treatise on Graphology Based on Analytical Psychology* (translated from the French), Scriptor Books, London, 1993, 288p.

In French :

J.Ch. GILLE-MAISANI, *Types de Jung et Tempéraments psychobiologiques. Expression dans l'écriture* [....] *Utilisation en psychologie appliquée*, Maloine, Paris, 1978, 196p.1

Monique GENTY, *L'Être et l'Écriture dans la psychologie jungienne*, Masson, Paris, 1991, 152p.

Catherine COLO, *Types psychobiologiques de Jung et Applications graphologiques*, Masson, Paris, 1992, 92p.

(e) On Szondi's vectors :

Fanchette LEFEBURE, Jean-Charles GILLE-MAISANI, *Graphologie et Test de Szondi. Tome 1 : Le Moi* (1976), 3rd ed., Masson, Paris, 1990, 182p.

Fanchette LEFEBURE, Jean-Charles GILLE-MAISANI, *Graphologie et Test de Szondi. Tome 2 : Dynamique des pulsions* (1980), 2nd ed., Masson, Paris, 1990, 230p.

Alex TULLOCH, "An Introduction to Szondi's Theory of Personality", *Graphology*, nos. 1, pp.4-8, 1987; 2, pp.1-32, 1987; 3, pp.24-34, 1988; 4, pp.29-43, 1988; 5, pp.5-18, 1988.

Alex TULLOCH, "Evaluation of a Handwriting : An Analysis based on Szondi's Theory of Personality", *Graphology*, no.6, pp.33-38, 1988, and no.7, pp.5-10, 1989.

(f) On psychobiological temperaments (related to the blood type) :

J.-Ch. GILLE MAISANI, *Tempéraments psychobiologiques et Groupes sanguins. Expression graphologique et artistique* (1978), new ed., Frison-Roche, Paris, 1991, 337p.

(4) On GRAPHOMETRY

Thea STEIN-LEWINSON, Joseph ZUBIN, *Handwriting Analysis. A Series of Scales for Evaluating the Dynamic Aspects of Handwriting*, King's Crown Press, New York, 1941, 147p.

H. de GOBINEAU, R. PERRON, *Génétique de l'écriture et Étude de la personnalité. Essais de graphométrie*, Delachaux et Niestlé, Neuchâtel, 1954, 215p.

Patrick GILBERT, Christian CHARDON, *Analyser l'écriture. Une démarche et un outil nouveaux en graphologie. Applications pratiques*, Editions ESF, Paris, 1987, 192p.

Jacques SALCE, "The Graphometric Test", *The Graphologist*, nos: *8*(2) : pp.1-26, 1990; *8*(3) : pp.1-25, 1990; *8*(4) : pp.1-25, 1990; *9*(1) : pp.1-37, 1991.

Marie-Thérèse PRÉNAT, *Graphométrie. Approche de la personnalité profonde*, Masson, Paris, 1992, 145p.

APPENDIX ON GRAPHOMETRY

The graphometrical analyses of Baudelaire, Mallarmé, Verlaine and Rimbaud were performed with the major help of Mme Marie-Thérèse Prénat. We give here a summary of her method to allow the reader to understand the charts of chapters 5 to 8. The method is explained in detail in her book, which is mentioned at the end of the bibliography.

The method, originally inspired by that of Th. Stein-Lewinson (1941) and elaborated in the 1960s by Jacques Salce, Marie-Thérèse Prénat and Fanchette Lefebure, consists in characterising a handwriting by the statistical distribution of a certain number of qualities laid out on an "expansion-concentration" scale of seven degrees, ranging from +3 (extreme concentration) down to -3 (extreme expansion), what is "normal" being represented by zero.

In practice there is a numbered list of twenty variables grouped into *four components* each of which having a certain graphic and psychological unity.

Here is the list.

Component I, instinctual (stroke) : the human "spark of life" and the impulses.

1) Variation in the width of the stroke : considerable spread (+) versus absence of relief (-).
2) Degree of pressure (relationship between the pressure of the stroke and that of the running hand, remembering their place) : noticeable spread (+) versus weak spread (-).
3) Edge of the stroke : clean edges (+) versus blurred edges (-).
4) Quality of the stroke : trenchant, viscous stroke (+) versus porous stroke (-).
5) Handling of the stroke : clubs, reversed pressure (+) versus slackening of tension (-).

Component II, rational (form, connection) : the kind of intelligence and the degree of rationality.

6) Complication (+) versus dissolution (-).
7) Personal shapes (+) versus copybook shapes (-).
8) Intermediary letters : stiffness (+) versus threading (-).
9) Connection between letters : elasticity (0), loss of elasticity through stiffening or rupture (+) or by downward displacement (-).
10) Degree of connection : juxtaposed writing (+) versus connected writing (-).

Component III, emotional (size, spatial layout) : the Ego in relation to itself.

11) Height of the middle zone : small (+) versus large (-).
12) Comparison of zone heights : prolonged lower extensions (+) versus prolonged upper extensions (-).
13) Direction of the lines : descending (+) versus ascending (-).
14) Sinuousness : sustained waves (+) versus brief waves (-)
15) Tangling : spaced out lines (+) versus letters tangling with the line above or below (-).

Component IV, relational (spatial layout) : the social Ego.

16) Spacing between letters : letters "glued" to each other (+) versus spread-out writing (-).
17) Width of letters : squeezed writing (+) versus wide letters (-).
18) Slant : leftward slanting writing (+) versus very right-slanted writing (-).
19) Variability of slant : weak (+) versus strong (-).
20) Spacing between words : wide (+) versus narrow (-).

Global histogram V, of adaptation (sum of the four components) : synthesis of the person, general integration and evaluation of balance, autonomy and efficiency.

The characterisation of a piece of handwriting is effected by counting up how many elements (strokes, letters, ...) are respectively to be evaluated by +3, +2, +1, 0, -1, -2 and -3, in conformity with a technique set up once and for all, affording an objective estimate. For each of the four components the results of the variables are added up, standardised and represented in a histogram. The inclusive fifth histogram represents the sum of the histograms of the four components, in other words, the sum of all the twenty variables.

The application of this method to Baudelaire, Mallarmé, Verlaine and Rimbaud appears respectively in charts 5.1, 6.1, 7.1 and 8.1 - namely the marks of +3, +2, +1, 0, -1, -2 and -3 of the twenty variables and the five histograms.

The *interpretation* rests mainly upon the comparison of each histogram with the "Gaussian" average histogram obtained from a population of contemporary, cultured French people. Note for reference that :

a) 0, +1 and -1 represent the *adaptability* zone (+1 : social and domestic habits, traditional educational values; 0 : efficient mastery by a conscious adapted self; -1 : empirical adaptation);
b) The expansive zone corresponds to an *excessive liberation* of instincts and desires (-2 : flight into action, avoidance of conflict; -3 : impulsiveness, actions performed without self-control, disintegration);
c) The concentrated zone corresponds to a *block* (+2 : difficulty in freeing certain emotions; +3 : inability to make use in real life of certain personality components).

The properties of the histogram of *sinuousness* give information particularly about the degree of *mastery over emotions*. It is often interesting to consider two histograms of sinuousness, obtained respectively from the beginning and the end of the text under examination : this has been done in charts 5.2 (Baudelaire) and 7.2 (Verlaine).

An *index of operational intelligence* or a *coefficient of efficiency* gives a figure which shows to what extent the variables as a whole are, for the particular script, close to or wide of the norm (in the sense of constriction or dispersal). It is the quotient of the scores 0 among the twenty variables divided by the sum of their scores differing from nought. It indicates to what extent the writer has compensated his struggles in order to free his energy and to conform, be "operational" : an index of 45% or higher is found mostly among writers of a highly organised intelligence (Mallarmé 49%); an index lower than 30% is a fairly certain sign of irregularity (Baudelaire with 31% and the young Rimbaud with 30% are at the morbid limit).

If x represents the sum of the 0 scores for the sum of the scores for the twenty variables, the sum of the scores -3, -2, -1, 0, +1, +2 and +3 is 2000 - x (because of the method of calculation in the histograms). The index of operational intelligence is by definition:

$$100 \frac{x}{2000 - x}$$

Here are the details of calculating for the Baudelaire example (Chart 5.1).

The sum of 0 scores for the twenty variables appears in the chart of the figures of the global histogram. This sum is 471, made up by the 0 scores of the four components :

$$110 + 172 + 90 + 99 = 471.$$

The sums of the scores -3, -2, -1, 0, +1, +2 and +3 are read off from the same chart. They are respectively:

129 322 320 285 373 100

and their sum is 1529. We therefore have:

$$471 + 1529 = 2000$$

The quotient for operational intelligence is therefore:

$$100 \frac{471}{1529} = 31\%$$

SOURCES OF THE EXAMPLES OF HANDWRITING

Abbreviations used :

B.L.	:	Bibliothèque littéraire Jacques Doucet, Paris.
B.M.	:	British Museum, London;
B.N.	:	Bibliothèque Nationale, Paris.

1.1 : B.M. (Egerton 2611f. 17r and 17v) .— 1.2 : B.M. (Egerton 2611 f. 22 and 129r). — 1.3 : B.M. Ashley B 2633 (Cat. XI-16), p. B2671r. — 1.4 : B.M. Ashley 4729 (Cat. XI. 23-24), f. 4r. - -1.5 : B.M. Ashley 5160 (Cat. XI. 38-39). — 1.6 : B.M. Ahsley 4753 (Cat. XI. 42-43), p. 2v.

2.1 : Houghton Library, Cambridge, (USA) — 2.2 : B.M. (Ashley 4869). — 2.3 : B.M. (Add. 34019 f. 11v°). — 2.4 : B.M. (Add. 34019 f. 31). — 2.5 : B.M. (Add. 34019 f.74).

3.1 : Archives de la Défense Nationale, Vincennes, the de Vigny file. — 3.2 : B.N. (N.A.F. 15503 p. 14 and 9856 Rotschild). — 3.3 : Bibliothèque de l'Institut, Chantilly. — 3.4 : B.N. (2814 N.A.F. 25086 f. 25r and 1885 N.A.F. 1305 f. 18). — 3.5 : B.N. (N.A.F. 25086 f. 94 and N.A.F. 24984 p. 156). — 3.6 *L'Autographe*, no.26, p. 223 (Dec. 15, 1864). — 3.7 : Bibliothèque de l'Institut, Chantilly.

4.1 : M. Ia. BASINA, *Gorod poeta,* Detskaia literatura, Leningrad, 1965, p.193; Abram EFROS, *Risunki poeta*, Academia, Leningrad, 1933, p.96. — 4.2 : B. MEILAKH, *Khudozhestvennoe myshlenie Pushkina kak tvorcheskii protses*, Academy of Sciences, Leningrad, 1962, pl. 1. — 4.3 : *Zhurnal psikho-grafologii, 1*(2), p.20 (October 1, 1903) and *1*(3) p.34 (November 1, 1903). — 4.4 : B. MEILAKH, *op. cit.*, pl. 13 and D.D. Blagov (ed.), *Pushkin v portretakh i illiustratsiakh*, Uchpedgiz, Leningrad, 1951, p.263. — 4.5 : *L'Autographe*, no.28, p.235 (January 15, 1865) and J.-L. BACKÈS, *Pouchkine par lui-même*, Seuil, Paris, 1966, pl. II. — 4.6 : A. EFROS, *op. cit.*, p.327. — 4.7 : A. Efros, *op. cit.*, p.319, 317. — 4.8 : B. MEILAKH, *op. cit.*, pl. 11, 12, 13 and S. BONDI, *Chernoviki Pushkina*, Prosveshchenie, Moscow, 1971, p.36. — 4.9 : A. EFROS, *op. cit.*, p.339.

5.1 and 5.2 : Claude Pichois's collection. — 5.3 Édouard de ROUGEMONT, *Commentaires graphologiques sur Charles Baudelaire*, Société de graphologie, Paris, 1923, facing p.16. — 5.4 : Claude Pichois's collection. — 5.5 : B.N. (N.A.F. 1485, p.4). — 5.6 : E. de ROUGEMONT, *op. cit.,*facing p.24. — 5.7 : B.N. (Facs 8°-225, p.38). — 5.8 : B.N. (N.A.F. 1485 p.9). — 5.9 : B.N. (Facs 8°-208 p.22v). — 5.10 : Archives des Affaires étrangères, Paris. — 5.11 to 5.15 : Archives de la Défense nationale (armée de terre), Vincennes.

6.1 and 6.2 : B.L. alpha 7248.4 and 7248.6. — 6.3 : Stéphane MALLARMÉ, *Autobiographie. Lettre à Verlaine*, facsimile edition "Les Manuscrits des maîres", Albert Messein, Paris, 1924. — 6.4 and 6.5 : *Écrivains des XIXème et XXème siècles. Éditions originales, manuscrits et lettres autographes,* catalogue no.56, Pierre Berès, Paris, without date, nos. 370, 380. — 6.6 : B.L., alpha 7248,7. — 6.7 : B.N., N.A.F. 14666, f. 33lr, 332. — 6.8 and 6.9 : *Le Manuscrit autographe, 1*(1), pp.10, 11 (1926). — 6.10 : Jacques SCHERER, *Le "Livre" de Mallarmé. Premières recherches sur des documents inédits*, 5th ed., Gallimard, Paris, p.40(A) and front page.

7.1 and 7.2 : Paul VERLAINE, *Fêtes galantes,* facsimile ed. "Les Manuscrits des maîtres", Messein, Paris, 1920, front page and f.13. — 7.3 : B.L. 922 H VII-4. — 7.4, 7.5 and 7.6 : Paul VERLAINE, *Sagesse*, facsimile ed. "Les Manuscrits des maîtres", Messein, Paris, 1913, pp.31, 29. 54. 79. — 7.7 : B.L. A IV 10-7203-356. — 7.6 : B.N. 9320 N.A.F. 23057 f. 10. — 4.9 (third signature) : B.L. A IV 10-7203-363. — 7.10 : B.L. 7203-2734 AN 10. — 4.11 : B.N. 9320 N.A.F. 23057 f. 70.

8.1, 8.2, 8.3, 8.5, 8.7 : Arthur RIMBAUD, *Poésies*, facsimile ed. "Les Manuscrits des maîtres", Albert Messein, Paris, 1919, respectively 1st (6.1, 6.2, 6.3), 2nd (6.5) and 4th part (6.7). — 6.4, 6.19, 6.20 : *L'Art vivant 6*, no.132 (June 15, 1936), pp.486, 485 (photograph B.N. f. V.5897). — 8.6 : Aurthur RIMBAUD, *Lettre du Voyant à Paul Demeny du 15 Mai 1871 avec le facsimilé de l'autographe*, Albert Messein, Paris, 1954. — 8.8 Henry de BOUILLANE de LACOSTE, *Rimbaud et le Problème des Illuminations*, Mercure de France, Paris, 1949, p.167. — 8.9 : H. MATARASSO, R. PETITFILS, *Vie d'Arthur Rimbaud*, Hachette, Paris, 1962, p.15. — 8.10 : Archives départmentales des Ardennes, Mézières (État-civil de Charleville, Mariages, 8 février 1853). — 8.11 Musée Rimbaud, Charleville. — 8.12 to 8.18 : B.L., respectively 7199-6 A IV-4, 7199-8 A IV-4, 7199-20 A IV-4, 7199-23 A IV-4 (last page), 7199-27 A IV-4, 7199-30 A IV-4 and 7199-60 A IV-4.

SOURCES OF THE PORTRAITS

Byron : portrait by R. Westall, National Portrait Gallery (4243), London.

Keats : portrait by W. Hilton, National Portrait Gallery (194), London.

Vigny : Bibliothèque Nationale (C 3033), Paris.

Pushkin : portrait by V. Propinin, Museum literatury im. Adama Mickiewicza (4105), Warsaw.

Baudelaire : Bibliothèque Nationale (B31401), Paris.

Mallarmé : Nadar/Archives photographiques, Paris/S.P.A.D.E.M. (MA 238-9021).

Verlaine : photograph, Musée Rimbaud, Charleville.

Rimbaud : photograph by Carjat, Musée Rimbaud, Charleville.